The World Bank
and the
Gods of Lending

The World Bank
and the
Gods of Lending

Steve Berkman

Kumarian Press
An Imprint of Stylus Publishing

The World Bank and the Gods of Lending

Published in 2008 in the United States of America by Kumarian Press, 22883 Quicksilver Drive, Sterling, VA 20166 USA

The text of this book is set in 10.5/13 Palatino.

Cover design by Laura Augustine.
Cover photo by Erica Flock.
Book design by Joan Weber Laflamme, jml ediset.
Proofread by Beth Richards.
Index by Robert Swanson.

Marc Roesch cartoon on page 249 reprinted with the permission of www.developmentart.com.

Printed in the United States of America by Thompson-Shore. Text printed with vegetable oil-based ink.

∞ The paper used in this publication meets the minimum requirements of the American National Standard for Information Sciences—Permanence of Paper for printed Library Materials, ANSI Z39.48–1984

Library of Congress Cataloging-in-Publication Data

Berkman, Steve, 1933–
    The World Bank and the gods of lending / by Steve Berkman.
        p. cm.
    Includes bibliographical references and index.
    ISBN 978–1–56549–259–2 (pbk. : alk. paper)
1. World Bank—History. I. Title.
    HG3881.5.W57B47 2008
    332.1'532—dc22

                                                                2008010159

This book is dedicated to the millions of poor souls
who have yet to find a better life
through economic development projects
and policy reforms funded by the World Bank
and the donor community.

Contents

Illustrations

Acknowledgments

This book would not have been possible without the help, advice, and encouragement of many of my friends and former colleagues at the World Bank. By helping me understand the dynamics of development lending, sharing their frustrations and years of experience, and offering moral support when needed, they have knowingly and unknowingly given me the motivation to reveal the inner workings of the Bank as I have witnessed them. Without question, I am grateful to all the project task managers, technical specialists, disbursement officers, and yes, even some in management, who shared my concerns about the direction the Bank had taken over the past several decades and what is needed to get it back on track.

From my time with the Africa Region Operations Group I am especially grateful to Paul Blanchet, Ken Sigrist, Nick Bennett, Benny di Zitti, P. C. Mohan, R. J. Gopalkrishnan, Kenneth Miller, Hovsep Melkonian, Sithamparam Sengamalay, Janet De Merode, Ebenezer Aikens-Afful, Bertrand Ah-Sue, David Howarth, Randolph Andersen, Manoucher Ashouripour, Alfred Nickesen, Eugene Boostrom, Gerard Boulch, Kevin Cleaver, Judith Edstrom, James Sackey, Michael Gillette, Snorri Hallgrimsson, Ian Heggie, John Kendall, Jean-Christoph Laederach, Colin Lyle, Uche Mbanefo, Peter Morris, John Nebiker, Alain Papineau, Max Pulgar-Vidal, Cesar Queiroz, Emmerich Schebeck, Mary Oakes Smith, David Steeds, Michael Stevens, Townsend Swayze, Bernard Veuthey, Heinz Weindler, Mulugeta Wodajo, and all the others who helped to show me the way.

Bridging my last years with the Africa Region and my later return to work with the newly formed Anti-Corruption and Fraud Investigation Unit I am deeply indebted to those in the Internal Audit Department who listened to my ranting about corruption and began the difficult process of addressing that issue: Allan

Newstadt, who circulated my paper on the impact of corruption to senior management; Graham Joscelyne, our auditor general, who listened and had the courage to do something about it; Skip White, who invited me back to work with our initial group of investigators and guided me throughout my tenure there; my first partner, Karl Krueger, whose sharp mind inspired me; Dzung Nguyen, who has always been there to hear me out and offer advice; Mike Kramer, the most dedicated investigator on the planet; John McCormick, former prosecutor, friend, confidant, and mentor, who really cares about making the world a better place; Al Sharp, Steve Zimmermann, Glenn Ware, Mike Richards, Terry Matthews, Peter Dent, Diomedes Berroa, and the rest of the gang who taught me so much about fraud investigation; and last but not least, Yannick Stephant and Dina-Maria Hack, who partnered with me on a difficult investigation in Cote d'Ivoire.

Many friends and fellow travelers outside the Bank also provided support and encouragement in the preparation of this book. Foremost is Jim Wesberry, whom I first met at the Bank. A former Georgia state senator, fraud examiner, special investigator, and lifelong opponent of corruption, Jim is widely known for his anticorruption expertise in Latin America. Through his network of contacts and with his extensive background in fighting corruption, he has provided me with immeasurable assistance over the years, and I owe him much for helping to bring this book to fruition.

Following his revelations of corruption in Indonesia during the mid-1990s, I had the good fortune to meet Jeffrey Winters, professor of political economy at Northwestern University. With shared perspectives on the use and abuse of aid to the Third World, Jeffrey has had considerable influence over the direction this book has taken. Bruce Rich, senior counsel for Environmental Defense in Washington, D.C., also provided much needed help in focusing on content and potential audiences.

Jack Blum, a former United States Senate staff attorney involved in numerous high-profile investigations, including the Bank of Credit and Commerce International and General Noriega's drug trafficking, is well known as an expert on money laundering and tax evasion. He has been a good sounding board for my thoughts and ideas throughout the preparation of this book, and his explanations of the movement of illegal funds through international financial systems have provided me with additional insights into the world of corruption.

George Ayittey, professor of economics at American University and president of the Free Africa Foundation has also provided me with sound insights into African cultures and the despotic regimes who govern the continent. Gerald Caiden, professor of public administration at the University of Southern California, has provided tremendous support in helping me to get my manuscript published. His encouragement and advice have been instrumental in getting over the last hurdles of this endeavor, and I am in his debt.

One would think that writing a book would be the most difficult part of the exercise, but for me, the hard part was finding the right publisher. I have been fortunate to have connected with Kumarian Press and Jim Lance, its editor and associate publisher. Jim has shepherded me through the publishing process as painlessly as possible, and I am most grateful for all his help.

Finally, these acknowledgments would not be complete without a few words for my lovely wife, Ellen. Putting up with me all these years has not been easy, and her patience and understanding during the preparation of this book are acknowledged and appreciated. Where would I be without you?

. . . AND AN APOLOGY

The quality of the documents reprinted in this book is very poor. They have been included nevertheless to provide a few visual examples of the kinds of fraud committed on World Bank–funded projects.

Acronyms

ACFIU	Anti-Corruption and Fraud Investigation Unit
ADT	average daily traffic
AFR	Africa Region (Operations Group)
AFT	Africa Region Technical Department
AFTED	AFT, Education Division
AFTHR	AFT, Human Resources Division
AFTPN	AFT, Population, Health, and Nutrition Division
ARPP	Annual Review of the Project Portfolio
ASP	agriculture services project
CAS	country assistance strategy
CD	country department
CFIU	Corruption and Fraud Investigation Unit
CY	calendar year
DANIDA	Danish International Development Agency
DFR	Department of Feeder Roads (Ghana)
DOSA	Department of State for Agriculture (The Gambia)
EAP	East Africa Projects (regional group)
ECN	Electricity Corporation of Nigeria
EDI	Economic Development Institute
ERR	Economic Rate of Return
FY	fiscal year

IADIU	Internal Audit Department Investigation Unit
IBRD	International Bank for Reconstruction and Development
ICB	international competitive bidding
IDA	International Development Association
ILO	International Labour Organization
INT	Department of Institutional Integrity
INTIU	Department of Institutional Integrity Investigation Unit
LC	letter of credit
LCB	local competitive bidding
LIB	limited international bidding
MTR	midterm review
NBTE	National Board for Technical Education (Nigeria)
NCB	national competitive bidding
NDA	Niger Dams Authority (Nigeria)
NEPA	National Electric Power Authority (Nigeria)
NIB	Nigeria International Bank
NUC	National Universities Commission (Nigeria)
ODA	Overseas Development Administration (United Kingdom)
OED	Operations Evaluation Department
OPEC	Organization of Petroleum Exporting Countries
OPS	Operations Policy and Strategy Group
PAFA	public administration financial audit
PAR	project audit report
PCR	project completion report
PIU	project implementation unit

PMU	project monitoring unit
PPF	project preparation facility
PREM	Poverty Reduction and Economic Management Network
PRT	project-related training
SA	special account
SAC	structural adjustment credit
SAL	structural adjustment loan
SAR	staff appraisal report
SOE	statement of expenditures
STD	sexually transmitted disease
TD	technical department
TI	Transparency International
USAID	United States Agency for International Development
VPD	vehicles per day

Introduction
· · · · · · ·

Broken Promises
and the Gods of Lending

Of the six billion people on our planet, it is the general consensus that roughly two billion live on less than a dollar a day and have no access to clean water, adequate sanitation, health services, or any of the other basic necessities for a decent and productive life. Of course, no one knows the exact number, but whatever it is, the human devastation caused by such widespread poverty is beyond comprehension as malnutrition, illiteracy, high infant mortality, health epidemics, and economic deprivation all take their toll on the lives of those who were unfortunately born in the "wrong" part of the world. But the unfortunates should not despair, for help is on the way as those of us from the "right" part of the world reach out to lead them to a better life. That is our mission, and that is our promise.

Gaining independence from the colonial powers in the 1960s, the newly formed nations of the Third World faced enormous challenges as they sought to become integrated into the world economy. Ruled by dysfunctional governments, plagued by corruption, denied basic public services, and lacking adequate infrastructure, the people of these countries have long suffered in poverty with little hope of improving their lives. Against this background, and with the best of intentions, international efforts to redress this condition have been made by the affluent nations of the West. Yet despite enormous inputs costing hundreds of billions of dollars, these efforts have achieved little in alleviating poverty and the deplorable conditions under which much of the world's population lives. While millions of innocent souls struggle to survive, the corrupt elites who govern them live in obscene luxury.

But what is it that prevents the poor from receiving the benefits of economic development? What is it that keeps them mired in poverty? Although these third-world nations began independence lacking a critical mass of human and financial resources, they have had more than four decades of assistance from the West. Hundreds of thousands of international experts have provided assistance in vain attempts to improve their standards of living. Hundreds of thousands of local government officials have been trained in public-sector administration at internationally renowned universities. Billions of dollars have been provided to improve national infrastructures, foster private enterprise, build schools and hospitals, develop agriculture, protect the environment, and all the other things that form the basis of a well-governed society.

Yet for the most part, it has all been for naught. White-elephant projects can be found everywhere, buildings are empty and crumbling, roads are not maintained, hospitals are built without medical supplies, schools are built without books, and no government service will be provided unless a bribe is paid. Against this reality, there appears to be little interest in the West to admit to, much less correct, the development failures of the past. Promises of progress and the alleviation of poverty have been repeatedly broken, while the business of lending money to corrupt and dysfunctional governments continues unabated.

And so, we are left with some burning questions. Why, after four decades, haven't the industrial nations been able to keep their promise to the poor? Why, with their enormous intellectual, technical, and financial capacity, haven't they been able to bring about the economic development that they have so loudly proclaimed? High on the list of unfulfilled promises are the complicated and symbiotic relationships between the donor institutions of the West and the recipient governments of the Third World. What began as a noble attempt to bring economic development to the poor soon became a mating dance in which the dancers' agendas took precedence over the needs of the poor. Leading the dance are the World Bank and the regional multilateral banks (MLBs) such as the African Development Bank, the Asian Development Bank, the Inter-American Development Bank, and their dance partners, the third-world governments to whom they lend money. But institutions are really the personification of the individuals who manage them, and this is where good intentions take a detour.

Having loaned more than half a trillion dollars for economic development over the past five decades, the World Bank is considered the leading institution in its field. With a staff of more than eleven thousand persons, it provides an average of $20 billion each year in development loans to its borrowers. Overseen by its shareholders through a board of directors, the Bank's primary mission has been to "alleviate poverty" in the borrower countries. But as the Bank has grown over the years, it has become ever more bureaucratic, ever more inwardly focused on the self-serving agendas of its management, and ever more averse to criticism. Fostering a culture of lending without regard to the risks of failure, the Bank's management has built a wall of misinformation around its lending operations, creating the illusion that all is well in the world of development, when it is not.

Thus, while responsible for the Bank's actions in principle, in practice, management has considerable freedom to do as it pleases and report as it sees fit. Those in Bank management are the gods of lending, and they can do no wrong. They have created the myth that they are at the "cutting edge" of development, while they hide the appalling number of failures within the Bank's portfolio—failures that enrich the governing elites of the Third World while creating mountains of debt that cannot be repaid. Singing their own praises, they lead the Bank ever further from its primary mission, ignoring their professional and fiduciary obligations as they advance their individual careers, while the people they have promised to help continue to live in poverty.

But the Bank is not dancing alone, nor can it take all the blame for the appalling conditions in the underdeveloped countries. In fairness, the blame must be shared equally, if not more so, with its dancing partners, the Bank's borrowers. And as the Bank is the personification of its management, so the governments of the Third World are the personification of their public officials. With personal agendas that are contrary to the best interests of the governed, these officials are, with rare exception, motivated by a single overriding objective: to keep their positions of power and authority for as long as possible so that they may enrich themselves and their associates with the spoils of office.

It is this single truth that exposes the hypocrisy of the whole business: the Bank pretends it is lending for noble purposes, while the borrowers pretend they will put the money to good use. This relationship serves both parties well, as Bank staff further their careers and government officials fill their personal bank accounts. How else can we explain the decades of assistance without any significant improvement in the lives of the poor? How else can we explain the billions loaned for improving governance with little to show for it? How else can we explain the billions loaned for health care and education that are never delivered, or are delivered so poorly as to be irrelevant? Why, for example, are donor funds given to dysfunctional government institutions that totally consume a nation's resources while providing nothing in return? Why are donor funds placed in the hands of officials with a history of looting national treasuries? How could the Bank and the other donor institutions have so carelessly given their shareholders' money to the corrupt regimes of Marcos, Suharto, Mobutu, and Abacha, to name just a few? How could they not know they were lending to thieves? Do they really believe that their dance partners are honestly committed to using that money to help the poor? Do they really care?

By the mid-1990s the Bank and the rest of the donor community could no longer ignore the existence of corruption and its impact on the poor. After decades of profligate lending in which billions of dollars were stolen by corrupt government elites, it was obvious that the Bank's dancing partners had not exactly been models of integrity. Faced with increasing public pressure, the Bank, for the first time in its history, attempted to deal with the corruption issue. Long overdue, this has been a good thing, although to date it has not been very effective in stopping the embezzlement of funds from its lending operations. Initially focused on the investigation and exposure of fraud committed against Bank projects and the debarment of firms dealing with corrupt government officials, management soon realized that such exposure created serious credibility problems for the Bank and provided damaging information that could be used by its critics. Aware that they could not put the genie back in the bottle, management officials shifted the Bank's focus from exposing corruption to studying it, writing about it, and talking about it. And this has worked well, for it has allowed them to continue to claim leadership in the fight against corruption while permitting them to continue lending to corrupt governments.

And so, while the rhetoric about the evils of corruption remains strong, corruption is alive and well. Government officials and their accomplices continue to plunder untold billions of dollars each year with impunity, while the Bank and the other donor institutions nibble at the edges pretending they are making a difference. The poor continue to live in abject poverty, while their leaders continue to live in luxury. But if we are to keep our promise to the poor, we must insist upon a different course of action. The individuals who manage the Bank and the donor community in general must honor their fiduciary responsibilities and ensure that the money provided for economic development is used to bring direct benefits to the poor. They need to lend less and supervise more. They need to study less and act more. They need to report honestly and completely about the failures in their lending programs. They need to use the full power of their institutions to press governments to investigate, prosecute, and punish corrupt officials, and to recover stolen funds and assets wherever possible, as would be done with any other criminals. The gods of lending can do no less if we are to keep our promise to the poor souls who were unfortunate enough to have been born in the wrong part of the world.

And this is where my story begins. In my sixteen years with the Bank, I would come to observe the true essence of the development agenda and the forces that sustain it. I would learn that nothing is black or white in the development business, and, to use an old saying, that the road to hell is paved with good intentions. Perhaps sadly, and most important, I would observe that the poor souls struggling to survive in the Third World have been, and are being, ill served by the alleged good intentions of the Bank and the donor community in general. That there are good, honest, hardworking, and dedicated individuals within the Bank is without question. That the Bank has within it an entrenched bureaucracy with its own agenda is also without question. Combine these conflicting factors with the pervasive corruption that exists within third-world governments and it is easy to see why the social and economic conditions in many of these countries are worse today than they were several decades ago.

My tenure with the Bank began in November 1983 and ended with my retirement in December 1995. Although initially hired to advise on training components within Bank-funded projects in the Africa Region, this function broadened into areas of public-sector management, and from that to issues of corruption. For it had, over the years, become quite obvious to me that all efforts at training, capacity building, and public-sector management were rendered totally useless in the corrupt environments within which we were working, and that many on both sides of the development-aid equation were feeding at the trough with little concern for genuine and long-lasting results. I was then and am still now convinced that billions of dollars of aid monies have been and are being diverted into private pockets each year, with little if any effort made to apprehend and prosecute the corrupt individuals in question, or, more important, to recover the funds stolen from Bank lending operations.

Despite the efforts of some concerned Bank staff to bring corruption issues to the forefront of the Bank's agenda, corruption continued to be a taboo subject until the arrival of James Wolfensohn, who served as president from 1995 through 2005. Within a short time after his arrival, the Bank began to investigate allegations of corrupt activities within its lending portfolio, and I returned from May 1998 through February 2002 to participate in the creation and operation of an Investigation Unit to deal with these issues.

What I describe in the chapters that follow are my observations of the management of the Bank's lending operations and the events leading up to the creation of the Investigation Unit. But that is only part of my motivation for writing this book, for the real issue is about the Bank's willingness and ability to return to its basic mission: to provide financial and technical assistance to those governments genuinely committed to improving the welfare of their citizens.

The World Bank has enormous potential for alleviating poverty and suffering in the underdeveloped nations of the Third World. I believe that over the past several decades it has needlessly squandered this potential due to a plethora of human, political, and bureaucratic factors that have played into the hands of corrupt individuals at the receiving end of the Bank's lending program. While the Bank has since taken some steps to address these issues, I believe it has yet to use the full power of its intellectual, political, and financial capacity to address the primary causes of its failure to bring substantive benefits to the average man, woman, and child on the African continent, and to the rest of the Third World as well.

The Bank has become a bloated bureaucracy with too many people doing too many things that have no bearing on its mission. It has become a vehicle whereby funds are loaned to third-world countries only to be returned to the donor community in the form of civil works contracts, equipment orders, and consulting assignments that seldom if ever translate into cost-effective benefits for the poor. And finally, it has become a cash cow for third-world politicians and public officials who manipulate the system for their own enrichment. In the end, the money is gone and nothing is left but corrupt and dysfunctional public institutions, decaying infrastructure, huge debts, and the dashed hopes of the indigenous populations.

In the pages that follow I aim to present my observations from the trenches of World Bank lending operations in Africa that have led me to these conclusions, and what I perceive to be the only way in which the Bank can return to its primary mission. To return to that mission, the Bank must drastically reduce its obsession with needless intellectual activities. It must drastically reduce the scope of its lending programs, lending programs that are far too aggressive to be absorbed by many of its borrowers and that frequently ignore the corrupt nature of the representatives of those governments with whom it negotiates. This in turn will require considerable downsizing of its bureaucracy and a tremendous amount of soul searching among the Bank's shareholders and management. Whether the Bank, and the individuals who make it work, have the courage to do what needs to be done remains an open question.

1
· · · · · · ·

Managing for Mediocrity

It was not unusual to hear Bank managers talking about the need for excellence—an excellence that was never defined specifically, but the use of the word seemed to encourage everyone to believe that this was the obvious solution for Africa's problems. If only we could bring excellence to Africa! One of the favorite topics in this regard was the concept of creating "centers of excellence" in Africa. These centers would be the seedbeds of intellectual activity whereby research into sector specific issues, and above all, economic policies, would lead to a better Africa. The unspoken implication was that the Bank could transfer the "excellence" of its own institution to the governments of Africa, and we were all pleased with ourselves in this knowledge. During these discussions there were times when, considering the bureaucratic chaos that existed within the Bank and the dysfunctional governments that we were dealing with, I would suggest that perhaps it might be more realistic if we first concentrated on establishing "centers of mediocrity." Somehow, this idea never received the support that I felt it deserved.

The International Bank for Reconstruction and Development (IBRD) aims to reduce poverty in middle income and creditworthy poorer countries by promoting sustainable development, through loans, guarantees and nonlending—including analytical and advisory—services. The International Development Association (IDA), is the World Bank's concessional window. It provides long term loans at zero interest to the poorest of the developing countries. IDA helps build human capital, policies, institutions, and physical infrastructure that these countries urgently need to achieve faster, environmentally sustainable growth. IDA's goal is to reduce disparities across and within countries, especially in access to primary education, basic health, and water supply and sanitation, and to bring more people into the mainstream by raising their productivity.[1]

With these noble objectives some eleven thousand professional and support staff[2] are employed by the Bank to carry out a wide variety of activities devoted to economic development and the alleviation of poverty in the Third World. Most are dedicated, extremely intelligent, hard-working individuals who believe in what they are doing and who are committed to achieving the Bank's stated objectives. The Bank, however, as with so many institutions, has evolved its own bureaucracy, which somehow has reduced this dedication, intelligence and commitment to the lowest common denominator. How this has come about, given the caliber of the majority of its staff and management, is something I have never been able to comprehend, but there is no question that this bureaucracy has, over the years, greatly impeded the effectiveness of the institution. The wasted efforts, the repeated mistakes, and the endless reinvention of "new" approaches, the myriad new slogans, and the periodic reorganizations are evidence enough of the paralysis that has engulfed the Bank in the past several decades. To understand this better, one must first understand how the Bank's management culture affects day-to-day tasks of Bank staff as they go about the business of lending money to third-world governments.

IF IT DOESN'T WORK, REORGANIZE

We trained hard—but it seemed that every time we were beginning to form up into teams, we would be reorganized. I was to learn later in life that we would tend to meet any new situation by reorganizing, and a wonderful method it can be for creating the illusion of progress while producing confusion, inefficiency, and demoralization. (Gaius Petronius, c. AD 50)[3]

Like Gaius Petronius, it took several years before I realized that in a bureaucracy, the appearance that one is managing is much more important than the act itself—management by smoke and mirrors. No one has escaped the uncertainty and turmoil caused by the Bank's management with its never-ending reorganizations, re-wiring, re-engineering, modifying, adjusting, rethinking, and fine tuning of the institution. These activities would occur in cycles that I often felt were connected to either a full moon or the realization by management officials that development wasn't "working" and if they didn't do something, anything, they might be held accountable. While this may appear to be a trivial matter, it is my observation that each cycle of reorganization has, in some ways, reduced the effectiveness of the Bank in carrying out its mission. One thing Bank employees can be absolutely sure of is that they will be reorganized. Maybe not next month, or even next year, but it will happen, and usually just about the time all members of the team are working well together. Why, one has to ask, couldn't they decide how they wanted to manage the place and stay with it? At least for a few years, so we could focus on the real work at hand. Please bear with me as I try to explain.

When I arrived at the Bank in 1983, lending operations for Sub-Saharan Africa were divided administratively into two regions: East Africa Projects (EAP) and West Africa Projects (WAP). Within the regions there were two groups: the project departments, divided into sector divisions; and the country programs departments, divided into country programs divisions. Project sector divisions covered agriculture, transportation, industrial development, finance, education, energy, water supply, and urban development. These were basically staffed with sector specialists, such as engineers, agriculturalists, educators, public-health specialists, financial analysts, and economists, who were responsible for the design, appraisal, negotiation, and supervision of sector lending operations.

The country program divisions covered specific countries and were staffed for the most part with economists, who were responsible for determining the lending programs for each of the countries in their portfolio. In addition to these groups there were centralized departments for transportation, water, education, industry, and urban development that conducted research, developed Bank sector policies, and provided technical expertise for regional lending operations. By all accounts this arrangement seemed to work, and in my first few years at the Bank I sensed an esprit and commitment that was shared by all my colleagues. I might have attributed this feeling to the fact that I was new on the job, but my previous thirty-five years of work outside the Bank led me to believe that this was, to a large degree, genuine.

My job as a project-related training (PRT) specialist was with the West Africa Projects Education Division (WAPED), and I was primarily assigned to assist project officers in the other sector divisions with the design and supervision of training components in their projects. This was fortuitous in that it afforded me a wonderful opportunity to work in all the sectors and most of the countries in the West Africa portfolio. From 1983 through 1987 the organizational structure remained stable, with some minor exceptions.

PRT was no small matter, as we usually had between two hundred and three hundred projects ongoing at any given time. There were very few projects that did not include training components, often costing millions of dollars. These were based upon the Bank's assessment of the borrower's lack of sector management capacity, and it was not unusual in any given year to have several hundred million dollars invested in these training components within the region. Needless to say, there was never enough time or resources to supervise these activities properly, but we were not alone; this was a common problem for all operations staff. Despite the Bank's generous operating budget, management could never seem to find adequate resources for the unglamorous work that was needed to address the myriad implementation problems we faced in the field, and although this problem was discussed at meetings and addressed in numerous reports, I found that nothing of substance was ever done to correct it.

Then came the great reorganization of 1987, with its attending confusion and demoralization of staff and managers alike. I have no idea who planted the seeds for this exercise, but the justifications we were given by management were perplexing to me, as they seemed to imply that the Bank had not been doing its job as effectively as it should have been. Lame explanations about responding to the changing needs of borrowers and filling the gaps in our knowledge of economic development were cited to justify this major upheaval. And while other rationalizations abounded, it seemed more an act of desperation on the part of management to draw attention away from the failures in our portfolio and the Bank's increasingly aimless mission drift.

Obviously, there will always be room for improvement in the management of any organization, but given the caliber of the majority of the individuals working in the Bank, their dedication, and the thousands of accumulated staff years of experience in the business, I had great difficulty accepting the reasons for this bungled exercise that created repercussions for several years afterward. It was stated that the administrative costs for the reorganization would be $101 million, with a total staff reduction of 390 positions;[4] these most certainly could have been used more effectively for our work in the field, which, after all, had not really changed in substance. Procedures may have changed, job titles may have changed, and who reported to whom may have changed, but the mechanics and logistics of getting money out the door continued as before. We still processed loans and credits for the same kinds of projects and, ever increasingly, for structural adjustment operations—the latter being a convenient way to increase our lending with less effort and accountability.

Behind the published justifications for the reorganization, rumors circulated that the real motivation for the exercise was alleged complaints from the Bank's shareholders that the Bank had become top heavy and that the real purpose of the reorganization was to reduce higher-level positions in the institution. At the end of the day, only 320 staff were made redundant. At $101 million, this comes to about $352,000 per redundancy, a rather expensive exercise for such paltry results.

But equally important were the time and effort expended by management and staff to effect this seemingly unnecessary upheaval. It was a game of musical chairs on a grand scale, full of behind-the-scenes maneuvering as managers and staff alike sought the plum jobs—or tried to keep the ones they had. For despite all the meetings, assessments, internal studies, staff reviews, disbanding of old units and creation of new ones, "retreats" to get the new teams acquainted with the new order, office moves,[5] and who knows what else, most of us were still lending money and managing projects just as we had before. At the end of the exercise, the only apparent administrative difference was that we now had two fewer vice presidents and there were different faces with different titles in different offices. In the newly formed Africa Region (AFR) we now had three more directors than the combined former East and West Africa regions, a number that gradually grew from thirty-three to thirty-nine by 1992. My colleagues and I still had the same projects to work on, traveled to the same countries, worked with the same borrower staff, wrote the same reports, and went to the same meetings. And those in management were satisfied that they had fulfilled their roles as managers.

With much publicity, the Bank was now said to be more effective and "in tune" with the needs of its borrowers. Ready to alleviate poverty, ready to meet the needs of the poor, ready to meet the rapidly changing requirements of our borrowers, ready to champion environmentally sustainable development, ready to be a center of knowledge, ready to work hand in hand with the beneficiaries of our loans, ready to get results on the ground, etcetera, etcetera, etcetera. What had we been doing before that? And by what stroke of magic was all this going to change things for the better? Interestingly enough, as noted in the excerpts below, the *World Bank Annual Report 1988*[6] hinted at some of the problems created by the reorganization, but in usual Bank style, these hints did not provide adequate details or state the severity of the problems.

> The short-term, intangible costs of the reorganization were perhaps higher than had been expected, but, by the beginning of calendar 1988, the issues that remained to be resolved had been identified, and constructive responses had been formulated to capture the full benefits of the reorganization in terms of greater relevance, heightened agility, and enhanced efficiency of the institution.

Note that there was no mention of how much higher the costs were, what issues remained to be resolved, or the nature of the constructive responses that had been formulated.

> Momentum was restored to its major work programs after an initial slowdown caused by the staff selection process.

No mention of how much momentum was lost, or the length of the slowdown.

> While much has been achieved, some transitional problems remain, and some further organizational adjustments may be necessary. Working relationships between some units have not yet been developed to their full potential.

What transitional problems remain, and what organizational adjustments are now necessary? Which units are not working to their full potential? Watch out! Here comes some more reorganizing.

These extracts are typical of the manner in which management decisions and actions were explained to both internal and external audiences. Problems, shortcomings, and failures were always described in such vague ways that the reader would never know exactly what went wrong, who was responsible, or how it was going to be corrected. I often found it amusing that when it came to explaining things, the Bank's management could dissect a problem a thousand ways, presenting the most minute and trivial details, as long as the problem was associated with our borrowers or some external economic policy issue. When the problem was associated with the Bank itself, the explanations suddenly became vague and so generalized that one could barely recognize there was a problem at all. And, of course, there was always an assurance at the end of the explanation that "we have formed a committee, or team, or task force, to study the problem" or "we are implementing measures to deal with the problem." Smoke and mirrors elevated to an art form.

I had never before worked in such a huge bureaucracy, much less an international one, so it took longer than it might have otherwise to adjust to an environment where obfuscation and hypocrisy seemed to be the primary modus operandi. Nothing was ever what it seemed to be, with myriad personal, unit, and regional agendas that never appeared to coalesce into a common force to achieve the Bank's stated mission. There was a lot of movement and activity, but we always seemed to come back to where we had started. I gradually became more and more disillusioned with the failure of the institution to deal seriously with the real issues facing our stated mission in Africa. The approach to management was alien to what I had experienced in my years prior to the Bank, when I had, at different times, worked in the manufacturing, construction, and petrochemical industries, with the latter on overseas projects—totally different environments where real results, not talk, were the primary objective. Where we focused on addressing problems directly and quickly without endless meetings, discussions, and studies ad nauseam. Where, when something didn't work, we didn't sit around wringing our hands trying to come up with ways to avoid the issue. Where, when things went wrong, people got fired, not transferred or promoted. Identify the problem and fix it, or clean out your desk!

One final observation regarding the attempts by management to show that they had streamlined the Bank. It is interesting to note that until 1986 the Bank in its annual reports had always reported total staff numbers; in 1986 there were 6,002 staff members. Since 1987, however, the Bank has not reported total staff levels in its annual reports, and it is not clear that it has presented these figures in any other public documents. In 2001 staffing levels were approximately 11,370,[7] representing a 90 percent increase over fifteen years. It also appears that the number of vice presidents rose from twenty-one in 1986 to twenty-seven in 2001, an increase of 28 percent, while the number of directors grew from fifty-two to over 150,[8] an increase of 188 percent. Until 1994 the annual reports included the number of directors; in 1994 there were sixty.

While pre-1987 annual reports contained a section entitled "Bank Management and Staff,"[9] which included a breakdown of staffing numbers and composition, and pre-1994 annual reports contained information about the numbers of directors, it is difficult for the outside observer to get any sense of the growth of the bureaucracy over the succeeding years. Considering the Bank's extensive efforts to encourage downsizing of the bloated government bureaucracies in the Third World, it is perhaps understandable that management would not wish to publicize its own bloated condition. More interesting is the fact that while staff levels have doubled over the past two decades, lending levels have remained more or less constant. This translates to roughly twice as many staff to move the same amount of money. How is that for an example of management efficiency?

With the 1987 reorganization, the East and West Africa regions were combined into the AFR, with six country departments (CDs) and a Technical Department (TD) that were supposed to replace the formerly centralized sector departments. Under this arrangement, country programs and project operations were combined within sector-based divisions, the only difference being, as far as I could see, that the project officers, now called task managers, didn't have to walk to another part of the building to meet with the programs people. For those of us working in the field, there was nothing different in the substance of our work. That doesn't mean, however, that we didn't have a different set of hoops to jump through in order to satisfy the bureaucracy.

I was relocated into the Education Division in the newly formed Technical Department (AFTED) and remained there until 1992, when we went through a reorganization of the TD. AFTED was disbanded and a new division (AFTHR, for Human Resources) was created that joined education with the AFT, Population, Health, and Nutrition Division (formerly AFTPN). Musical chairs and uncertainty again as staff sought to protect their careers. In 1994 there were more changes. We went from six CDs to five, and within the TD I was transferred to AFTCB (for Capacity Building), which had been created in 1993 from the former AFTIM (for Institutional Development and Management), which in 1992 had been created from the former AFTPS (for Public Sector Management). This, I came to realize, was what the Bank meant when it talked about change!

Throughout all these organizational moves my basic work with PRT never changed, although by the early 1990s I had become more and more concerned about public sector management and corruption issues that, to me, appeared to be at the heart of our failures in Africa. After all, it was so obvious, who could miss it? We had funded training for thousands of African civil servants, and they had more degrees than many of our own staff, yet after several decades governance on the continent was as dysfunctional as ever. How was training going to solve these problems when our borrowers had other agendas? Is this what management is all about? Is this how we define excellence?

NOTES

1. The World Bank's website, accessed April 2003.

2. Approximate staff strength as of 2001, taken from the Bank's directory. This number has grown steadily; it was roughly fifty-six hundred when I joined the Bank in 1983.

3. I never knew if this was actually written by a first-century Roman or was just another example of office humor. It is, however, an accurate description of the circumstances we continually faced at the Bank, and I kept it pinned on my office wall for many years.

4. *World Bank Annual Report 1987*, p. 25.

5. In my sixteen years at the Bank I occupied eleven offices, obliging me to pack and unpack my files every eighteen months on average. It was not unusual for each move to consume at least two weeks of my time. Add this to the cost of moving furniture, phone and computer relocations, and other support services, and one can readily imagine the impact such moves had on our budget. A budget, I might add, that never seemed to be sufficient for effective supervision of our lending operations.

6. See *World Bank Annual Report 1988*, pp. 45, 46.

7. Taken from the Bank's 2001 directory.

8. Ibid.

9. See the *World Bank Annual Report 1986*, p. 32.9

2

. . . .

The Economist Managers

While sorting through some documents back in the early 1990s, I came across the following bit of wisdom, spelling mistakes and all, that had been inadvertently left behind by one of our summer interns who had been working on a paper for a Ph.D. degree in economics:

> The problem of inteligent action maybe stated as follows: Given an agent whose action repetoire is A:{a1...an}, whose current perceptual input ranges over the possible observable properties of the world W:{p1...pj}, and whose goal is to bring about a world state satisfying G:{g1...gk}, determine what to do next. The problem is challenging because typically it will take a sequence of actions to bring about G, so it is not obvious what action to perform first.

I confess that I haven't a clue what he was talking about. But then again, I must confess that there were numerous occasions when I didn't have a clue as to what some of my economist colleagues were talking about either when it came to economic development or anything else connected with our work.

Now I'm really going to get into trouble with many of my good friends who are economists and for whom I have tremendous respect both personally and professionally—individuals who are able to combine the practical with the theoretical, who understand what is possible and what is not possible, and who, when there is a job to be done, try to cut through the crap to find workable solutions. But it is obvious to me that when you staff an institution with a disproportionate number of individuals coming from one discipline, you run the risk of having a one-dimensional institution. In the case of the Bank, I've come to believe that the disconnect between the intellectual fantasy world in which too many of the Bank's economists live and the real world of Africa has largely contributed to the Bank's failures there.

Now this is no small matter, as I've become convinced that much of the Bank's aimless mission drift in Africa, and the rest of the world, has been due to its reliance on the leadership of a cadre of bureaucratic and academically oriented economists who have learned the rules of career progression and have risen accordingly in the system. Not because they have accomplished great things, but because they have played the game well in a system created by themselves.

Trust me, I do not mean that all the Bank's managers fit this mold, but there is most certainly a critical mass of those that do, and they have caused great harm to the Bank's mission. Let's face it, economic development for Africa is not rocket science. What the African man or woman on the street wants are the basic essentials that we all want: adequate food, shelter, sanitation, health care, education for their kids, and a chance to live their lives without being oppressed by their own governments. It is obvious to me that neither the Bank nor the other donors providing aid to Africa have been able to get African governments and power brokers to accomplish these basic objectives in real terms over the past forty years. Not because of the complexities of the task, but because the African leadership had other agendas and were in no way committed to doing anything to benefit the masses at the expense of their own enrichment. By avoiding the reality of African politics, power, and corruption, the Bank's economist managers have done a great disservice to Africa and to the Bank.

How have I come to these conclusions? I'm sure my observations will be challenged from certain quarters with all kinds of statistics, data, and excuses, but I believe it can be demonstrated that the economist managers of the Bank go to great lengths to cloud the issue when it comes to telling the world what the Bank has done, or is doing. For example, a February 1993 report[1] discusses the Bank's role in Africa as follows:

The overriding mission of the World Bank is to help countries alleviate poverty, and its agenda for Africa's development aims first and foremost to assist African governments improve the quality of life for the majority of Africans who live in abject poverty.

A noble mission statement, but the key phrase here is "to assist African governments," for that is where the whole business takes a detour. It would all make sense *if* the African elites who run their governments were sincerely interested in improving the quality of life for the majority of Africans. But this is the rare exception rather than the rule, and the truth is that the Bank has poured billions into the hands, or should I say pockets, of government functionaries who have shown little interest in improving the quality of life for anyone except themselves and those in their immediate circles. The report continues:

Almost everything the Bank does in Africa is related to poverty. The Bank's lending in structural and sectoral adjustment serves to promote economic growth—with growth, everyone benefits. But growth alone is not sufficient to reduce poverty. The pattern of growth is as important as the rate of growth. The Bank's strategy is to encourage efficient, labor-intensive growth which provides employment and income for the poor. The Bank's small-holder focus in African agriculture, for example, serves to empower the rural poor who comprise the majority of Africa's citizens. The promotion of an enabling policy environment, technology creation and transfer, rural infrastructure, and natural resource management has a decisive impact on the performance of the rural poor. The Bank also invests directly in people: it helps provide social services, especially primary education, basic health, family planning, and nutrition, to improve living conditions and to increase the capacity of the poor to respond to income opportunities arising from economic growth. Protecting the environment is another important element in the Bank's poverty-reduction strategy.

Even with all these efforts, it will take longer for some of Africa's poor to participate in growth and social investments, and some will not participate at all. Therefore, an important part of the Bank's agenda includes targeting particularly vulnerable groups, especially women who play a critical role in African development.

How could one possibly find fault with these wonderful platitudes? But do they tell us anything of substance? Are we really helping countries alleviate poverty? Sounds great, except that after more than four decades we really haven't made a dent in that problem, and as I will discuss at greater length later, the only poverty we have alleviated has been that of those in power who have plundered Bank-funded projects along with their national treasuries and anything else they could get their hands on.

In real terms, African men or women in the street have less today than they did decades ago, while African civil servants and politicians have filled their personal bank accounts with untold billions. And how is this for being disingenuous? "Almost everything the Bank does is related to poverty." The Bank spends millions studying poverty, talking about poverty, holding conferences about poverty, writing reports about poverty, compiling statistics about poverty, creating slogans about poverty, interviewing those living in poverty, interviewing those who have something to say about poverty, and discussing poverty with the corrupt civil servants and politicians who are the primary cause of poverty among the masses. So yes, I guess we could say that everything the Bank does is related to poverty, everything, that is, except to alleviate it among the poor. Certainly, the results of all that effort are nothing to brag about: the money has disappeared with very little to show for it, and the continent is deeper in debt than it was before.

Now in fairness to the Bank, its staff, and its managers, in many cases this condition has been exacerbated by forces either partially or totally outside of their control. Nonetheless, the Bank's management must admit that the many billions of dollars loaned or granted to African governments over the years have never reached the man or woman in the street. The same report also has this to say:

> Finally, and most significant, economic and political mismanagement in most African countries has led to inefficiency, low productivity, and limited investment in human capital and institutions. The results are weak or dysfunctional institutions, a paucity of skilled and trained manpower, and economic growth that has barely kept ahead of population growth. (p. 2)

A little further on it states:

> Lending to Sub-Saharan Africa has doubled over the last four
> years to roughly $4 billion in 1992. . . . Furthermore, the Bank
> has however unintentionally, assumed the dominant intel-
> lectual role on African economic issues . . . [and] . . . it is
> involved in 90 percent of the analytical research on Africa.
> (p. 2)

What are we to make of all this? On the one hand, the report is
telling us what a wonderful job the Bank is doing fighting poverty in Africa. On the other hand, it is telling us that it has doubled
its lending over four years to $4 billion to governments that are,
by its own accounts, dysfunctional, inefficient, mismanaged, and,
one must assume, otherwise incapable of implementing the economic policies that the Bank, in its "dominant intellectual role,"
has put forth. Does this mean that the more dysfunctional a government is, the more money it gets?[2] And, of course, nowhere in
this document do we find any mention of the rampant corruption throughout the region, which has permeated every single
government institution and has been the root cause of Africa's
plight.

In my opinion, with the exception of natural calamities, much
of Africa's present condition—the civil wars, the ethnic conflicts,
the decaying infrastructure, and the lack of basic services—can
be traced to the wholesale looting of national treasuries. Or, in
the case of the civil wars and ethnic conflicts, who gets to be in
charge of the wholesale looting. But this, of course, was a taboo
subject at the Bank and, with the exception of some intellectual
papers written about the subject,[3] was never seriously dealt with
by management. This critical issue certainly did not affect the
level or substance of the Bank's lending program, which continued as if corruption did not exist. It was not until the appointment of James Wolfensohn as president in 1995 that the corruption
factor became mainstreamed at the Bank, and even then there
were, and continue to be, those in the bureaucracy who would prefer to return to the old ways of "see no evil, hear no evil, speak no
evil."

Finally, again from Jaycox's report, we have an example of the
Bank's "modesty" in the following self-congratulatory statement:

Overall, the Bank can claim a number of achievements in promoting economic reform in Sub-Saharan Africa. It has helped in creating a group of economic managers on the continent who are knowledgeable and confident about what has gone wrong and what is required to fix it. It has encouraged broad-based economic growth. (p. 8)

Really? Now, while "policy reform" is something very dear to the hearts of the Bank's economist managers, I believe their claim of achievements can be challenged. It has been my experience that we often required our borrowers to accept policy reforms and other economic measures in order to get the Bank's approval for a particular loan or credit. The borrowers would accept our conditions during negotiations and would sign the loan or credit agreement accordingly. We would then say that the borrower was implementing policy reforms and take due credit for it. Whether these reforms were the right thing or not under the circumstances, I cannot say, but I do know that in too many cases the borrowers had no intention whatsoever of carrying out the policy reforms and would effectively stonewall the whole business after the loan or credit was approved.

Once the loan or credit was approved and "under implementation," the Bank's task managers would report on the status of the policy reforms, along with other aspects of the project. More often than not, these reports would cite delays, reversals of policies, changes in local administration, continuing dialogue, lack of capacity, and numerous other reasons to explain why the policies, whatever they were, were not being implemented. Depending upon the integrity of the task managers, or the pressure they were under from management, these issues might, or might not, be assigned the necessary level of importance in evaluating the overall project. At the end of the day, the project would be completed, that is to say, the funds would have been disbursed, but the conditions the project was meant to resolve were still present—and in some cases were worse than before.

As for "creating a group of economic managers on the continent," I cannot resist a few comments of my own. It is here that we come back to my previous observation about the institution being one dimensional. As a non-economist at the Bank, I was periodically reminded by my superiors of my obvious inability to

grasp the full essence of economic development and all the nu-
ances of the economic process. They were probably right, as I was,
after all, just a technical specialist, and while specialists could only
advise on their specialty, economists could advise on anything they
damn well pleased because they were economists and had the inside track on everything. They were the economic managers, and
their solution to the world's problems was to produce more economic managers. And so the Bank would fund all sorts of training
(Ph.D. degrees in economics being one of the more popular approaches), conferences, seminars, workshops, and whatever, to that
end. The economists at the Bank were in essence cloning themselves, and they seemed to be quite pleased with the whole business.

To further that end, funds were often included in projects to
create or strengthen ministries of economic planning, departments
of economic planning, and economic planning units in every other
ministry in government. Worse, entire projects were dedicated to
that purpose.[4] Not that I have anything against planning, but to
plan for things that you obviously can't implement is, to me, the
tail wagging the dog. We had plans at the Bank, the borrowers
had plans, there were plans for plans, there were discussions about
the plans, there were meetings about the plans, there were reports
written about the plans, yet for the most part, when completed,
those plans just sat in file cabinets or were stacked on shelves,
never to be touched again. One could be sure of one thing though:
sooner or later some economist manager would realize that we
"needed a plan," and the process would repeat itself. And while I
have observed that the economist managers love to plan, I've also
observed that they seldom have any genuine interest in seeing
things through beyond that point. One of the reasons for this lack
of interest, I believe, is a subconscious fear that once beyond the
planning stage, their plans might prove to have been made in error, and that would expose the planners to criticism. And that
would be intolerable.

Beyond the Bank's infatuation with economic planning, I have
always wondered what "economic management" is anyway. Can
anyone really and truly manage the economy? Isn't this what
the Soviet Union tried, and failed, to do? Until I came to the Bank,
I had never heard of education economists, agriculture economists, highway economists, social economists, and all of the other

economist titles that abound at the Bank. Now, I can understand that there could be a need for expertise in these specialized areas of economics, but in such overwhelming numbers? Since when can a bunch of intellectuals really manage an economy? Hard as they may try, and as much as they may think they do, the influence of economists on the economic decisions and actions of the general population is, I believe, greatly overrated. Please don't misunderstand me here. The field of economics most definitely has its place in the scheme of things, but the extent to which it has become a cult at the Bank has perverted the Bank's role in the development process.

NO PROBLEM

I recall a regional management meeting in 1995 during which we were reviewing "problem projects" in our lending portfolio for Africa. We had at the time over five hundred ongoing projects in an $11 billion portfolio[5] that required supervision by Bank staff to ensure that implementation was on track, loan agreement conditions were being met, and that project objectives would be achieved. As my PRT work had morphed into institutional development and public-sector management, and I had been doing skills-mix analyses for many of our borrower institutions, I decided, prior to our meeting, to examine the skills mix of our regional staff to see if this might have any correlation to our portfolio problems. Lo and behold, it seems that we had roughly 300 economists of various persuasions, 10 financial analysts, 10 public-administration specialists, and roughly 150 technical specialists (engineers, architects, educators, health services specialists, and so forth).

I raised this matter at the meeting and inquired how we could effectively handle the financial and institutional management issues, which were our major problem areas, with only ten financial and ten public-administration specialists on our staff. I also asked what project-management expertise three hundred economists were adding to our ability to supervise our portfolio adequately. In fact, I specifically recall asking what we needed 300 economists for in the first place. After all, hadn't we studied, analyzed, scrutinized, hypothesized, and theorized all there is to know about

African economies over the past forty years? What more could our economists possibly do that they hadn't already done? What great unknown wisdom remained to be discovered about Africa? My queries were met with a period of silence, and then our regional vice president replied that he "hadn't realized" we had that many economists in the region. He said nothing more. My other questions went unanswered, perhaps because they were inappropriate in the first place—or perhaps because there was no answer. Needless to say, the ratio of economists to financial and public management specialists did not change, nor did the status of our portfolio.

The passages quoted above from the 1993 report are not exceptions to the style and substance of the Bank's published pronouncements, and I could cite numerous other Bank documents that similarly mislead and obfuscate the reality of the Bank's failures in Africa and other parts of the world. For the most part, and despite the intensity with which the Bank's economic managers immerse themselves in these esoteric exercises, it is difficult to find any evidence by which one could reasonably judge whether, in fact, the Bank has accomplished anything at all. Nowhere, prior to 1995 and the beginning of the Wolfensohn era, could one find a serious discussion of the total lack of concern by African politicians and government bureaucrats for the common good, or most important, of the cancer of corruption that has perverted economic development everywhere.

THE TRUTH BE TOLD

But while dishonest and self-congratulatory statements about the Bank's successes were being presented to the public, what was being said internally? Were there, within the Bank, individuals who saw the hypocrisy between the image we were projecting to the outside world and the reality of our failed mission? For me, it was often puzzling to note the degree of honesty that could sometimes be found within the institution as shown by the following excerpts from an internal memo, dated March 26, 1993, reporting on statements made by Lewis Preston, the Bank's president at the time, at a senior management retreat held that March:

The President spoke first and criticized the Bank for being elitist, resistant to change, reluctant to listen to criticism and reluctant to acknowledge its mistakes. . . . He also stressed that consensus was all too often used as a substitute for leadership . . . and the perceived failure of the Bank to trigger self-sustaining development in Africa.

The memo went on to describe inconsistencies in the management of the institution of which four were most revealing about the management culture:

What we say is often what is politically correct but not what we really feel or do. . . . Bank managers are disinclined to manage (the intellectual side is more fun). . . . Bank managers prefer to work on new initiatives rather than do necessary maintenance and follow-up. . . . There is no accountability for failure.

In terms of the issues addressed here, nothing could be closer to the truth. Yet business went on as usual. This was consistent with all I had experienced in previous years, and what I would experience in succeeding years. Internally, at least, senior management would periodically experience moments of truth and reveal what most of us already knew. The bureaucracy would acknowledge reality, new slogans would be invented, new acronyms created, reports would be written to support the new wisdom, and, within a year or two, it would all be forgotten as a new cycle of institutional reinvention would begin. As for Mr. Preston's comments, it remains to be seen whether the Bank has shed its image of being elitist, resistant to change, and reluctant to listen to criticism or to acknowledge its mistakes.

Truth could also emerge at lower levels within the bureaucracy, as witnessed by the following paragraph on governance written in an internal draft "Country Strategy Note" for Nigeria dated February 2, 1994:

The public sector in Nigeria lacks transparency and accountability. Pervasive corruption robs the economy of resources that otherwise might be used for poverty reduction, adds to the cost of doing business in Nigeria, and undermines confidence in the public sector—even as its beneficiaries swell the ranks of the constituency for bad economic policies. Deficiencies in governance manifest themselves in a number of ways. First, although the oil sector has been governed by pragmatic policies that have protected Nigeria's position as a low cost/high quality oil producer, oil revenues typically cannot be accounted for. The failure to establish full control over the government's statutory oil revenues, particularly transfer payments from NNPC [Nigeria National Petroleum Corporation], has obstructed proper fiscal management. Second, control mechanisms are ineffective in halting unauthorized extra-budgetary spending for political and non-productive programs. Third, the public investment program is biased towards large projects with opportunities for kick-backs to civil servants from contractors. Fourth, the quality of public service delivery, including utility and infrastructure services is appalling, undermining Nigeria's competitiveness. (p. 6, para. 18)

Elsewhere in this document was the interesting observation that "Nigeria needs to make a fundamental shift from policies and institutional arrangements that promote opportunities for rent-seeking behavior by vested interests" (p. 5, para. 15).

In the specific case of Nigeria, it was around this time that management was beginning to realize that there was no longer any way to escape the realities of the corrupt state of affairs within the country. While the above statements indicate the growing awareness that things were not going well with the Bank's Nigeria portfolio and presaged a dramatic reduction in Bank assistance, this document, like others addressing the subject, said nothing about the Bank's support, through its lending program, to those in power during the previous decades—support that allowed the Nigerian dictators, politicians, and civil servants to pursue their corrupt agendas. For the Bank had, in the previous three decades up to 1994, loaned Nigeria approximately $7.1 billion, of which approximately $4.6 billion had been loaned between 1984 and 1994, the period of the most rampant corruption and governmental dysfunction in Nigeria's history.[6]

And so, here we have this admission that all was not well in Nigeria, yet one can find no admission that perhaps the Bank shares some culpability in the matter. It was not, after all, a condition that had appeared overnight. The problem should have been obvious to anyone with an IQ over fifty who spent more than a few days in the country, yet the Bank's management had been content to continue lending as if their Nigerian counterparts were seriously interested in bettering the lives of all Nigerians. The Bank's economic managers had, in their great wisdom, abandoned all pretenses of fiduciary responsibility as they shoveled the money out the door and into the pockets of corrupt Nigerian officials year after year.

At the operational level, one could also find numerous examples of Bank staff who were not averse to honest reporting of the abysmal condition of the region's lending portfolio. A case in point is the following from an internal memo from the Bank's resident representative in Cameroon to his director.

> The assessment in the report confirms the serious magnitude of problems confronting the portfolio, highlighting, inter alia, the country's inability to ensure good management of public resources and the precarious socio-economic environment as serious obstacles to effective project execution.
>
> On project specific issues, the report indicates that for the 12 projects examined by the consultant, organization was unsatisfactory in 80 percent of the projects and 70 percent of them lacked a "sense of direction" in implementation. Close to 67 percent of technical assistance was poorly utilized, and a majority of project staff were either inadequately trained or lacked motivation. More than 80 percent of the projects lacked counterpart funds. Procurement procedures were unsatisfactory in about 83 percent of Bank funded projects, while some 67 percent did not have acceptable financial management systems. Accounting systems and financial reporting were inadequate in about 83 percent of the projects, and the same number lacked project implementation and operation manuals. Finally, financial and technical control functions existed in theory but were not being exercised in more than 80 percent of the projects. Such lack of control led to poor quality audits and laxity towards financial covenant requirements in over 66 percent of the projects.[7]

Suffice it to say that this kind of specific information would never find its way outside the institution, for, if it did, it would certainly be in conflict with the success stories publicized by the Bank. No, the Bank would merely describe these as "problem projects" and let the reader try to figure out what the problems were. In the case of Cameroon, a notoriously corrupt country, the Bank funded ninety-four loans and credits between 1967 and 1995 for a total amount of approximately $1.82 billion. As was the case with Nigeria, it had become increasingly obvious to even the most casual observers in the decade prior to 1995 that the government was completely corrupt and dysfunctional, yet the Bank's management continued to push its lending agenda to the tune of roughly $950 million during that decade. Coincidentally, as with Nigeria, this amount was roughly half of all the loans and credits issued by the Bank in the decades prior to 1985, which I consider to be another indicator of the Bank's obsession with increased lending targets during that period. Again, as in the case of Nigeria, the Bank had reached a point where the problem could not be ignored and, while there was a reduction in lending for a while, the Bank was still able to lend the government roughly $500 million between 1996 and 2001. Old habits are hard to break.

Even more precise examples of internal institutional honesty can be found in specific project reports such as the following project review conducted by the Bank's Operations Evaluation Department (OED), which identified the following significant project shortcomings:

- No monitoring indicators or quantified outputs were reported to demonstrate the progress of the Project.
- There was no recorded inventory of procurement (e.g., 13 vehicles, 1000 mattresses, essential drugs) under the Project.
- The status of studies (e.g., prevalence of malaria, a review of hospital finances and operations, hospitals' action plans, an inventory of health facilities, and assessment of rehabilitation needs) funded by the project is unknown.
- Management capacity was not strengthened; various units (e.g., Managing Committee and Planning Unit at MOH [Ministry of Health]) were not operational.

- The lack of reaction by Bank management to the lapses in project supervision indicates an institutional weakness of the Bank. Problems remained even though all (but one) of the ten supervision missions had reported violation in legal and financial covenants.
- Service delivery for the Priority Health Programs did not improve:
  1. Endemic malaria persisted in Bioko Island where the Malaria Control program was to be piloted.
  2. Four newly constructed health centers, meant to improve Mother Child Health/Family Planning, were under-utilized, and physically deteriorating.
  3. The National STD [sexually transmitted disease] control center, which the Project funded, was no longer in operation.
  4. There was a shortage of essential drugs in the entire public health system that was started with US$0.65 million of the project's funding.
  5. Despite the costly rehabilitation of drug warehouses, they were practically empty (Malabo and Bata), and their physical conditions were deplorable (Malabo).

In a section of the review entitled "Significant Outcomes/Impacts" the only, I repeat, the *only* claim made was this:

> The project funded the preparation and publication of a useful booklet on treatment of Sexually Transmitted Disease (STD), and copies were seen in clinics during ICR [implementation completion report] mission.[8]

If one takes this at face value, it would appear that the STD booklets—and note that the number produced was not identified—were the only positive results to come out of this $5.5 million IDA credit. In terms of achieving project objectives, the review found that

> the project's objectives were generally not achieved except for a partial fulfillment of staff training. Some training took place for nurses, birth attendants, and hospital administrators, but

anecdotal evidence suggested that the trained personnel were no longer in the same communities. Tangible project achievements were limited to the construction of four health centers, the extension of the health school in Bata, and the rehabilitation of MOH buildings and drug warehouses, but all of these were found to be under-utilized and deteriorating.[9]

Not a very encouraging assessment! But how can we reconcile this with all the glowing success stories the Bank puts forth each year? Is this just an aberration, or is it the proverbial tip of the iceberg? Unfortunately, I believe it is the latter, for I have worked on far too many projects that had similar results to believe otherwise. What I could never understand, however, was how our management could pretend that African governments were sincere in seeking the Bank's help, when their lack of integrity, lack of commitment, and lack of national purpose were so obvious. Now I must interject here that when I say government, I mean those individuals, those government functionaries, and those bureaucrats with whom we were dealing directly, and not some faceless entity called government. So, how could the Bank's management, in the above case of Equatorial Guinea, pretend that this notoriously corrupt government was serious? How could management, in negotiating with these charlatans, pretend that the government would implement the project as agreed? Or even try?

Sadly, I believe that many managers within the Bank, in their heart of hearts, often knew full well with whom and with what they were dealing, but they did not have the courage to challenge the system and disrupt the flow of money to these corrupt governments. That would be heresy and would certainly bring reprimands, if not censure, from above. But is this good economic management? Is this encouraging economic growth? Is this alleviating poverty? And so, while some Bank staff and managers have had the courage to report honestly about the deplorable state of affairs in the Bank's portfolio, somehow, as this information works its way up through the system, it becomes whitewashed or otherwise reduced to pablum that is then fed to the outside world. Meanwhile, business is conducted as usual. What does that say about economic management?

NOTES

1. Edward (Kim) Jaycox, "Africa: From Stagnation to Recovery," World Bank internal document, February 1993, pp. 3, 4. Jaycox was vice president of AFR at that time. The title alone leads to false assumptions.

2. One only has to look at the lending to Nigeria during the 1980s and early 1990s to see this rationale in action.

3. These papers gently described corruption as "rent-seeking" and, to my constant amusement, usually contained economic formulas and graphs to rationalize why people steal or are otherwise corrupt. But there was never any recognition of the fact that these were criminal acts carried out by criminals.

4. According to the *World Bank Annual Report 2002* (Table 5.1), during the ten-year period between 1993 and 2002, $1.515 billion was loaned to Africa specifically for economic management. How much of that translated into a better economic existence for the average African will never be known.

5. *Africa Region News* (November 27, 1995).

6. There were ninety-eight loans and credits between 1964 and 1994, of which fifty-two were between 1984 and 1994.

7. Internal Bank memo regarding a report on the management capacity of Bank-financed projects in Cameroon, August 11, 1995.

8. OED, project review for a health project in Equatorial Guinea, January 10, 2000, p. 2, para. 4.

9. Ibid., para. 3.

3

• • • • • • •

Confucius and the Bank

The essence of knowledge is, having it, to apply it. (Confucius, 551–479 BC)

Some years ago, my daughter Nancy gave me a drawing of Confucius that contained the above caption. It was very appropriate to what I perceived was going on at the Bank, and it hung on my office wall for all to see. As you may have guessed by now, I had gradually developed an aversion to the endless intellectualizing at the Bank, and activity that not only seemed to fly in the face of reality but also appeared to prevent anything of substance from ever being accomplished. So much of what we were doing was superfluous to our mission, which was, I thought, to help the people of Africa achieve some degree of economic well-being. But not being an economist, who was I to judge what was needed and what was not? And how was I to know that the key to it all was in the acquisition of knowledge? If we only had knowledge, we could solve all of Africa's problems, and the rest of the world's as well.

And so I watched as management became more and more obsessed with the quest for knowledge. A quest that meant untold hours, days, weeks, months, and years of all-consuming research, analyses, meetings, seminars, reports, and treatises on every imaginable subject known to man. Enough to keep us gainfully employed for a very long time. Strangely, management's increased focus on the quest for knowledge seemed to be directly

proportional to the growing rate of failure within the Bank's lending portfolio. Could it be that management was trying to quietly
divest itself of any responsibility for those failures? After all, there's
no risk whatsoever in accumulating and disseminating knowledge,
and it clearly beats trying to make things work in Africa, or anywhere else for that matter.

> A formidable enemy of intuition is ANALYSIS PARALYSIS,
> a condition caused by too much inquiry. Constantly accu-
> mulating new information . . . without giving the mind a
> chance to percolate and come to a conclusion intuitively, can
> delay any important decision until the time for action ex-
> pires. This is substituting study for courage.[1]

The above quotation shared a spot on the wall with the one from
Confucius, and it summed up my feelings about where we were
headed with the Bank's growing desire to become an even bigger
repository of knowledge than it already was. The fact that the Bank
had, over the past four decades, already accumulated every con-
ceivable bit of knowledge about underdeveloped countries did
not seem to deter its quest for more. The fact that the Bank had, in
the professional knowledge and experience of its staff, thousands
of years of combined expertise in every imaginable aspect of economic development was also ignored by the proponents of this
new agenda. Had anyone ever taken an inventory of all the reports, papers, studies, assessments, analyses, reviews, and assorted
publications produced by the Bank about Africa and the rest of
the Third World? Apparently not, for if anyone had, it would have
been evident that we already knew more than we needed to know
about the subject.[2] Need some examples? Try the following "Ab-
stracts of Current Studies" taken from the World Bank website on
July 24, 2003.

"THE ECONOMICS OF ETHNICITY
AND ENTREPRENEURSHIP IN AFRICA"

Recent contributions to the literature on cross-country differences in economic performance suggest that ethnic diversity

is associated with slower growth and poorer macroeconomic management. In particular, Sub-Saharan Africa's dismal growth record over the past three decades has been linked to its relatively high ethnolinguistic fractionalization. But the reason for this association remains unclear. . . . Aimed at generating hypotheses for further work on these questions, the study estimated productivity, growth, and wage determination equations based on the fifth wave of the Ghanaian Manufacturing Enterprise Survey and the first and second waves of the Addis Ababa Industrial Enterprise Survey in Ethiopia. (abstract text)

Again, I reveal my ignorance of economics, but will someone please explain how this helps the millions of impoverished souls trying to eke out a living in their little workshops and stalls along the African roadsides? Notice that we only "suggest" an association among ethnic diversity, slow growth, and macroeconomic management, and that the reason for this "suggested" association "remains unclear." Not exactly cutting edge research, is it? Notice also that this study was "aimed at generating hypotheses for further work." After all, if a study does not lead to further studies, what good is it? Or, how about the following study?

"USING SEMI-PARAMETRIC METHODS FOR THE EVALUATION OF SOCIAL PROGRAMS AND POLICIES"

Econometric work to evaluate the impact of social programs and policies typically assumes that the impact is the same throughout the distribution of the indicator under review— for example, throughout the distribution of income. This assumption stems from the fact that in a traditional regression setting, parametric methods of estimation yield one parameter estimate for the impact, whether the program or policy is captured in the data through a continuous or a categorical (for example, dichotomous) variable. (abstract text)

Is this really necessary? Or is this just another self-perpetuating activity to provide work for the economists? Weren't they hired because they were supposed to know all this stuff? How does this translate into a better life for the billions of people living in poverty? Want another example?

"THE GLOBAL BENEFITS OF PER-MILE AND PER-GALLON ACCIDENT PREMIUMS"

The more people drive, the more accidents occur. But if people were made to pay the full economic cost of driving an extra mile, through an insurance scheme based on miles driven, they would drive less—resulting in not only fewer accidents and fewer injuries and deaths but also less congestion and lower emissions. . . . This study estimates and compares the benefits of introducing per-mile and per-gallon automobile insurance in the United States and in developing countries. (abstract text)

Are they serious? Will someone please tell me what this has to do with the pressing issues facing developing countries, the Bank, or anyone else, for that matter? Will someone tell me what this has to do with the Bank's mission in Africa? Couldn't the money and effort expended for this mindless nonsense have been used more appropriately to alleviate poverty? Finally, I can't resist one more example.

"A NEW APPROACH TO VALUING MORTALITY RISK REDUCTIONS: WHAT ARE OLDER PEOPLE WILLING TO PAY TO REDUCE THEIR RISK OF DYING?"

In most industrial countries the mortality benefits of environmental programs accrue primarily to older people. In the case of air pollution controls the age distribution of statistical lives saved parallels the age distribution of deaths, implying that 75 percent of people saved are over 65 years old. Yet the most common method of valuing these risk reductions is to use compensating wage differentials from the labor market. . . . To remedy this difficulty, this study has

developed a survey that asks people ages 40–75 what they
would pay to reduce their risk of dying. (abstract text)

Are they for real? What does this have to do with anything? Is
this what the search for knowledge is all about? Does this represent the wisdom of Confucius? Multiply this by the thousands
of reports produced by Bank staff each year, and you will understand how this endless intellectual self-gratification distracts the
Bank from its mission. What we needed then, and now, is to take
Confucius's advice and apply what we do know sensibly. But
somehow, this logic has never been acted upon by management.
Meanwhile, Bank staff are still being gauged by the number of
loans and credits processed each year, while the guiding intellectual elements within the bureaucracy continue to distance
themselves from any responsibility by wrapping themselves in
the protective cloak of "knowledge," as witness the following
statement:

> The Bank needs to operate more as a knowledge based or-
> ganization where knowledge is used as a source of com-
> petitive advantage and a means of differentiation and profits
> are derived from the Bank's intellectual capital. Within the
> Bank we need to move from "structured" work which is
> predictable, linear, standardized, planned and focused on
> cost, schedule and quality, to "knowledge" work which is
> unpredictable, non-linear, unique, more strategic, and fo-
> cused on innovation.[3]

Could their intentions be any clearer? Let's move away from
"structured work," meaning lending with measurable development objectives, and instead pursue knowledge, for which there
is no accountability. So what does all this mean? Are these just
the misguided observations of some disgruntled former Bank
staff member who doesn't understand the deeper aspects of economic development? Or, could it be that something is seriously
wrong with the way the Bank has been managed? As I have noted
previously, there were, and still are, others within the Bank who
have been able to see through the smoke and mirrors:

After spending the better part of our first 50 years pretending that we know it all, can solve any problem, and the hell with the critics, we seem to be swinging to the other extreme now: we can't do anything right, we have failed in Africa, our structures and processes are inadequate, nobody loves us, let's advertise and improve our image, etc. There is truth in all of the above. . . .

The bureaucratic, defensive, self-justifying answers will look for the odd project that has worked well, the odd country (one so far, Mauritius) that has doubled per capita incomes in a decade, the increases in school enrollment and reductions in mortality rates here and there, etc., as evidence that things are not as bad as the critics say. . . . *Overall, however, one has to be blind and intellectually dishonest not to see that over the past three decades Africa's (and by association our) performance has been generally poor.*[4] (emphasis added)

Other evidence of this schizophrenic condition within the Bank abounds; on the one hand glowing self-praise of the Bank's accomplishments to the outside world, and on the other hand, internal doubt and apprehension as to whether the Bank is accomplishing anything all.

All this has led me to conclude that the Bank, an institution with so much potential to alleviate poverty and suffering in the Third World, has been aimlessly adrift in the pursuit of its mission, periodically reorganizing itself as it searches endlessly for just the right management structure to implement its agenda but never quite satisfied with the results. Constantly moving the goal posts by which its accomplishments can be measured by the outside world, and by which it could be held accountable. Frequently substituting intellectual elitism for old-fashioned common sense. Always placing its own bureaucratic survival above that of its shareholders and borrowers.

Now I admit that these are harsh accusations, and there is no question that the Bank, its staff, and its managers do accomplish good things at times. But in the final analysis, despite the high caliber of its staff, and despite the enormous resources at its disposal, I do believe that its failures have far outweighed its successes. This is certainly the case in terms of substantive and measurable results on the ground, or, more specifically, the lack thereof. One only has to look at the state of economic development in Africa today after four decades of the Bank's "intellectual leadership." How effective were the policies it pushed upon uncommitted borrowers? How often were loans and credits provided to dysfunctional and corrupt governments? How can we explain the huge indebtedness of the African people without the concomitant benefits that were supposed to accrue to them in the process?

Those who disagree with this assessment will undoubtedly cite some showcase examples where varying degrees of progress have occurred, such as Botswana, Mauritius, and Ghana, and certain sector initiatives such as the Onchocerciasis (river blindness) Program and the Volta River Authority, but these are by far the exception. Between 1951 and 1995, the Bank funded over twenty-two hundred lending operations in Sub-Saharan Africa, totaling over $54 billion (not adjusted for inflation). And try as I might, I could never get any of the old Africa hands to identify more than ten projects that they personally deemed a success, and they all usually referred to the same projects.

Nothing exemplifies more the unexplainable willingness of the Bank's management to lend to dysfunctional African governments than the case of Nigeria, the biggest borrower in the Bank's Africa portfolio. In the decade between 1984 and 1994 the Bank funded fifty-two projects in Nigeria, totaling $4.6 billion, yet an internal review of civil service reform and capacity building[5] rated all of the following categories of Nigerian governance as *poor*: governance environment, size and cost of civil service, capacity for resource management, capacity for public service delivery, financial accountability and transparency, and participation in civil society. What were they thinking? How could the Bank's management continue to allow its funds to be placed in the hands of such incompetent and corrupt governments? What does this say about the Bank's own management and its respect for, and commitment to, the Bank's mission and its fiduciary responsibilities? Why do we continue to contemplate our navels when there is work to be done? With all our knowledge, why haven't we done better?

NOTES

1. Roy Rowan, *The Intuitive Manager* (Boston: Little, Brown, and Company, 1986), p. 91.

2. For example, in 1995, I did a brief review of operational reports and studies done for Sub-Saharan Africa and found over seventy-six hundred documents produced up to that date.

3. Minutes of a departmental management meeting, May 25, 1995.

4. Internal memo, July 3, 1995.

5. Working paper, October 4, 1995.

4

Feeding the Beast

The International Bank for Reconstruction and Development (IBRD) Cumulative Lending (1945–2002): $371 billion
The International Development Association (IDA) Cumulative Lending (1960–2002): $135 billion[1]

With billions of people living in poverty, the need for funding to support economic development in the Third World is enormous. But concurrent with this need is an ever-present risk: the temptation for greedy individuals to abuse the system in order to enrich themselves. And herein lies the dilemma, for while the needs are obvious, the risks are also obvious, thus presenting the donor community with the challenge of filling the maximum need while keeping the risk to a minimum.

How can we alleviate poverty for the masses without enriching corrupt government officials and their accomplices? How can we ensure that donor funds are used for the noble objectives described in all the loans, credits, and grants made to governments that are known to be egregiously corrupt? How can we feed the "beast" without having it devour us? For the World Bank, these questions are not easily answered, but if we are to address this issue, it is necessary to understand the mechanisms by which the money moves from its headquarters in Washington to the governments of the Third World. For in many cases it is through the manipulation of this process that the Bank's mission of alleviating poverty for the masses becomes transformed into alleviating poverty for the ruling elites.

THE PROCESS TRUMPS RESULTS

Emphasis on Loan Approval: The uncontrollable—i.e., global—causes and the deficiencies in national policy, regulatory frameworks, and institutional capabilities are critical determinants of project performance. However, there are also aspects of Bank practice that either may contribute to portfolio management problems or are insufficiently effective in resolving them. Underlying many of these aspects is the Bank's pervasive preoccupation with new lending. In the eyes of borrowers and co-lenders as well as staff, the emphasis on timely loan approval (described by some assistance agencies as the "approval culture") and the often active Bank role in preparation, may connote a promotional—rather than objective—approach to appraisal. . . . As a result, the quality of projects at the time of their entry into the portfolio—quality being defined to include inter alia implementability and sustained local commitment—is not always what it might be.[2]

It took me a while to realize that there was one overriding objective in our work at the Bank, and that was to get as much money out the door as possible. Of course, this was never stated openly, and it was both interesting and at times unsettling to observe the dynamics of this process and the effect it had on Bank staff and managers. One could easily observe the differences between those who were sincerely dedicated and committed to improving conditions in Africa and those whose primary focus was on the advancement of their careers. For the latter, this meant moving money. If projects succeeded, so much the better for career advancement, but if they failed, as was so often the case, such staff and managers chose to ignore it, cover it up, and put as much distance as possible between the failure and themselves—a human characteristic unfortunately demonstrating a lack of courage, professionalism, and fiduciary responsibility. After all, weren't we supposed to ensure that the money be used effectively to alleviate poverty and promote economic development? And weren't we supposed to ensure that it was not to be used to enrich politicians, government bureaucrats, and their accomplices?

The Bank shall make arrangements to ensure that the proceeds of any loan are used only for the purposes for which the loan was granted, with due attention to considerations of economy and efficiency and without regard to political or other non-economic influences or considerations.[3]

This contradiction between those Bank staff and managers who were devoted to trying to make things work in Africa and those who devoted their efforts to advancement within the bureaucracy created a constant tension that tended to resolve itself in favor of the bureaucrats. In order to understand how these dynamics played out, one must first know a little about the rules of the game and how the Bank goes about getting the money out the door. This process is the basis by which all is measured within the Bank, and what really matters is that the process is followed according to the rules laid out by the bureaucracy. If the process is followed correctly, careers will be advanced. If it is not, we will have to go back to the drawing board and do it again, and again, until we get it right.[4] Whether the project succeeds or is realistically able to achieve the desired results is not nearly as important, despite management's claims to the contrary.

"The Project"

In the beginning was the Project, and then arose the Assumptions. And the Project was without form and the Assumptions were void. And darkness was upon the face of the Implementers. And they spake unto their manager, and their voices said, "It is a crock of shit, and it stinketh."

And the manager went to the 2nd level manager, and he spake unto him, saying, "It is a crock of excrement and none may abide the odor thereof."

And the 2nd level manager went to the 3rd level manager, and he spake unto him saying, "It is a container of excrement, and it is so strong that none may abide before it."

And the 3rd level manager went to the Headquarters Director, and he spake unto him, saying, "It is a vessel of fertilizer, and none may abide its strength."

And the Director went to the Divisional Vice President, and he spake unto him saying, "It contains that which aids plant growth, and it is very strong."

And the Vice President went to the Division President, and he spake unto him saying, "It promoteth growth, and it is very powerful."

And the Division President went before the Executive Board, and he spake unto them saying, "This powerful new project will promote the growth of the company."

And the Executive Board looked upon the project, and saw that it was GOOD.

—Author Unknown

Somewhere earlier in my career I found this bit of wisdom and kept it pinned on the wall along with the rest of my office graffiti. When I came to the Bank in 1983 the project was, and still is, the main vehicle by which funds are provided to third-world governments, and I soon learned that the processing of the project was a very serious business. It was, in a sense, a precisely choreographed ballet in which each project team member had a specific role to play and outputs to deliver against a schedule orchestrated from above. When the ballet was performed smoothly, everyone was happy, merit increases were given, people were promoted, and another lending operation was added to our portfolio. Once the loan (IBRD) or credit (IDA) was approved and implementation began, however, interest in its success sharply declined as management began its search for new loans to process, as acknowledged by the following:

Treatment of Risks, Sensitivity, and Implementability in Design and Appraisal: The pervasive emphasis on loan approval is not matched by equal emphasis in implementation planning and identification and assessment of major risks to project performance. Sensitivity/risk analysis is limited, and virtually no attention is given to macroeconomic risks. The project concepts are not always well calibrated to the implementation capacity of executing agencies.[5]

Management and Motivation: Although managerial behavior varies, signals from senior management are consistently seen by staff to focus on lending targets rather than results on the ground. A telling example is the almost exclusive preoccupation with lending programs in the performance contracts underlying the budget process.[6]

PROJECT IDENTIFICATION

I never knew exactly just when, where, or how it was determined that a loan should be made for a particular project in a particular country.[7] In my early days at the Bank I had assumed that our lending was demand driven, that government officials would determine that they needed to improve their infrastructure, the delivery of services to their citizens, or make some other public investments for the benefit of the general population. I assumed that in the pursuit of funding for such endeavors, the government would prepare a proposal, which it would submit to the Bank to support its request for a loan. It would then be the Bank's responsibility to evaluate the government's proposal to ensure that the investment was viable, and either approve the loan, with or without modifications, or reject it. In this manner the government's commitment, an absolutely essential requirement, would be more or less assured, and we could assume that the government had thought it through at both the technical and political levels. After all, if the government was not genuinely committed to the project, why on earth should we finance it?

I soon realized that these were naive assumptions. It soon became clear that projects and loans were conceived at the Bank, by the Bank, and for the Bank, and while they appeared on the surface to be the creations of government, that was rarely the case. In reality, the government was often just a willing bystander, allowing the game to be played out to the Bank's satisfaction as long as it could eventually get its hands on the money. In order to get the money, government officials had little choice but to follow the

Bank's lead throughout the process. And while, externally, the Bank went to great lengths to maintain the facade of government commitment, internally, management made no effort to conceal its obsession with generating lending operations according to its own agendas, as witnessed by the following excerpts from an audit report of twenty lending operations between 1988 and 1992:

> In at least two of the projects reviewed we found evidence that the Bank had proceeded on with project preparation despite reservations expressed by borrower representatives about the justification or appropriateness of proposed projects. In one of these cases, the borrower advised the Bank that it was not in accord with the project design and that a much larger project was needed. The Bank persisted with its own design and, as a result, project preparation was marked by long intervals where the project's supposed sponsors ceased work on the project only to resume after pressure from the Bank. Later, project implementation was very slow and problematic.[8]

Note that this finding concerns "at least" two projects, implying that the number might be greater, even within this small sample. It is also quite likely that similar circumstances surrounded other projects, but that the "borrower representatives" chose not to raise a stink for reasons that I have noted above. But the reality here lies in management's written response to the above finding:

> Regional management advises that a persistent lack of commitment on the part of the borrower is not always sufficient basis for dropping a project.[9]

Well, whose project is it anyway? No doubt about intentions here, for while the Bank's management would have us believe that borrower commitment is essential to project success, internally we see that it is not going to let "a persistent lack of commitment" stand in the way of processing a loan. You will take this project and you will take this loan whether you like it or not, whether you believe in it or not, whether you are committed to it or not! The borrowers, cunning devils that they are, will say to the Bank, "Yes, we will take this loan under your conditions," and to themselves they will say, "And we will see to it that your money finds a good home." And this is how the game is played.

And so, after various economic studies were conducted and country assistance strategies (CASs) written, endless meetings would be held and numerous memos would be circulated until a decision was made on lending targets for each country during each fiscal year. A country lending program would be determined and amounts would be allocated for each sector of the economy. The stage was set, and we could then proceed to "identify" projects that would satisfy our lending program. As the lending cycle progressed, Bank staff had to be sure to adhere to each step of the process as spelled out in the Bank's *Operational Manual on Bank Procedures*—procedures that provided for every eventuality that might occur during the process except for the recognition of past failures, lack of borrower commitment, dysfunctional government institutions, corruption, and anything else that might jeopardize getting a loan approved by the board.

And finally, to maintain the facade of demand-driven lending, there was the matter of obtaining a formal request from the borrower for assistance in preparing the project. Yes, we had figured out just what it was that the borrower needed and how much we would lend, but now we had to present it in such a way that it would appear to have been conceived by our clients. This feat was often accomplished by Bank staff or consultants who would draft the letters requesting Bank assistance. Government officials would then copy the letters on their own stationary, submit them to the Bank, and the lending process would be set in motion. Thus we would gently but firmly lead the borrower down the path to a new loan.

After several decades of Bank involvement, a particular project was often nothing more than a continuation of previous projects in one way or another. For example, it was not unusual to be on an identification mission in Nigeria, Ghana, or anywhere else, laying the groundwork for a power project that would be the fourth, fifth, or sixth project with the Ministry of Energy. What was interesting in these cases was that if one reviewed the earlier projects there would often be repeated assessments of the issues to be addressed, repeated proposals to solve those issues, and repeated assumptions that the issues would be resolved through another lending operation.

While the physical nature of these projects might differ—for example, from dam building, to generating stations, to transmission and distribution grids—the underlying rationale for the projects would always be to strengthen the government agencies involved so that they could do a better job of providing electric power to the general public. The same rationale would apply to infrastructure projects, whether they involved road rehabilitation, water supply, or urban development. Ditto the health, agriculture, and education sectors. On the surface there would always be logical explanations for investing in these endeavors, but beneath it always lurked the reality of dysfunctional public institutions that hadn't a chance of carrying out even the most basic tasks needed to achieve project objectives.

The inability of these institutions to carry out the planning and preparation of any project proposals was evident from the beginning of each project cycle. It was indeed the rare occasion when local government staff would actually gather the necessary data and define the project objectives, physical and financial requirements, and the scheduling required for subsequent management of a project. Instead, in most cases expatriate consultants would be employed to perform these tasks, either with funds from an ongoing project, bilateral donors, consultant trust funds,[10] or even from the Bank's own operating budget.

And so, the process would begin with Bank staff and external consultants on center stage carrying out the substantive work while the locals were relegated to supporting assignments. Of course, it was always made to appear that it was the local authorities who were leading the process and that the consultants were working for the locals. In reality, it was the other way around, and I cannot recall even one instance where an identification mission report, or any other report for that matter, was prepared, written and submitted to the Bank by local government staff in a manner that was acceptable to the Bank. Better to let the consultants do it.

PROJECT PREPARATION

Once a project had been identified, the real work would begin and the tempo would pick up considerably. Internally, teams would be assigned and processing schedules would become increasingly important as everyone became focused on that day when the loan would be submitted to the board of directors for approval. A day that would demonstrate to their superiors that they could deliver loans, a day that would bring them closer to their next promotion. Whatever happened to the project after that, they were secure in the knowledge that they would not be held accountable, and it often amused me to reflect upon the track records of certain individuals who had risen through the ranks to become managers, directors, and vice presidents as a result of the ill-conceived projects they had presented to the board.

They had followed their marching orders diligently, they had prepared loan documents that defied reality and common sense, they had hidden the truth about dysfunctional and corrupt governments, and in the final moment, they deceived the board. But the irony is that this was exactly what it took to succeed in the Bank's bureaucracy. And for those who doubt my observations, one only has to look at the lending history of those Bank employees who have achieved management status in the Bank to understand what I am talking about. How many bad loans were processed, how many projects failed, and how much third-world debt was incurred during the tenure of these managers, directors, and vice presidents, past and present? And who has been held accountable for that?

And so, depending upon the size of the anticipated loan and the importance of the country in the Bank's lending program,[11] a team would be dispatched to assist the government with the preparation of the proposed project. Naturally, the more complex the project, the larger and more diverse the team's composition. It would not be unusual to have an economist (*always* an economist), a sector specialist (highway engineer, agronomist, educator, urban planner, etc.), a financial analyst, a public-sector administration specialist, an architect (often doubling as a procurement specialist), a training specialist, and any other category of expertise that might be deemed necessary.

The team members would arrive with their leather cases—long since replaced by laptops—filled with documents, papers, plans, cost tables and all sorts of background data that would form the basis for the proposed project. It often seemed as if we were working backward from the initial loan amount that been established before the mission, and I can recall numerous occasions when we would arrive in the field with a rough draft of what the project would encompass and would then proceed to fill in the blanks with the necessary data. Whether the data was accurate, credible, wishful thinking, or contrived was seldom a top priority as long as it cleared the way for subsequent approval by the board of directors. A practice universally known as "cooking the numbers" was seldom, if ever, seriously questioned by management.

One example of this was the treatment of counterpart funds that were the government's contribution to the project. These funds would be used for day-to-day operations and were, in effect, the project's lifeblood.[12] Although these amounts were small in comparison to the overall cost of the project, they were nevertheless included in the Bank's calculations with complete disregard for the fact that the government had never been able to provide those funds adequately in previous project operations and would most likely not be able to do so in the upcoming project. This was not an isolated occurrence; it applied to every project in every country in Africa in which I worked. Worse, the problem had been frequently recognized in numerous Bank memos and reports as the following shows:

> The shortages of counterpart funds seriously affect the implementation of the portfolio, particularly in Infrastructure, Agriculture, and Human Resources. The main causes of the shortages are inefficiencies in budgetary allocation, delays in the release of allocated funds, and weak government commitment to the sectoral priorities supported by the projects.[13]

Yet, despite the obvious, appraisal reports continued to present counterpart funding figures in a positive light. Other examples of cooking the numbers included anticipated revenues from charges to the public for electric power, water supply, telecom services, and so forth. And finally, there were the Bank's all-important economic rate of return (ERR) figures, which were endlessly tweaked in order to smooth the way for board approval.

Projects Subject to an ERR Test: Evidence
   Although some SARs (Staff Appraisal Report) acknowledge that the macroeconomic environment is important for determining project outcomes, macroeconomic variables,

along with assumptions about governments implementation capacity, and the availability of local cost financing are not explicitly taken into account in calculating ERRs. True, these factors are frequently cited in the risk section of the SARs and are sometimes considered in sensitivity analyses. But even the best SARs do not quantify the risks—to project costs and benefits—of slippage on the macroeconomic, financial, and institutional capacity/implementation fronts, notwithstanding they are prominent sources of failure. The result is an upward bias to ERR estimates, which are supposed to describe the expected value—that is, the statistical mean of possible project outcomes. This neglect largely explains the so-called ERR gap—that is the difference between the ERR at appraisal and the ERR at the time of project completion. Given an appraisal ERR based on "everything goes according to plan" and a completion ERR based on the cold reality of project implementation, it is not surprising there is a gap. Nor is it surprising that, in a period of macroeconomic decline, it has widened considerably in recent years.[14]

The substance of this paragraph could be stated more succinctly if it just said that the Bank, despite its self-described leadership in the field of economics, has an abysmal record of assessing economic rates of return, a record that has led to the approval of many loans that would have otherwise been unacceptable to the board. So, we were either too dumb or too incompetent to get the data and projections right, or we intentionally misled the board into believing that our proposed projects had a reasonable chance to succeed. In either case, the results were the same. The loans were approved and the projects failed.

Now I must digress a bit here to explain what I mean by failure, because there will be those apologists within the Bank who will point to all sorts of reports and evaluations claiming empowerment of the beneficiaries, best practices, lessons learned, progress made in policy dialogue, and anything else that would imply the success of Bank-funded projects. These claims, by their very nature, are intangible and disingenuous because they can't be measured. Of course, there are always some bits of success that can be measured in most, if not all, projects. The question is, how much success versus how much failure? Or, how much success at how much cost? If one spends $100 for $10 worth of success, is that worth the effort? If a health clinic is built and equipped but cannot function because the government cannot, or will not, provide an adequate operating budget, should that be considered a success?

The example cited in Chapter 2 herein concerning the OED report on a health project in Equatorial Guinea is the kind of success versus failure situation I am talking about, and there are too many similar project results in my experience to assume that this is the exception rather than the rule. When the policies incorporated into the loan agreement are ignored or subverted by the government, when the civil works are not completed or are in a state of deterioration, when the equipment provided by the project is broken or otherwise not in use, and when large sums have been embezzled from the project accounts, it is inconceivable that such a project could have succeeded. This is what I mean by failure.

PROJECT APPRAISAL

The project-appraisal process was divided into two or sometimes three phases: pre-appraisal, appraisal, and, if necessary, post appraisal. In an honest world one would expect that the Bank's appraisal of the borrower's project proposal would be just that. The Bank, as the lender, would appraise the borrower's request for a loan to ensure that the borrower would use the funds appropriately, that the proposal had merit and was justified, and that the borrower was capable of implementing the project successfully. In reality, however, and despite all the rhetoric about dialogue with the borrower, the Bank was appraising its own lending program, its own project plans and schedules, its own estimates, and its own assessments of project viability. This is not to say that the borrowers had no involvement whatsoever, that they were not included in the process, or that they had no input into project design. But, as noted earlier, theirs was a passive role in comparison to that of the Bank. Under these circumstances it is hard to imagine that Bank staff and managers would ultimately reject a lending operation they themselves had created. In fact, with the exception of rare cases that involved major disagreement with the borrower or catastrophic conditions such as civil war, they never did.

Following the preparation mission, and adhering as closely as possible to the predetermined project-processing schedule, the pre-appraisal mission would embark. By now, the scope of the project was pretty much determined, with objectives, activities, physical and financial requirements, and basic supporting data put down on paper. The purpose of the pre-appraisal mission was to solidify the work done to date and, most important, to ensure that the following appraisal mission did not run into any problems. *Problems* meant anything that would delay board approval, such as recalcitrant government bureaucrats with other agendas, the obvious inability of the government to implement the project, potentially weak supporting data, abysmal results from previous loans, and so on. All these had to be dealt with in such a way that their projected impact on project success was reduced—at least on paper, where the whitewashing of project risks was the order of the day.

Finally, with the identification, preparation, pre-appraisal, and appraisal tasks done, we could be assured that nothing would stop the loan from becoming a reality. Yes, we had to tweak the numbers here and there. Yes, we had to have the appraisal report vetted by those who knew the subject matter, and those who didn't. Yes, we had to sit through endless meetings to discuss the whole business. And yes, it really didn't matter if this project was going to work or not. This thing was going to be approved by the board one way or another, and we were all comfortable with that.

NOTES

1. *World Bank Annual Report 2002.*
2. Portfolio Management Task Force Report, September 1992, p. iii, D.vii.
3. The Bank's Articles of Agreement (as amended in 1989), Art. III, section 5 (b). This requirement was consistently ignored and violated by both borrowers and the Bank.
4. I cannot recall any project appraisal report that did not go through revision after revision as it made its way through the bureaucracy until every noun, pronoun, verb, adjective, colon, comma, and period had been properly vetted by everyone but the janitors.
5. Portfolio Management Task Force Report, September 1992, p. iii, D.viii.

6. Ibid., p. 23, para. 60.

7. Henceforth, I will use the term *loan* to include credits also.

8. "Report on an Audit of Loan Processing in the Africa Region," February 1994, p. 9, para. 17. The first case referred to touches on another aspect of the dynamics of Bank/borrower relationships whereby the borrowers would often push for grandiose projects that defied logic. The motivation for this could usually be traced to political agendas and, of course, the opportunity to embezzle larger sums through increased expenditures. I will present more on this later.

9. Ibid.

10. Consultant trust funds are funds that are provided to the Bank by bilateral donors who usually require that the funds be used to employ consultants from the donor country.

11. A proposed hundred million dollar loan would, of course, be of much higher priority and would be more conducive to career advancement than a ten million dollar loan, and a project in Nigeria would be a lot more important than a similar project in Benin.

12. I often compare counterpart funds to the gasoline needed to drive a car. There is no sense in borrowing money to buy a car if you don't have the money to pay for the fuel.

13. "Africa Region FY91 Annual Report on Implementation and Supervision," December 9, 1991, p. 5, para. 27.

14. Portfolio Management Task Force Report, September 1992, p. 15, para. 2.

5

· · · · · · ·

Groping in the Dark

The extent to which risks are ignored during project appraisals is exemplified by the Bank's lending to the National Electric Power Authority (NEPA) in Nigeria. I first became involved with the Bank's NEPA projects in 1984 and continued to work with them through 1989. From 1964 through 1989 the Bank provided loans for seven projects, totaling slightly over $470 million. While the first three projects,[1] undertaken in the early days of Nigeria's independence, were for the construction of much needed power-sector infrastructure, later loans became more complex and dubious as they increasingly encompassed institutional and sector policy issues. The following is a brief summary of those projects.

TRANSMISSION PROJECT (POWER I) 1964

The total project cost was $42 million, of which $30 million was financed by an IBRD loan for the construction of electric transmission and distribution lines in conjunction with the construction of a new hydroelectric dam at Kainji. The implementing agency was the Electricity Corporation of Nigeria (ECN). Although this project was based upon obvious energy needs for Nigeria at that time, it was also clear that local capacity to implement the project was seriously lacking. And while the appraisal report contained some brief and innocuous implications of organizational problems within ECN, it avoided any discussion of institutional risks of the kind that would plague Nigeria's power sector throughout the coming decades. The only hint of problems to come was contained in the following lone sentence: "ECN has agreed with the Bank on the necessity of strengthening its organization and appropriate steps are being taken."[2] And so the symbiotic relationship between the Bank and the Nigerian power sector began, a relationship that would advance the careers of Bank staff, provide employment for untold numbers of consultants and foreign advisors, fill the order books of foreign equipment suppliers, and enrich beyond all measure the personal fortunes of key public officials.

KAINJI MULTIPURPOSE PROJECT (POWER II) 1964

This project was in parallel with the Power I project. The total cost was $207 million, of which $82 million was financed by an IBRD loan to cover part of the foreign exchange costs for the construction of the Kainji dam. The implementing agency would be the Niger Dams Authority (NDA), which was in the process of being organized during appraisal. Although the appraisal report contained no institutional assessment of NDA's ability to implement the project, this did not deter the Bank from approving the project. Nor was the Bank deterred by the appraisal team's marginal assessment of the economic justification for the project:

> The economic evaluation of the Project, made by comparing the cost of Kainji with the cost of thermal plants over a 60 year period, indicates that the Project's benefits represent an acceptable, *though marginal*, justification for building it at this time. When the hydro station is fully developed and loaded the cost of generation will compare favorably with that available from alternative sources." (p. 22, para. 86) (emphasis added)

And so, a second loan was made without any serious consideration of the institutional capacity to implement such a project successfully. Nor was there a serious assessment of the inherent risks associated with such an endeavor, given the lack of experience among the Nigerians. Yes, the project would be managed by a cadre of senior foreign experts who would shoulder all the work and responsibility and who would achieve the civil works as planned. But at the end of the day, there was the larger-than-life risk that the exercise would, in later years, prove to have been overly ambitious due to incompetence, negligence, other agendas, and the ever-present cancer of corruption. And so it was.

SUPPLEMENTARY LOAN FOR KAINJI MULTIPURPOSE PROJECT (POWER III) 1968

Due to cost overruns and the inability of the government to provide sufficient foreign exchange, an additional $37 million was required to complete the Kainji dam project. With minimal need to reappraise the project, the Bank approved a supplementary loan of $14.5 million to help meet these costs. By this point the Bank had approved loans worth $126.5 million in the first four years of its involvement with the Nigerian power sector.

NATIONAL ELECTRIC POWER AUTHORITY (POWER IV) 1972

The total project cost was $126 million, of which $76 million was financed by an IBRD loan. The Bank's relationship with the Nigerian power sector was now eight years old, and during this period Bank reports raised the idea of consolidating ECN and NDA into one institution. It took several years to convince the government of the merits of these recommendations, which were finally implemented under this project.

While the concept of a single power-sector institution was, and is, completely rational on paper, it was not so on the ground. ECN and NDA had not performed as anticipated during the previous three Bank loans, yet the Bank assumed that by merging the two into a single institution, these shortcomings would be resolved. And while two defective parts do not make a functioning whole, this did not deter the Bank from approving another loan. Thus, NEPA was born following an appraisal report that, with the typical ambivalence of most Bank reports, made every effort to appear positive about NEPA's chances for success while at the same time alluding to serious unresolved institutional problems:

The project, for which a loan of US$76 million is proposed, would help Nigeria meet the rapid growth in the demand for power experienced since the cessation of the civil war in 1970, and would also help improve the management of the power sector, which has appreciably worsened since the first power loan to ECN in 1964. ("Summary and Conclusions," para [i])

The report continued:

The main problem facing the power sector is the physical and financial deterioration that has been taking place for some years now. In an effort to ameliorate the present condition of the sector, the Government is creating NEPA by merging ECN and NDA, and will appoint top management personnel acceptable to the Bank and engage a team of highly qualified advisors to assist the Nigerian staff. (para [ii])

Could things be any worse than that? Isn't the appointment of top management personnel and "highly qualified" advisors exactly what had been applied to the previous projects? Are the "experts" there to assist the Nigerians, or are they really there to do the work and ensure that the project at least survives through to completion? Have they made any attempt to identify the causes of the physical and financial deterioration? What guarantee was there that this approach would work when similar efforts had failed in the past? And what do we make of other telling hints of disaster contained in the report? In reviewing the results of the previous Bank-funded projects, the appraisal team stated:

Despite the cost overrun, which was the basis for the second loan to NDA, the execution of both previous Bank projects was successfully completed; however, the institutional objectives of these projects were not achieved.

ECN's and NDA's past financial performance has been poor. . . . Their accounting is seriously in arrears and their records are inaccurate. As a result it has been impossible to gather any financial information which can be considered up-to-date or accurate. (paras. [iv], [v])

But in the very next paragraph, the report says:

NEPA's future financial situation looks considerably brighter. Rapidly growing sales at relatively high tariffs will yield sufficient revenues to enable NEPA to reach a minimum rate of return of 8% on the net fixed assets in operation in FY 1973, generate enough funds to finance about 53% of its expansion program, and also complete reductions in existing tariffs in a few years. (para. [vi])

After admitting the dysfunctional state of affairs within the sector, how could the Bank's appraisal team consider possibly such an optimistic turnaround through the creation of NEPA? By what magic did it suppose that a new name on the door and a new organization chart would overcome the deeply rooted inertia, incompetence, and corruption that plagued the sector? Reorganizing defective institutions changes nothing, and as for the inertia, incompetence, and corruption, best to let sleeping dogs lie in order to get the project to the board. And these are not the only indications of serious unresolved issues contained in the SAR, as witness the following:

ECN, the older of the two Government agencies in the power sector, had shown a steady deterioration in its management and operation for some years now. NDA has also been facing a similar predicament. . . . Coordination of planning, design, construction, and operations between the two entities has been practically non-existent, with neither agency doing very much to bring about an improvement. (p. 1, para. 1.03)

Because of the fragmented condition of the sector and the dearth of competent personnel, much of the basic work involved in the definition of the project, the preparation of cost estimates and load forecasts, the establishment of the project's justification, and the preparation of a financing plan was done by Bank staff during pre-appraisal missions to Nigeria in March/April and October, 1971. (p. 2, para. 1.06)[3]

And finally, with complete assurance that they would not be challenged by the board, the appraisal team and its management admitted that no feasibility studies had been conducted, studies that would have provided a baseline for the measurement of project success at completion:

> Feasibility studies would have helped improve the quality of the load forecast, ascertain the accuracy of the cost estimates, establish with a higher precision priorities among all the possible electrification schemes, select the best routes for transmission lines, and determine the optimum timing of the various items composing the project. However, *despite the absence of feasibility studies and despite the approximations that had to be made to prepare an investment program, the proposed project warrants the Bank's assistance.* (p. 9, para. 4.02) (emphasis added)

> *The appraisal team, with the help of ECN and NDA prepared a six-year (FY1973–78) investment program.*[4] (p. 9, para. 4.03) (emphasis added)

And so, without a clue whether this thing would work or not, another project was approved by the board.

LAGOS POWER DISTRIBUTION PROJECT (POWER V) 1979

The total project cost was $222 million, of which $100 million was financed by an IBRD loan for the construction of transmission and distribution grids in the Lagos area. Although NEPA had now been in existence for seven years, its performance record was far short of that envisioned during the appraisal of the previous project. Further, although the Bank appeared to be aware of these shortcomings, this did not deter management from pushing through another loan. In describing NEPA's operational performance, the appraisal team wrote:

> NEPA's power system is subjected to frequent unscheduled interruptions, caused by a wide variety of incidents, most of them originating in the transmission and distribution systems. Although some records exist regarding causes, location and duration of power failures, they are not a suitable

basis from which to carry out a systematic analysis, which would permit the taking of measures to improve service reliability in a rational manner. Furthermore, the existing record system would not permit satisfactory evaluation of improvements in system reliability in the Lagos area, which are likely to result from the proposed Bank project. (p. 5, para. 2.05)

While this might not appear to be a serious matter at first glance, one must keep in mind that NEPA, along with its predecessors, the ECN and the NDA, had already enjoyed the guidance of the Bank through four projects and $202.5 million in loans during the previous fifteen years, and there were *still* no reliable procedures in place to deal with endemic power outages. Despite the Bank's involvement, and the parallel involvement of bilateral donors, twinning arrangements with experienced power-sector utility companies, and other forms of technical assistance, it should have been obvious to the Bank that these problems went beyond systemic shortcomings. Power outages and their frequency are, after all, something by which government and the public can most readily judge the institution's ability to function effectively, and one would think that if NEPA's management had seriously wanted to find the causes to these outages, it could have and would have done so. Clearly, NEPA's management was not really interested in or committed to reducing these outages, a condition mockingly described in the local media as "groping in the dark."

The outages were more than just a minor issue; they were an indication that much deeper problems within NEPA precluded it from attaining institutional viability. And what about the rosy predictions of improved financial performance made during the appraisal of the previous project? In assessing NEPA's financial status, the appraisal team found that

accounts are kept in accordance with generally accepted accounting principles, largely following United Kingdom practice. Each year, NEPA publishes well presented accounts as part of an attractive, colorful and informative annual report. Within NEPA's headquarters, sound procedures are used for the preparation of annual recurrent and capital budgets and long term financial forecasts. Well established budgetary controls exist. (p. 10, para. 2.20)

Statements like this always amazed me, for they tended to white-wash the true financial conditions of the government institutions we dealt with. Accounting principles and procedures had been prepared by internationally recognized consulting firms as part of past Bank-funded projects or bilateral donor assistance.[5] The rules were there, and NEPA's senior financial managers had the necessary training and credentials to see that they were followed.

Yet underneath this veneer of acceptability lay widespread financial chaos and corruption that should have been obvious to even the most inexperienced observer. Lengthy and unacceptable delays in recording transactions, large gaps in accounting entries, improper purchase order and invoicing documents, and unexplained cash transfers all pointed to serious problems. All were classic red flags of fraud and corruption. But then, following brief praise for NEPA's accounting system, colorful reports, and budgetary controls, the SAR, in apparent contradiction, goes on to say:

> However, the efficient operation of systems depends upon a reasonable degree of competence among all levels of staff. Unfortunately, below the level of senior management, the staffing problems affecting NEPA as a whole seriously undermine the systems of financial control. Senior management itself has numerous vacancies for qualified accountants, throwing almost impossible burdens upon other managers. Thus, lacking adequate supervision, the less senior financial and commercial staff do not carry out their responsibilities in an efficient and timely manner. This is particularly evident at district level, where much of the day-to-day commercial and financial operations are transacted. Meter reading and meter inspection are inefficient, billing is tardy and cash collection poor. . . .
>
> As an indication of the inefficiencies at district level, NEPA's outstanding consumer receivables practically doubled from March 1977 to March 1978. About Naira 64.0 million (US$100.0 million equivalent) is now outstanding representing about six months' sales. . . . Despite strong management pressure, there has been, so far, little sign of improvement. (p. 10, paras. 2.21, 2.23)

So, after being told that NEPA keeps its accounts properly and submits "colorful" reports, we learn that it suffers from a serious lack of competent personnel who are not adequately supervised and who have been unable to collect $100 million from its customers over a one-year period. Another telling statement is found further in the report in the Bank's assessment of future financial performance:

> The clear preference of NEPA's management, at present, is for virtually all capital finance to be provided by the Federal Government. Indeed, in the short run, there is very little alternative, because NEPA's unsatisfactory and hitherto deteriorating financial performance could not have supported the raising of capital finance from local or foreign private source. (p. 40, para. 7.14)

With the admission that NEPA's financial performance is unsatisfactory and deteriorating, it would seem that this matter should have received more attention from the Bank than it did. The truth is that a good portion of this "uncollected" $100 million most likely had found its way into the pockets of NEPA employees at the district level and above. Under-reporting billing collections, falsifying meter-reading reports, overlooking illegal service connections in return for bribes, and reducing customer invoices in return for kickbacks were common scams. They were perpetrated not only by NEPA employees but also were typical of the corrupt practices encountered in the power and water sectors where monies are collected from the public.

But let these things not deter us from recommending this project. For we have seen NEPA, and it is good. At least good enough to push another loan to the board.

POWER TRANSMISSION AND DISTRIBUTION PROJECT (POWER VI) 1981

The total project cost was $218 million, of which $100 million was financed by an IBRD loan and was appraised only two years after the Power V Project to cover further expansion of transmission and distribution systems in the Lagos area. With $6.7 million of the project costs allocated to studies, training, and management support, the first stated objective in the SAR was this: "To continue the strengthening of NEPA's organization and capability through support for its manpower development program and specific assistance for known areas of weak management" (p. 18, para. 4.01[1]).

It had now been nine years since NEPA was created out of the ineffective ECN and NDA, and during that time the institution had received a wide range of technical assistance from several European and Canadian power utilities. These companies had extensive experience in the power sectors of underdeveloped countries, and, despite their inputs in the management and operation of NEPA, there had been no measurable improvement in NEPA's ability to manage its affairs. In fact, things seemed to get worse instead of better. No matter how much money and expertise were thrown at NEPA it continued to be a dysfunctional institution. It remained this way because those in government, and those within NEPA, had other agendas that had little, if anything, to do with providing electric power to the general population. Yet despite these failed efforts, the Bank continued to maintain the facade that NEPA's problems were somehow manageable and that NEPA could be turned into an efficiently functioning organization. All we had to do was lend it more money.

On another issue that was indicative of NEPA's failures, it is interesting to note that in the appraisal of the Power V project, the Bank had made brief mention of the increasing use of privately generated electricity by consumers: "Data on power generated by self suppliers are scarce but there are indications that such consumption has increased substantially during the last year due to power shortages" (p. 2, para. 1.03). Two years later, in the appraisal of the Power VI project, the Bank again addressed the problem with a single sentence: "Private power generation for both industrial and residential use increased considerably during 1977/78 due to persistent power shortages in NEPA's system" (p. 8, para. 2.11). Further on in the same report, brief mention of this issue was also made in the section on the supply and demand of electric power. It stated: "Assuming non-NEPA supply were to remain at 5% of total consumption and based on growth forecasts per capita consumption would reach 240 Kwh by 1987" (p. 8, para. 2.11).

Once again, there was only passing mention of an issue that has serious consequences for the power sector in general, and for NEPA in particular. These statements seem to contradict each other, however, as the undefined "increases," on the one hand, are not logically compatible with the rather non-threatening assumption of a stable 5 percent figure, on the other hand. This figure was in disagreement with what Bank staff were saying in private by a factor of ten when, during after-hours talk while on mission, we would occasionally discuss this issue. During those discussions the general consensus among us was that by the early 1990s about half of Nigeria's electric power consumption was being produced privately. Interestingly enough, the Project Completion Report (PCR) for the Power IV project, in a section dealing with NEPA's operating performance problems, stated: "As a consequence, customers installed an inordinately high amount of captive plant, recently estimated to exceed 600 MW [megawatts]" (p. 17, para. 4.01).[6] An amount of installed capacity that equaled roughly 49 percent of peak demand in 1980, the year the Power IV project was completed.[7] A figure very close to our after-hours discussions. Further confirmation of this condition can be found in the Project Performance Audit Report of the Power IV project prepared by the OED in July 1985:

> Almost every manufacturing firm and medium and large-sized commercial establishment must have auto-generators. These sets are being used frequently and have replicated a major part of public investment in the electricity supply industry. (p. 5, para. 10)

This had to be obvious to even the most casual observer, for one only had to walk the streets during a power outage to hear the crescendo of noise as the private diesel-generator sets started up and kept things running for their owners. How could this have escaped the Bank's attention during the appraisals of two loans? Given the economic significance connected with the replication of public investment, as noted above, it is telling that the appraisal reports, despite their inclusion of all sorts of mundane statistics about the sector, made no attempt to analyze this issue. Why, with the Bank's overriding obsession for data and detail, didn't they seek to shed additional light on this? After all, it would seem that this could have been accomplished quite easily with a few customer surveys. And it was certainly a subject worth pursuing if the Bank were seriously concerned about NEPA's ability to serve the public. But then again, exposing an issue of this magnitude would certainly not help in getting the loans approved, so it is best left alone.

This cavalier attitude about power outages and private generation occurred at a time when NEPA supposedly had more installed capacity than it could deliver. In fact, those who took the time to study the data contained in the SAR would see that available capacity in 1979 at the time of the Power V project appraisal was about 50 percent higher than peak demand, and in 1981, at the time of the Power VI project appraisal, it had risen to 70 percent, thus demonstrating that NEPA had much more capacity than it needed (Annex 1.01, p. 3). A strong indication that NEPA had engaged in an overextended program of poorly planned expansion, with its lucrative opportunities for bid rigging, kickbacks, and bribes, resulting in a physical plant that was considerably beyond its financial and managerial capacity to operate. Yet nowhere were these issues factored into the Bank's decisions to continue lending to NEPA. Nigeria needs electric power, NEPA is the institution that provides it, and the Bank has the financing to keep NEPA afloat. What could be simpler? Except that it never worked!

POWER SECTOR MAINTENANCE AND REHABILITATION PROJECT (POWER VII) 1989

The total project cost was $150 million, of which $70 million was financed by an IBRD loan. The objectives of this last major Bank-funded project[8] were to carry out the maintenance and rehabilitation of NEPA's deteriorating physical plant and to "strengthen" the institution so that it would be a "commercially viable entity." In presenting the benefits of the proposed project, the SAR[9] stated:

> The Project will help (a) improve the efficiency, availability and reliability of power supply in the country; and (b) relieve

power shortages, and reduce the high cost of private autogeneration, and thereby, contribute to industrial growth. The Project will also contribute substantially towards institution building to improve the efficiency and management of NEPA, and help establish it as a commercially viable utility. ("Project Summary," p. 3)

Given NEPA's past history, could this have been perhaps a bit optimistic? How could the appraisal team possibly conclude that this was going to come about given the Bank's involvement, which had now spanned a quarter of a century, six projects, and roughly $400 million thrown down a rat hole? Let us first look at what this latest SAR had to say about "autogeneration," referred to in previous reports as "captive plant," "power generated by self-suppliers," and "private power generation":

In recent years, the quality of NEPA's service to its customers has been poor. As a result, a large autogeneration capacity by consumers, unable to obtain adequate and reliable supply of power, has been built up in the country. (p. 2, para. 1.08)

Then, further on, we learn:

As a consequence of the unreliable electricity supply, substantial captive generating capacity has been established in the country. While no precise estimates are available, data on licenses issued for new autogeneration capacity, plus renewals of existing licenses, for the past three years alone, all of which cover only a portion of the total captive sets available in the economy, indicated the presence of a minimum of 500 MW of captive generating sets with commercial and more affluent households. Actual autogeneration availability, as estimated in the Bank's Energy Assessment for Nigeria (1983), may well be as high as 1,500 MW. (p. 4, para. 1.16)

Could this have been true? Was it possible that NEPA's customers now had almost as much generating capacity as NEPA's peak-load demand? On the same page that shows an estimated private capacity of 1,500 megawatts, the report also states:

Nigeria's installed generating capacity is substantial, and, on the face of it, more than adequate to meet its current peak load. Yet, the country has faced constant problems of supply for more than a decade due to relatively unsatisfactory levels of capacity availability reflected in considerable inoperable capacity and a low level of system reliability. Current installed capacity is about 4,700 MW. . . . Although current peak load is about 1,900 MW, there have been constant supply shortfalls. (p. 4, para. 1.14)

So, let's consider this. In 1989, NEPA was said to have about 4,700 megawatts of electric power generating capacity, yet its peak load was only 1,900 megawatts, and it apparently couldn't even deliver that on a reliable basis. The report further predicted that NEPA's capacity would increase to "over 5,800 MW" in the coming three years (p. 4, para. 1.15). This despite the fact that it couldn't deliver 1,900 megawatts and, shame on it, that its customers could almost meet the peak load demand on their own. Keep in mind also that the private capacity of 1,500 megawatts was estimated in 1983, six years prior to the report under discussion; it would be realistic to assume that this figure had increased in the interim. In fact, it would seem that many consumers were ignoring NEPA in their own plans for electrification:

To some extent, the declining trend of commercial and industrial consumption reflects the somewhat lesser dependence of these groups upon the relatively unreliable supply of electricity from the grid, and the correspondingly greater usage of captive generation sets. (p. 6, para 1.26)

At this point, one has to ask why the government and NEPA persisted in continuing to expand generating capacity. NEPA already had two and a half times more generating capacity than its peak demand and was in the process of increasing that ratio even further. In many cases the answer lies in the large contracts awarded to international suppliers. A new power-generating station can cost hundreds of millions of dollars, and that translates into large kickbacks for those in government who can facilitate contract awards, and smaller kickbacks for those involved

in supervising the civil works and procuring supplies and equipment. It can also result in lucrative subcontracts for shell companies owned by government officials, their relatives, and close
associates—subcontracts in which payments are received for services not rendered or for material and equipment supplied at
grossly inflated prices.

Never mind that the new plants won't operate effectively because of myriad managerial, technical, and operational problems.
Never mind that the transmission and distribution grids are not
adequate for the job. Never mind that NEPA is totally incapable of
operating all this efficiently or economically. Never mind that the
Bank, other international donors, and numerous consultant studies have all recommended against further expansion until existing problems are overcome. Never mind that the government has
blatantly ignored the logic of these recommendations. Never mind,
because this is how we enrich ourselves at the expense of Nigeria's
economy.

Now, let's revisit the issue of power outages that were to have
been ameliorated at least partially under the Power V and
Power VI projects. While this problem was alluded to in previous
appraisal reports, it appears that it had gotten worse since NEPA's
inception seventeen years earlier:

> NEPA's public image has deteriorated rapidly in recent years
> due to poor quality and unreliability of service. There were
> 22 total system blackouts and at least 11 partial system col-
> lapses in 1987. Average consumer outages are in the range of
> some 500 to 600 hours per year—over 100 times the level of a
> typical rural system in developed countries. These opera-
> tional problems, the most apparent to consumers, are the re-
> sult of poor management, the lack of staff motivation and
> insufficient foreign exchange for spare parts, vehicles and
> repairs. Other serious contributory factors have been inad-
> equate preventive maintenance programs, cumbersome and
> slow contract approval within FGN [Federal Government of
> Nigeria], lack of proper training, poor maintenance supervi-
> sion, and even suspected sabotage. Belatedly, NEPA's man-
> agement has recognized the seriousness of the situation,
> especially the financial crisis, and has begun to tackle some
> of the major problems. (p. 12, para. 2.04)

Well, that's certainly a revelation! NEPA's management has at last recognized the seriousness of the situation, and it only took seventeen years to do so. They can't be serious! Could we possibly add anything worse to this list of complaints? Is there anything positive one could have said about the institution, its management, or its ability to serve the public? Could anyone have confidence that NEPA was capable of changing after this abysmal track record? It was, I believe, an insult to one's intelligence to gloss over the issue with such obviously disingenuous statements. Would NEPA really "tackle" some of the major problems? Don't hold your breath!

There is no need to dissect every paragraph in the forty-five-page appraisal report, but let me briefly highlight one last revelation from this exercise:

NEPA suffers from poor internal communications and the lack of timely information critical to effective management. Poor accounting and financial reporting systems preclude performance setting and cost control monitoring. Lack of management information systems, particularly at the corporate level, results in confusion, uninformed decision making, increased costs, loss of control, no confidence in the reliability of information, and a slow, reactive style of management. By any measure, NEPA's operating environment is complex. Yet, most of the generally accepted information systems in a typical power utility are either non-existent in NEPA, or where provided, unreliable. Major automated systems that are lacking include payroll, general accounting, materials management, budget management, fleet management, personnel data, accounts payable, property plant and equipment. (p. 15, para. 2.11)

What happened to all the rosy predictions emanating from the appraisal reports of the previous projects? Predictions that failed to materialize. And why were they so conveniently ignored as we prepared yet another loan? Is there any private commercial entity that could survive for long under these conditions? How could the Bank's management look at this and then conclude that further lending to NEPA was a good idea? How could the Bank be so cavalier about project risks when it stated: "There are no unusual risks associated with the proposed project" (p. 43, para. 4.09).

How could the Bank's management continue to deceive itself, its board, its shareholders, and the rest of the donor community with such biased and misguided appraisals? NEPA had been a sham since its inception, kept as a cash cow by the vested interests both inside and outside the institution, and certainly by the completion of the Power V project it should have been considered an unacceptable lending risk by the Bank.

In the preceding brief examples of just one series of loans to one sector in one country, I have tried to show the way in which appraisal reports were produced in order to ensure board approval. Lengthy discourses on technical and financial issues filled with needless details and data that have meaning only for those who wrote them, while an occasional paragraph is devoted to weak management and other serious institutional issues. To solve these institutional problems, we will finance some training programs and bring in some technical assistance despite the fact that these remedies had failed in the past and despite the fact that there was no logical reason to conclude that they would succeed in the future.

In the end, the SARs were, for the most part, meaningless. They created the illusion that the institution benefiting from the Bank's loan was viable, or at least had the potential to become viable. They created the illusion that the government officials responsible for implementing the project were committed to the it, and that it would indeed benefit the general population. In too many cases, however, these illusions proved to be wishful thinking, at best, and blatant deception, at worst. Most important, no one—no Bank staff, no Bank manager, no consultant—ever included statements about the pervasive corruption that robbed these institutions of their ability to function effectively. Corruption, a chronic cancer that destroyed all efforts to bring economic development to Africa, was never factored in to the Bank's appraisals of project feasibility. To do this would have exposed the entire process for the fraud that it was. And so, we deliver another well-written appraisal report with mind-numbing information about irrelevant facts, while important issues are glossed over. Another project taken to the board, another office party to celebrate, another promotion for Bank staff, and now let's move on to more loans.

NOTES

1. These projects were undertaken with NEPA's predecessors, the Electricity Corporation of Nigeria (ECN) and the Niger Dams Authority (NDA).

2. Staff appraisal report (SAR), "Summary," para. iv. Hereafter, page and paragraph numbers for quotations from various SARs will be cited in the text.

3. Note the reference to the Bank's role in creating the project despite the obvious lack of participation by the Nigerians.

4. This is a good example of "cooking the numbers."

5. These accounting principles and procedures were usually prepared in conjunction with local affiliates, who did the work while retaining the cachet of the international company.

6. This PCR was dated November 1984, three years after the appraisal of the Power VI project.

7. This is according to the Power VI SAR, Annex 1.01, p. 3.

8. No further loans were made through 2000, although preparations were being made to resume lending at some time in the future.

9. References to this SAR were taken from a draft report dated January 23, 1989.

6
• • • • • • •

And Darkness Was
upon the Face
of the Implementers

It always amazed me that no matter how flawed or misconceived our projects were, the loans were always approved. The process was a complete charade, and I often wondered why we spent so much effort writing the "perfect" appraisal report when we knew it would be approved no matter what. It was at this point that we faced our moment of truth. We had made all those glowing assessments and wonderful promises, and now we would have to make it all work. And that knowledge brought fear and trepidation to those left with the task.

Once the project was approved and became "effective"—essentially, the starting date for the project—the demeanor of Bank staff and management would change from unbridled optimism to guarded caution. Worse, there were times when it seemed that everyone was running for the hills, trying to distance themselves from that which they had created. Now, we have to make this thing succeed as we had predicted, and it's not going to be easy! The days of wishful thinking were over, and the time for smoke and mirrors was beginning. Forget about getting measurable results on the ground! Let's just concentrate on ensuring that the funds get disbursed on schedule and that our supervision reports minimize implementation problems as much as possible. And so the nightmare would begin. Project task managers were now faced with disbursement profiles, procurement issues, supervision missions, reporting delays, and the often futile efforts to salvage whatever they could from the optimistic promises made during appraisal. But above all, we had to be sure that the money got out the door.

THE TELLER'S WINDOW

During the ten-year period between 1986 and 1995, the Bank disbursed approximately $15 billion against IBRD and IDA projects in the Africa Region. In addition, approximately $11 billion was disbursed against structural adjustment loans and credits (SALs and SACs). SALs increasingly became the Bank's vehicle to promote economic policy reforms, address balance of payments, and other macro economic issues. But as I am not qualified to discuss them, and as I was never involved in their implementation, I will have to leave that aspect of the Bank's lending program to others. My only observation on structural adjustment lending is that it seemed to me to be an excellent device to move a lot of money with a minimum of effort and without any accountability afterward. Billions of dollars shoveled out the door and nobody seemed to know exactly where it all went.

Contrary to the laissez-faire disbursement of SAL funds, the disbursement of project funds was conducted according to a rigid system of procedures. These procedures had to be strictly followed by the Bank's disbursement officers, who individually processed hundreds of payments each month amounting to many millions of dollars. Each disbursement officer would be responsible for project disbursements within one or more countries, and the work was both frustrating and thankless. Payments had to be made against withdrawal applications submitted by the borrower's project management staff. If the payments were for Bank-approved contracts, one had to ensure that they were made in accordance with that contract. If the payments were for approved goods and services, one had to ensure that the Bank's procurement guidelines had been respected, that bidding procedures had been followed correctly, that supporting documentation was in order, that funds were being withdrawn against the correct disbursement categories, and that the payments were eligible under the Bank's rules. These and other disbursement regulations had to be accomplished in such a short time as to preclude serious examination.[1]

The volume of work requiring intimate knowledge of the project, procurement regulations, and the idiosyncrasies of the borrowers was often overwhelming. In addition, the pressure to get the money out the door sometimes created an adversarial relationship with certain task managers who saw any delay in disbursements as an obstacle to their own agendas. Needless to say, this did not work in favor of ensuring that the Bank's fiduciary responsibilities were adhered to. But be assured that it did work in favor of those local project officials who quickly learned that the system's safeguards could be easily breached through the submission of fraudulent documents to support the withdrawal applications.

The money would normally leave the Bank through two basic processes: the first covered direct payments to the contractors, consultants, and suppliers; and the second involved the replenishment of revolving funds kept in special accounts. Contract award limits were established in each loan agreement to define the demarcation between those awards that required prior Bank approval and those that did not. For example, the approval limit for a civil works contract might be $500,000. For consultant contracts the award limit might be $100,000. For goods and services, it might be $50,000. In principle, all contracts below these amounts were subject to review by the Bank after the fact, but in practice this rarely happened.

For international contractors, consultants, and suppliers, the payments would be made directly into their foreign accounts upon the submission of the appropriate supporting documents attached to Bank withdrawal applications. The withdrawal applications and supporting documents would be prepared by the local project implementation unit (PIU)[2] and sent to the Bank's disbursement officers to be processed. While these procedures were completely rational and seemed to protect the Bank's fiduciary responsibilities, in practice they depended completely upon the integrity of those managing the process—and this is where things would fall apart.

The second method of disbursement, the replenishment of revolving funds in the special accounts, posed even greater problems for the disbursement officers. These accounts were established to provide local project officials with funds for day-to-day operations. The process would begin with an initial deposit of US dollars into a local commercial bank account established by the PIU. The initial deposit amount was determined according to the estimated budgetary needs of the project, usually on a monthly basis. The PIU was required to make these expenditures according to Bank procedures and submit a withdrawal application each month for reimbursement of the amounts spent during that month. The withdrawal application would have an attached statement of expenditures (SOE), and the PIU was required to maintain all the supporting documentation for the SOEs available for review by the Bank. Such reviews were the responsibility of the Bank's project supervision teams, but these reviews were seldom carried out due to other perceived priorities.

As I intend to demonstrate later, the rampant abuse of the special accounts has been one of the root causes of the Bank's fiduciary failures, an oversight that clearly demonstrates the Bank's lack of understanding of project management, for how can one oversee a project if one does not know where the money is going? As with the system of direct payments, the special-accounts process made sense on paper, but it also depended completely upon the integrity of the local project managers, a quality that was often lacking in the corrupt environments surrounding these projects. Fraudulent documents, overpricing, bid rigging, payments for goods and services never delivered, undocumented travel expenses and stipends, and every possible form of embezzlement have been carried out through the special accounts, as I will discuss in greater detail in the following chapters.

THE FORTY PERCENT PROBLEM

NOTED: Even with much experience handling procurement matters, in some cases it is almost impossible to detect misrepresentation/fraud (estimated at 30–40%).

The above comment was the consensus of the Nigeria Country Team as recorded in the minutes of a meeting held on January 10, 1995, to discuss ways to reduce fraud in Bank procurement. This single sentence contains both a basic error, and a revealing truth. The error of course, was that rather than being impossible, fraud on Bank-funded projects was extremely easy to detect with only a minimum of effort and a little common sense, provided one wanted to look for it. The revealing truth was that after several decades of pretending the problem of corruption in Nigeria did not exist, the topic was finally being discussed openly. Of course, Nigeria was not unique in this regard, as the problem was just as pervasive in the rest of the Bank's portfolio. But it was nevertheless a revelation to hear team members actually call it fraud and provide a percentage figure for the record.

Despite the fact that it was a very considerable sum, no one dared mention exactly how much this percentage represented in dollars. This omission was typical of Bank meetings where it was more common to refer to "leakage," "rent seeking," and other non-threatening terms when discussing the corruption issue. For despite the Bank's obsession with numbers and statistical data, no one ever wanted to put a dollar figure on this problem. In this particular case, during the three prior fiscal years (FY92–94), the Bank had disbursed approximately \$950 million in Nigeria[3] which, if we are to use the team's own assessment, would mean that somewhere between \$280 million and \$380 million had been stolen from Bank-funded projects, or roughly \$100 million per year.

What was also not mentioned at the meeting was that we were really discussing probable criminal acts by our Nigerian counterparts, the very people we were constantly negotiating with, and interacting with, in the management of our Nigeria portfolio. Stealing public funds through fraud, embezzlement, and other forms of deception is, after all, a crime. But it was not good politics to call our clients criminals, so we were content merely to discuss ways in which we could perhaps reduce the possibilities of fraud through stricter application of the Bank's procurement guidelines. And although this meeting was indeed a positive first step at the operational level, its recommendations were merely reiterations of the various oversight practices and common-sense guidelines that Bank staff should have been following all along.

The Bank's procurement guidelines are defined according to the types of bidding procedures specified in each loan agreement.

In keeping with Article III of the Bank's Articles of Agreement, their purpose is to ensure both the most efficient and economical procurement for the execution of each project and the transparency of the process. Clearly spelled out on paper but impossible to oversee due to the shortage of procurement specialists and the enormous volume of transactions requiring Bank review. Under these conditions it is difficult to understand how management could so blithely ignore the impact this weakness in procurement oversight had on our mandate to ensure the transparency of the process. For, contrary to management's claims of the integrity of the Bank's procurement guidelines, in reality the whole process was conducted by harried and overworked individuals under such pressure to move things along that it was all too easy for corrupt individuals to take advantage of the system. We shall see in later chapters just how pervasive this could be. For now, let us take a brief look at the different categories of procurement that also define the parameters for fraud by project officials and their accomplices.

INTERNATIONAL COMPETITIVE BIDDING

Introduction: 2.1   The objective of International Competitive Bidding (ICB), as described in these Guidelines, is to provide all eligible prospective bidders with timely notification of a Borrower's requirements and an equal opportunity to bid for required goods and works.[4]

In principle, ICB guidelines are designed to provide the most transparent and economical method of procuring goods and works from qualified international and national suppliers and contractors. They define the types and sizes of contracts permitted in this category, how the borrower is to notify and pre-qualify bidders, how bids should be prepared and validated, how technical specifications and pricing are to be presented, and all the other necessary details common to international procurement. Most important, the guidelines clearly specify how bids are to be evaluated and contracts awarded, and it is in this area that things would often fall apart. The large foreign-exchange components of ICB contracts would attract government officials like flies to honey, with no end to the schemes they would create to pad the contracts for their own enrichment.

NATIONAL COMPETITIVE BIDDING (NCB)

NCB may be the preferred method of procurement where foreign bidders are not expected to be interested because (i) the contract values are small, (ii) works are scattered geographically or spread over time, (iii) works are labor intensive, or (iv) the goods or works are available locally at prices below the international market. NCB procedures may also be used where the advantages of ICB are clearly outweighed by the administrative or financial burden involved.[5]

NCB[6] suffered from the same failings as ICB in that the transparency of the process depended entirely upon the integrity of those managing it. Because the bidding primarily involved local firms, there was increased opportunity for local government officials to influence the submission of bids, their evaluation, and final awards. It was not unusual to find that friends, relatives, or outside business associates had information that was not available to other bidders or were otherwise given special treatment that ultimately led to the award of a contract. It was also not unusual to find instances where shell companies had been set up by government officials for the sole purpose of receiving contracts for locally procured vehicles, office equipment, building materials, and other items. The contracts awarded by the PIU would always be considerably above the true market value of the goods and services being procured and, amazingly, this particular form of embezzlement was never considered to be an issue worth noting in project audit reports. Nor did it appear to be of much concern to the Bank.

In addition to the ICB and NCB procedures noted above, there were other variations on the process including limited international bidding (LIB) and modified ICB. But despite all the procurement guidelines' precisely worded requirements and the harried efforts of Bank staff to keep things transparent, it all boiled down to how the government officials, either with or without complicit suppliers, were going to embezzle funds from the project accounts.

SHOPPING (INTERNATIONAL AND NATIONAL)

Shopping is a procurement method based on comparing price quotations obtained from several Suppliers, usually at least three, to assure competitive prices, and is an appropriate method for procuring readily available off-the-shelf goods or standard specification commodities that are small in value.[7]

As one might imagine, the further away the Bank's procurement guidelines go from the close oversight requirements of ICB to the looser arrangements of "shopping," the greater the risk for abuse by corrupt individuals. And while the abuse of ICB procedures frequently resulted in the loss of large sums over a relatively few transactions, the abuse of shopping procedures resulted in the loss of smaller sums on a large number of transactions. Coincidentally, over the years I observed that while the manipulation of the large ICB awards was usually orchestrated by the higher-level officials at the ministerial level and above, the manipulation of the lesser ICB, NCB, and shopping awards was usually orchestrated by lower-level officials within the ministry, the PIU, and other project agencies. In this manner project funds were embezzled both from the top down and from the bottom up, giving the project absolutely no chance of succeeding.

MISSION IMPOSSIBLE

Although the Bank's unwritten agenda was to get as much money out the door as quickly as possible, the management of its portfolio consumed a considerable amount of staff time and effort. Prior to loan approval we conducted economic studies at the local, provincial, national, and regional levels. We studied transportation, agriculture, rural development, water supply, electric power, education, health services, urban infrastructure, labor markets, financial systems, government institutions, and every other subject known to man. Then we prepared our country assistance strategies and determine when, where, and how we would lend to each country.

Once the appraisals had been completed and the loans approved by the Board, we would go into project-supervision mode. We were, after all, required to ensure that the project lived up to the promises and expectations presented in the appraisal reports, and to assist the borrowers in this endeavor. This was almost always impossible to achieve and was a frequent cause of staff frustration, especially for those of us who had to try and make it all work, while others, intent on promotions, moved on to generating more lending operations for the Bank.

Staff resources for supervision missions would be allocated by management each fiscal year, and in contrast to the generous resources allocated for appraisals, we were always far short of what was needed to do the job properly. Supervision missions would comprise one or more individuals, depending upon the size of the project and other task assignments. In many instances the team would also be working on the preparation or appraisal of the next lending operation, and this would usually take priority over supervision. Supervision itself always seemed to be a game of "catch-up," and we were always behind.

Things that were to have been accomplished by the PIU and the other project agencies were seldom done, while key local staff were either away for lengthy overseas training courses or had not yet been appointed by the government. We would often find that the government had neither provided counterpart funds as stipulated in the loan agreement nor implemented relevant policies that were essential for the project to succeed. Disbursements would be far behind original projections, while procurement was mired in bidding and contract irregularities that caused further delays. Too much time was spent socializing with the minister, too little time was spent checking the books to see what was happening to the money, and I could never understand why the latter was such a low priority for the Bank. Money is, after all, the lifeblood of any project, and how it is managed has a direct correlation with the project's success. Somehow this has never been truly understood by the Bank's management.

Bank procedures required that each supervision mission produce an "aide memoire" before returning to headquarters. The aide memoire provided a record of the mission's findings regarding the status of project implementation, tasks that were to be accomplished by the next mission, and problems and issues that needed to be addressed. A draft aide memoire was reviewed with PIU and ministry officials prior to a "wrap-up" meeting in which agreements were reached on future tasks and courses of action. Disagreements and outstanding issues were duly noted, and the document was signed by the mission leader and the appropriate PIU or other government officials.

Previous agreements notwithstanding, we would usually find that very little had been accomplished when we returned on the next supervision mission. As was often the case, the mission was either understaffed or had too little time to conduct an effective supervision of the project. Supervision in the field involved hurried visits to project sites, lengthy meetings with PIU and government officials, and late-night mission team review sessions to refine the aide memoire and plan for the next day. Project sites that were scattered around the country, or in remote locations, often were not inspected due to time or travel constraints, and often were never seen during the life of the project. All this was crammed into a few days, a week, or sometimes more, coupled with lengthy trips around the country by road or by air and overlapping assignments on other tasks and other projects. Under these conditions, and given the other agendas that frequently distracted the PIU and government officials, adequate supervision, and the protection of the Bank's fiduciary responsibility, was an impossibility.

Yet despite these obstacles to the implementation of our portfolio, project status reports emanating from within the Bank usually painted a picture of project success that was both deceptive and disingenuous. After each supervision mission, task managers were required to submit a boilerplate supervision report, with performance ratings graded from one (excellent) to four (poor),[8] and brief written evaluations were also recorded. The aide memoire and other supporting documents were submitted to management, and there was often a distinct difference between the information contained in the aide memoire and that presented in the numerical evaluation. With such a small spread between one and four, it was difficult to give a mathematical value to the serious problems that often plagued the projects we were funding. So, while the aide memoires would frequently describe pervasive problems with project management, counterpart funding shortfalls, disbursement delays, poor accounting and auditing practices, and other issues, the numerical ratings would typically indicate a much more benign situation.

A portfolio review in 1993 revealed the extent to which the contradiction between ratings and reality was recognized by some and yet ignored by management:

> **Contradictions**. We find that numerical supervision and reporting data do not always provide a complete picture of the realities in the field, while comparisons with other sources of information and firsthand reports from task managers do, at times, point to contradictions in the assessment and monitoring process. In addition, we recognize substantial differences in our expectations and assessments of project outputs (short term) versus project outcomes (long term) which complicates our overall measurement of the achievement of project objectives. A few typical examples help to highlight this problem:
>
> a. In the FY93 Semi-Annual Implementation Review, one Country Department stated that shortages of counterpart funds did "serious damage to our operations," while ratings for the availability of funds averaged 2.44 for the Department's sector activities. If this is the case, and 2.44 represents "serious damage," then one must conclude that the spread between (roughly) 2.5 and 1 represents pretty much the entire range of assessment in this category, and that 3's and 4's add little assessment value to the monitoring process. If this observation is valid, we may find that some projects with a 2 rating are also facing serious to moderately serious problems with counterpart funding.[9]

Yet, despite this admission of a failure in the rating system, management continued to hide reality with a bunch of fuzzy numbers, as evidenced by the FY94 review submitted the following year. And this was not just an isolated case in the PHR (population and human resources) sector, but was the modus operandi for the Africa Region and the rest of the Bank as well. Admitted by management but not acted upon, as seen by the following statements concerning an Operations Policy Research Department and

Operations Evaluation Department (OPR/OED) study on the disconnect between the annual review of the project portfolio (ARPP) ratings and the ratings in the project completion reports (PCRs) and project audit reports (PARs):

> The study was prompted by concerns expressed by Executive Directors in recent years about the lack of credibility of the Bank's project supervision ratings (Form 590). Antedating the criticisms in the Wapenhans report of the Form 590, these concerns were based mainly on the observed wide divergence between project performance assessments during supervision, as reported in the annual portfolio reports (ARPP), and at completion, as reported in OED's annual reports on evaluation results based on PCRs and PARs. Prior to 1984, the percentage of "unsatisfactory" projects reported in the OED annual reports generally exceeded the percentage of "problem" projects reported in the ARPP by a small margin; since then the gap has been much wider, averaging about 18 percent from 1989–91. . . .
>
> Finally, the study casts serious doubts on the quality of ARPP ratings during the initial years of project implementation and of those given to development objectives. ARPP ratings on both overall status and development objectives were excessively optimistic during the initial years of implementation, reflecting not only lack of information at that stage but also a failure perhaps to realistically assess risks at project entry or recognize early signs of future problems (e.g., long delays in effectiveness). ARPP development objectives ratings were also generally much more positive than already optimistic overall status ratings. This over optimism about development effectiveness was also observed in the FY92 portfolio.[10]

Do I need to go on? The Bank's management obviously knew about the failure of its rating system, but it preferred not to make any substantive changes to it. Yes, it was tinkered with at the edges, but it was never truly changed to the extent that it would honestly report on the status of the portfolio. To do so would, after all, expose the underlying agenda of the Bank's management, which was to get the money out the door and take no responsibility for what happens to it afterward.

NOTES

1. As presented during a February 1994 implementation workshop, withdrawal submissions during the early 1990s were averaging over seventeen thousand annually for the Africa Region alone. Adding to the problem was the fact that many applications were for multiple transactions, at times numbering in the hundreds, that were impossible to verify. As a rule, applications were being processed within four to seven days of receipt, an impossible time frame if one is to do the job properly.

2. Also called the project monitoring unit (PMU) on different projects.

3. *Annual Report on Portfolio Performance FY1994*, vol. 1, table 89.

4. *Guidelines: Procurement under IBRD Loans and IDA Credits*, rev. January 1999, p. 10.

5. Ibid., p. 33, para. 3.3.

6. In earlier days NCB was called local competitive bidding (LCB).

7. *Guidelines: Procurement under IBRD Loans and IDA Credits*, p. 33, para. 3.5.

8. These ratings were later changed to "highly satisfactory," "satisfactory," "unsatisfactory," and "highly unsatisfactory," which clouded evaluations even further.

9. "PHR Sector FY93 Portfolio Review" (ARPP), October 22, 1993, p. 1, para. 3.

10. Memo dated July 20, 1993, paras. 2, 11.

7

• • • • • • •

A Very Special Account

In our March 1976 audit report we drew attention to the need for Bank Management to develop means of assuring that funds disbursed against Statements of Expenditures (SOE) without supporting documentation were being used as intended. Efforts since that time to improve supervision techniques where SOEs have been used have proved to be largely ineffective. This is a matter that merits the attention of the Vice-President, Operations and other Vice-Presidents as appropriate. *The Controller's Department has estimated that SOEs will be used on about 14.0% ($876.5 million) of disbursements on loans and credits signed during FY77 ($6,245.0 million).* (emphasis added)

In paragraph 8 of the March 1976 report we stated that a January 1976 report by the Controller's Department showed that *approximately $1.7 billion or 9 percent of Bank and IDA commitments for FYs71–75 had been or would be disbursed against Statements of Expenditures (SOE) without supporting documentation. It was projected that the same 9 percent factor could result in unsupported disbursements of $4.9 billion in the FY76–80 period.* It was generally conceded at that time that field review of such documentation either by Bank staff or by independent auditors was largely non-existent. As a result, the Bank was not fulfilling its obligation to ensure that the proceeds of loans and credits were being used only for the purpose for which the loan or credit was provided. *A more recent estimate by the Controller's Department shows that SOEs are likely to be used on about 14 percent of disbursements on loans and credits signed during FY77.*[1] (emphasis added)

While preparing to give a workshop presentation in 1995, I came upon an internal audit report written seventeen years earlier pointing to serious issues surrounding the use of special accounts (SAs) and the reliance on SOEs as proof that funds had been spent in accordance with loan agreements. In essence, the report stated that between 1971 and 1975 approximately $1.7 billion, or roughly $340.0 million a year, had been disbursed without adequate documentation. This was projected to increase to $4.9 billion, or $980 million a year during the next five-year period, FY1976–80. The report caught my interest immediately because I was convinced that special accounts were the source of widespread fraud and embezzlement by our borrowers. Here was clear evidence that the issue had been raised many years before at the most senior levels of the Bank, but management had chosen to ignore it. Although the Internal Auditing Department (IAD) had expressed concern about SOE disbursements reaching 14 percent by 1977, by 1993 this percentage had risen considerably higher, as noted in a subsequent review of special accounts:

As of June 30, 1993, 1,861 special accounts (SA) were in operation with a total advance of $5.14 billion outstanding. During FY93, about $6.98 billion or 37% of total disbursements were channeled through SAs.[2]

So much for the concerns of the Bank's auditor general and controller! Ignoring their warnings, management continued to push money out the door with complete disregard for fiduciary responsibility. By FY93, annual SOE disbursements had reached $6.98 billion, an eightfold increase over the projected FY77 estimate of $876 million. This is not merely playing with numbers; the end result of the ever-increasing flow of funds through the special accounts has been a further reduction in the Bank's oversight of the money. This in turn has made it easier for corrupt officials to siphon funds from project accounts through a variety of schemes that are so simple and blatant that it is impossible to understand how the Bank's management could have allowed this condition to exist for the past three decades.

While the above figures represented the special account situation Bank wide, the problem was even greater in the Africa Region. Of the 1,861 active special accounts in 1993, 893 were in Africa; they added up to about two billion dollars.[3] But enough about abstract figures. Let us see what happens when special accounts are managed by corrupt individuals working within corrupt systems. How local project managers and their superiors can pervert the system to enrich themselves. And how all this is ignored in financial audits and Bank supervision. It is here that we shall learn the ugly truth about the special accounts.

EIGHTEEN CUPS OF TEA

It was my first mission as the new task manager for the project, and while visiting the offices of the National Board for Technical Education (NBTE) I asked to review its expenditures for a study that was one of the project sub-components. The NBTE had received a substantial advance in local currency[4] to employ consultants for the study, and I wanted to learn why their first draft report was almost one year overdue. The project accountant provided me with access to the account ledgers, and I sat down in a corner of the office to go over them.

I came across an entry showing a twenty thousand *naira* payment to a local roadside stand for eighteen cups of tea and snacks. At the current exchange rate, that translated to roughly $2,200 or $120 dollars per cup of tea. Astounded both at the cost and at the fact that Bank funds had been used for these refreshments, I first thought that this was some sort of entry error. But further examination revealed that it was not a mistake. The NBTE had actually paid $2,200 for eighteen cups of tea! And although this payment had come through the special account, it would never be revealed for what it was. The SOE would merely show it as a "reimbursement to NBTE for miscellaneous expenses," lumped together with other expenditures.

I discussed this matter with the accountant, who, although he had authorized the purchase order himself, said he would look into it without the slightest trace of concern that anything was wrong. This was crazy! And suddenly, it all became clear to me. Ever since I joined the Bank, I had been seeing more and more instances of fraud and corruption on the projects in our portfolio, but somehow, until this moment, I had never put all the pieces together to form the big picture. But now, the obscene price, paid with Bank funds for those eighteen cups of tea, brought home to me just how pervasive the problem was and how absurd it was for the Bank to pretend that we were on some sort of noble mission in partnership with dedicated government officials. But I am getting ahead of myself, so let me start at the beginning.

THE PROJECT

Approved in 1988, the loan for the Technical Education Project was for $23.3 million, with the government of Nigeria agreeing to provide an additional $3.4 million in counterpart funds, and the British Overseas Development Administration (ODA) providing $1.2 million in co-financing. In comparison with other projects in the Bank's Nigeria portfolio, this was a small operation. Its objectives were (1) to improve the quality of instruction at five technical schools, and (2) to strengthen institutional capacity for planning and coordinating technical education. Approximately $11.5 million of the foreign currency provided through the loan was to be used for the procurement of school workshop equipment, and the Bank's appraisal team leader had wisely insisted that this component be handled by outside procurement specialists. One million was allocated for textbook procurement, $1.7 million for technical assistance,[5] $400,000 for vehicles, and $340,000 for overseas training fellowships for staff members of the Ministry of Education, the PIU, and the five technical schools. Approximately $6.0 million in foreign exchange was provided for recurrent costs, and $2.1 million was set aside for contingencies.

EVEN WHEN YOU THINK
YOU'VE COVERED ALL THE BASES

It was a calculated move by the appraisal team to minimize procurement problems by insisting that the PIU use a reputable procurement agent. To this end, a contract was awarded to the International Labour Organization's (ILO) procurement branch, EQUIPRO. But the process did not always go as planned, and the frustrations experienced by the EQUIPRO consultants kept them awake many a night due to obstructions caused by PIU officials seeking to extract whatever personal benefits they could from a situation in which they were no longer in control of contract awards. The problems began immediately with the applications for letters of credit that were processed by the PIU:

> *Conversion of Dollars to Local Currency and Diversion of Funds.*
> The first expenditure from the Special Account was in the amount of $102,827 which was converted to *naira* (969,215), transferred to the Project Account, and used to pay the cost of opening nineteen letters of credit (LC) with Nigeria International Bank (NIB). Based on information provided by the PIU, the LCs were improperly drawn up and did not correspond to the contractual arrangements with the suppliers. As a result, fifteen LCs were not used and the Bank was informed that NIB agreed to refund roughly half of the fees incurred. This refund was made in the amount of 490,391 *naira* back into the Project Account where it was disbursed as noted in paragraph 2 above.[6] In this instance, two actions were taken that compromised the purpose of the Special Account:
>
> i. Despite the Bank's instructions to pay NIB directly in dollars from the Special Account, dollar funds were withdrawn, converted to local currency, and deposited in the Project Account which is the Government's vehicle for the disbursement of counterpart funds only.
> ii. The repayment of unused fees was returned as *naira* to the Project Account and used in non-compliance with Special Account regulations from which these funds originated.[7]

Now, why should this be considered anything more than bureaucratic bungling? Well, first, the PIU officials withdrew $102,000 in cash from the special account and deposited it several days later in the project account as *naira* at the official exchange rate. At that time the black market rate for dollars was roughly 50 percent higher than the official rate. Thus, there was the opportunity to sell the dollars on the black market and then deposit *naira* at the official rate into the project account while pocketing the difference. And how do we come to that conclusion? It's not too difficult, as both the special account and the project account were held in NIB, the same bank that was being paid to draw up the letters of credit. So what else could explain the fact that the funds were physically withdrawn as cash from one account one day and deposited in the other account several days later? And this, despite the Bank's instructions to pay NIB directly in dollars from the special account—a transaction that could have been executed internally without any cash passing through the teller's window!

Second, despite specific instructions from EQUIPRO, the PIU and NIB officials botched the paperwork required for the letters of credit. Of the nineteen letters of credit submitted to NIB, fifteen were rejected. And while this represented about 80 percent of NIB's fees, the PIU showed little interest in seeking a refund. It was only upon pressure from the Bank that NIB returned 50 percent of these fees, leaving some thirty thousand dollars unreturned and unaccounted for. So the project paid roughly fifty thousand dollars for four letters of credit that should have cost about five thousand dollars each. It was hard not to conclude that the PIU officials had pocketed an unknown amount of *naira* on the black market, while an additional thirty thousand dollars somehow disappeared. Meanwhile, EQUIPRO obtained the letters of credit at its own cost to protect its contract and its reputation.

Similar problems plagued EQUIPRO and the foreign suppliers throughout the process, as the PIU officials pressed continually for unnecessary trips overseas to "inspect" the suppliers' facilities, which, according to verbal reports received from the suppliers, were more about pressure for kickbacks than anything else. In all, four officials conducted nineteen trips for a total of 171 days over a four-year period at a cost to the project of roughly $200,000.[8] Other problems were caused by improper processing of customs clearance papers, delays in the reception and inventory of goods, and delays in the authorization of withdrawal applications for payment. On a final note, when the equipment did arrive, much of it languished in the school warehouses for years due to inertia within the school administrations, shortages of counterpart funds, and the overall lack of commitment that pervaded the Ministry of Education.

THE SPECIAL ACCOUNT

The Bank's Articles of Agreement require that loan proceeds be used to meet expenditures as they occur. However, to ensure an adequate flow of currency to finance the Bank's share of eligible expenditures with a minimum of administrative delay, the Bank may disburse funds before expenditures are made. The Borrower maintains advance disbursements in a separate special deposit account (SA) operated on terms and conditions satisfactory to the Bank.

The borrower submits replenishment applications at regular intervals specified by the Bank (usually intervals of one month, but not more than three months). If the SA is inactive for six months, the Bank notifies the borrower that it will request a refund of the outstanding balance unless, within 90 days, the borrower submits satisfactory evidence of eligible expenditures financed through the SA.[9]

The special account was opened with an initial deposit of $2.0 million in April 1989 and remained idle for twenty months until the first expenditures occurred in January 1991. As noted earlier, the purpose of this account was primarily to provide the PIU with access to foreign currency to facilitate project operations. It had been estimated during project appraisal that the $2.0 million would be needed to carry out the various project activities and would be replenished on a monthly basis as expenses were incurred. Yet the account was left untouched for more than a year and a half due to inertia at the ministry and the PIU, but perhaps more to the point, because it was earning interest that, as we shall see shortly, could be moved elsewhere, beyond the scrutiny of the Bank. Despite repeated pressure from the Bank to get the project rolling and to utilize the account, it wasn't until the payment for the letters of credit for the EQUIPRO contract that the account became active. Thus began an organized and thinly veiled program of embezzlement and fraud that continued throughout the life of the project, as documented in a special account review:

> The last two withdrawals from the Special Account in the amounts of $180,000 and $47,400 were made on October 12th and December 16th, 1992. Documents submitted for the recovery of these funds [SOEs used to justify the use of remaining special account funds at the end of the project] have been examined and found to be unacceptable for the reasons noted below:
>
> For the withdrawal of $180,000 recorded on October 12th:
>
> a. This amount was converted to *naira* at the rate of 19.37 and deposited in the Project Account [the separate account used for counterpart funds]. The *naira* amount deposited is shown as 3,486,834 yet the total amount of invoices claimed under this application is 5,224,865 naira. At the conversion rate used, this amounts to a discrepancy of $89,722 more than the amount withdrawn from the Special Account thus preventing a proper reconciliation of these funds.
>
> b. Despite widely different conditions at the five project locations and widely different specifications on the 23 contracts covered by this withdrawal, there are highly unusual similarities in the contract prices. Fifteen contracts were priced between 249,900 and 250,000 naira, two were around 240,000 and three were for 200,000. Given the differences in services and goods provided, it would be impossible for different suppliers in different locations to all arrive at nearly the same figures for these contracts. For example: (i) the provision of 2 video cassette recorders and 2–24" TVs for Afikpo cost 249,999 while (ii) the "refurbishing of library furniture and equipment" (details not specified) at Ado-Ekiti also cost 249,999 and (iii) the "refurbishing and installation of library audio-visual aids" at Bida cost 249,998.
>
> c. Despite widely different conditions, contract specifications, and project locations, *ALL* 23 contracts were awarded, signed, and invoiced over periods not exceeding 11 working days. Of these, (i) 10 contracts were

awarded on August 27th (at 2 different locations) with contracts signed August 28th; (ii) 8 contracts were awarded on August 28th and signed the same day; (iii) 15 invoices (from 4 different locations) were submitted on September 10th, 10 working days after the contracts were signed, while 3 invoices were submitted *one day* after the contracts were signed; and (iv) one invoice was authorized for payment four days *before* it was submitted by the contractor.

As noted in (b) above, given the differences in goods and services to be provided, and the different locations, it would be impossible for all these awards, contracts and invoices to be processed simultaneously and within a time frame that contradicts all local experience to date.[10]

As you can see, the devil is in the details. So let's try to interpret this. First, the PIU transferred $180,000 from the special account to the project account, where it will no longer get the same scrutiny that the Bank would apply to the special account. Then, in their rush to account for these funds, they provided invoices that totaled more than the amount transferred, without any rational explanation. Did they exchange the dollars for *naira* on the black market, or did they just throw in a bunch of invoices to cover the special account transfer without regard to the totals? I was never able to get a definitive answer to this question, but it was consistent with accounting patterns I had observed throughout the project—a total disregard for accuracy, transparency, or fiduciary responsibility. Just enter anything in the ledgers, produce invoices, any invoices will do, and don't worry because no one will conduct a serious examination of the books anyway. Neither the auditors, nor the government, nor the Bank.

Next, if we follow the transfers to the project account, we see that there was a mad rush to award contracts for vague and unsubstantiated purposes such as "maintenance of library furniture" and minor civil works, none of which was specified in the appraisal report or the loan agreement. Among these contracts we find that two VCRs and two 24-inch TVs were purchased for 249,999 *naira,* or $12,900 at the official exchange rate! Total street value for the same four items was confirmed at about $1,000.

Another red flag was that the limit for local procurement without Tender Board approval was 250,000 *naira*. How convenient that all these bids just happened to fall at, or below, that figure! As for the maintenance of library furniture, visits to several of the sites where this had supposedly occurred revealed the same broken chairs, tables, and bookshelves that had been seen on previous missions.

In sum, there was absolutely no evidence that any goods or services had been received as stated in the SOEs. And it was no surprise to me when, several years later, as part of a review of the now-closed project accounts, the Bank's auditor commented on unexplained "expenditure fluctuations," which included, among other things, $609,826 for the "maintenance of office building and equipment" during the final months of the project.[11] Of course, other than this one comment, no further action was taken to determine exactly why over half a million dollars was invoiced for such questionable expenditures. So, with no serious oversight by the Bank, and no oversight by the Tender Board, the PIU officials engaged in a final feeding frenzy at the end of the project. A brief look at one of the SOE sheets is all one needs to see the sheer audacity of the PIU officials in their rush to divert the last remaining funds from the special account after first transferring them to the project account (see Figure 7–1).

THE CHECK IS IN THE MAIL

Although lengthy delays in processing procurement were the norm on Bank-funded projects, whenever these transactions happened quickly, it was a sure sign that something was afoot as public officials sought to manipulate the process. Meetings with each potential bidder are held to ensure that the most cooperative bidder will get the contract award. Meetings among the officials are held to determine how the proceeds will be divided. More time is taken as the PIU corresponds back and forth with uncooperative bidders as it tries to deter those who might compromise the scam. And then, there are the time consuming communications back and forth with the Bank to obtain the Bank's approval or "no objection" to the procurement. Once contracts are awarded, there are two time tracks for payment against invoices. If the integrity of

Figure 7-1. Embezzlement of $180,000

Date	Name of Beneficiary	Purpose	Income	Expenditure	Balance
12/10/92	A/c No 0153547014	Cash Deposit	1,250,000.00	$180,000	4,947,416.85
9/10/92	"	Funds transfer	3,486,834.00		8,434,250.85
7/10/92	M/S Alfex Ltd	Minor Civil Works		250,000.00	8,184,250.85
"	M/S Tech Ltd	Mtce of lib. furn/Equipt		200,000.00	7,984,250.85
"	M/S K.L. Engineering	Mtce of lib.furn/Equipt		250,000.00	7,734,250.85
"	M/S El'tano Ltd	"		250,000.00	7,484,250.85
"	M/S GRace Ent.	Minor Civil Works		250,000.00	7,234,250.85
"	M/S M.O. Agene	"		250,000.00	6,984,250.85
"	M/S Nwabuwanne Ent.	Equipt. Installation		200,005.00	6,784,245.85
"	M/S Lizato Nig. ent	Mtce of lib.furn/Equipt		250,000.00	6,534,245.85,
"	M/S Graceland Ltd	"		200,001.00	6,334,244.85,
"	M/S Rume Nig. Coy.	Minor civil Works		250,000.00	6,084,244.85
"	M/S De-Far Fields Ltd	Mtce of lib furn/Equipt		200,000.00	5,884,244.85,
"	M/S Zion Grace Ent.	"		240,000.00	5,644,244.85
"	M/S Oye Gever Coy	"		130,003.00	5,514,241.85,
"	M/S Tola Bola Ent.	Minor Civil works		200,000.00	5,314,241.85,
"	M/S MidBell Ventura			250,000.00	5,064,241.85,
"	M/S Oluw Investment	Mtce of lib furn/Equipt		250,000.00	4,814,241.85
"	M/S Tunde Oderinde	"		250,000.00	4,564,241.85

the procurement process has been maintained, and there is no indication that fraud is involved, it usually takes forever for the PIU to process the payment documents.[12] The following fax requesting a payment for shipping services is an example:

> Subject: Outstanding payment of P____'s invoice covering port rental and container demurrage charges in the amount of Naira 357,762.
>
> I refer to your telephone conversation with Mr. G.____ on 30 August 1993 concerning the above-mentioned subject. The forwarder P____ has sent us several complaints over the past nine months about the outstanding payment because the invoices were certified by ILO/EQUIPRO and submitted to the PIU of the Federal Ministry of Education in Lagos.
>
> ILO/EQUIPRO and the ILO Office in Lagos have tried on numerous occasions to convince the PIU of their obligation to pay the amount due to P____. Therefore, I should be grateful if you would verify the request by Mr. E.____ (ref. AP/CON/65/193 of 8 July 1993) to settle this long outstanding

payment of Naira 357,762 through your disbursement division.[13]

In situations such as this, worn out and in desperation, the supplier would eventually agree to accept a lesser amount than that which was owed. Typically, the government officials would feign sympathy and understanding for the supplier's plight and state sadly that they had done everything they could to expedite the payment. They would then suggest that the payment could be pushed through the system if the supplier would agree to a "commission" for those officials higher up who could authorize the release of the funds. The higher officials were themselves, of course, and the matter would be resolved with another small victory for corruption.

The second track for payments against invoices was exactly the opposite. Where their personal enrichment was involved, PIU officials would move heaven and earth to ensure that the money was paid immediately. After all, at about the same time that the PIU began stalling the payment of 357,000 *naira* to the shipping company for clearly legitimate expenses, it was paying out roughly 3.5 million *naira* against 250,000 *naira* contracts that were clearly fraudulent. So, whereas there had been lengthy delays in processing payments for the suppliers connected with the EQUIPRO procurement management contract, the high-speed processing of payments to draw down the special account at the end of the project was alarming to me. Ten contracts awarded on August 27 and signed the very next day? Eight contracts awarded and signed the same day on August 28? At the end of August? When everyone was usually away on vacation? Hardly likely! And then we have fifteen invoices submitted within ten working days after contract signing, while three were submitted the day after signing? Last, we have one invoice that was authorized for payment four days before it was submitted by the contractor? This certainly had all the earmarks of fraud and embezzlement to me, and further investigation of the various goods and services allegedly delivered proved this to have been the case.

Then there is the matter of the final $47,400 withdrawn from the special account. When asked to return the unused funds from the special account, the PIU immediately transferred them into the project account under the pretense that it was to be used to pay NBTE for the study noted previously. A study for which, among other things, $2,200 had been paid for eighteen cups of tea! A study that merely required the consultants to travel around the country to gather basic data, compile it, and present their findings and recommendations in a final report. A study that never made it beyond a draft form. A study that proved to be useless:

STATUS OF LEGAL COVENANTS
Loan Schedule 6, Section C:
    NBTE to conduct study of relevant technical and vocational education issues including the cost and financing of this sub-sector and an action plan for the phased implementation of the main recommendations. This study to be completed and provided for Bank review no later than 6/30/90.
    Draft study was received 10/91 and reviewed by Bank. Study does not provide serious analysis of sector issues and proposes strategies without examining implementation or cost effectiveness issues. *The Bank considers the study to be of such poor quality that revisions will not be helpful.*[14] (emphasis added)

This brief assessment of the study should have been sufficient to cancel the exercise. In effect, the PIU did just that, for although it reported that it had withdrawn the $47,400 to pay the NBTE, it did not do so. Instead, the funds were held in the project account through the end of the project. And although the special account was officially closed with this last withdrawal, the funds remained available to the PIU through this tactic. No adequate or acceptable documentation was ever provided to substantiate this withdrawal, and the issue faded from view. In two interesting comments in the aide memoire of the final project supervision mission, the mission leader stated:

Project sustainability is now in doubt as FME had not fully complied with the agreements reached with the Bank.
    NBTE has not prepared an outline for the needs of the institutions as agreed at project inception. The project institutions seem to have an idea of what they require and have shown greater determination to survive. However, government's own commitment appears too weak to assure anyone of a

brilliant future for technical education in the country. A follow up project may help to correct this situation.[15]

Typical Bank logic! The project is not sustainable, and the government is not committed. By all means, we should have a followup project. Let's give them some more money, and let's open another special account.

NOTES

1. Internal Auditing Department, "Report on an Audit of Bank Loans and IDA Credits," September 29, 1978, p. 2, para. 5; p. 22, para. 67.

2. Loan Department, "Report of the Working Group for Review of Special Accounts," September 8, 1993, p. 2, para. 2.

3. Ibid., table 1.

4. The *naira*, which had an official exchange rate of about 9 to 1 against the dollar at that time.

5. Technical assistance was provided by the British Council through the ODA funding.

6. *Author's note:* Paragraph 2 referred to questionable procurement, including overpayment for goods and services, the use of unqualified suppliers, improper fund transfers, and unacceptable auditing.

7. Steve Berkman, "Case Study of Financial Management and Accounting Practices," September 3, 1993, p. 4, para. 4.a.

8. The ILO maintained offices in Lagos, and EQUIPRO staff members were in Nigeria frequently, so these trips were totally unnecessary.

9. *The World Bank Operational Manual,* "Operational Policies," OP 12.20 (May 1994), para. 1, 6.

10. Steve Berkman, "Nigeria—Technical Education Project, Special Account Review," July 1993. Submitted to management. This extract is only a partial list of ten different types of scams discussed in the review.

11. Internal memo dated April 28, 1994.

12. This would give the PIU officials one last opportunity to extract kickbacks from desperate suppliers seeking payment.

13. Fax, September 1, 1993, from ILO/EQUIPRO to the PIU. Names have been omitted to protect identities.

14. Attachment to internal memo dated September 23, 1993.

15. "Implementation Completion Report," mission aide memoire, October 27, 1995.

8

· · · · · · ·

Playing with the Books

THE PROJECT ACCOUNT

The Borrower shall: (i) pay into the Project Account an initial amount of three million Naira (N 3,000,000); and (ii) thereafter pay into the Project Account semi-annually amounts sufficient to meet the Borrower's contributions to the costs of the Project. The said semi-annual payments shall be based on estimates of project expenditure which the Project Office shall: (A) prepare each fiscal year for the immediately following fiscal year, and (B) furnish to the Bank for its review no later than June 30 of the fiscal year in which the estimates are to be prepared.[1]

The project account was established for the management of the government's counterpart funds. These funds were to be used primarily for the installation of the workshop equipment procured by EQUIPRO. Sadly, of the initial three million *naira* placed in the account, only fifty thousand *naira* were used for this purpose. The project account was also established to pay for the costs of administering the project and any other general overhead expenses. Over the life of the project, however, two factors prevented the account from serving this function. The first factor was the government's inability and/or unwillingness to provide the amount of counterpart funds stipulated in the loan agreement. This was a common occurrence in our Africa Region portfolio, and I was always amazed at the naive and unrealistic assumptions presented in our appraisal reports concerning a government's ability to meet its counterpart funding commitments. Time after time and project after project we would begin with assurances that these funds would be provided, yet in the end they rarely materialized in sufficient amounts to affect the project.

Second, the project account provided a conduit for diverting foreign exchange from the special account, and no stone was left unturned as project officials sought to manipulate each and every transaction for their personal enrichment. While some transactions appeared legitimate, most were contrived for the purpose of creating the necessary paperwork needed to justify payments made to complicit suppliers, consultants, contractors, friends, and associates. Who would suspect that these were not transparent transactions? After all, the process had been followed, documents had been properly signed, and all was in order. An island of probity in the midst of one of the most corrupt governments in all of Africa. But what will we find beneath the surface?

> 2.a. Despite extreme shortages of funds for the project schools, the PIU (with only 8 senior staff) procured the following items for its own use at a cost of 1.74m *naira* (or approximately 25% of all counterpart funds to that date): (i) one switchboard and sixty telephones, (ii) two copying machines, (iii) two duplicating machines, (iv) fourteen paper shredding machines, (v) one radio communication system, and (vi) furnishings for two rented apartments.
>
> For the four polytechnics, the PIU procured the following items at a cost of 2.0m *naira* (an additional 29% of counterpart funds): (i) four radio communications systems, (ii) eight copying machines, (iii) eight typewriters, (iv) eight file cabinets, (v) eight cooking stoves, (vi) forty-eight air conditioners, (vii) four freezers, and (viii) twelve refrigerators.
>
> The polytechnics were not consulted on this procurement, and none of the above items had any impact on the preparation of school facilities for the delivery of teaching aids and workshop equipment essential to achieving project objectives.[2]

Returning from a supervision mission, the above was included in my back-to-office report. Just to give you some idea about how the PIU officials embezzled funds transferred from the special account to the project account, let's take a look at some of these transactions.

MORE SHREDDERS THAN THE CIA

Given the small size of the PIU and the nature of its operations, the procurement of shredding machines seemed strange. This was an eight-person office, and all documents had to be retained on file for Bank supervision purposes, not to mention the record retention requirements of the government. Clearly, the need to shred documents did not exist. But this did not deter the project director from ordering ten machines at 25,000 *naira* each. The total amount of 250,000 *naira* was conveniently below the limit for Tender Board review

With that information, I went to an office equipment store in Lagos seeking to confirm that the PIU had at least obtained the best possible price. Using the same specifications contained in the PIU documents, I obtained a quotation of 9,000 *naira* per unit. How about that! A difference of 16,000 *naira* per unit, or 160,000 *naira* for ten units. An overcharge of 178 percent that, translated to dollars, came to roughly $16,000 at the time. Several months later the PIU purchased four more units at the same price, bringing the total to fourteen shredders for the eight-person office. Fourteen shredders of which only four could be found in inventory.

DO YOU HEAR ME NOW?

Another suspicious transaction was the purchase of short-wave radio equipment. Without consulting the project schools, the PIU had decided that reliable communications were needed between the schools, the NBTE, and itself. The fact that throughout the life of the project there was very little interaction between the PIU and the schools was irrelevant. It was also irrelevant that the schools had a more serious need for funds to prepare for the arrival of the equipment procured by EQUIPRO. In fact, the only thing that appeared to be relevant was that paperwork had to be generated to facilitate the disbursement of funds from the project account.

And so, in June 1990 a contract was awarded for slightly less than one million *naira* (approximately $100,000) to install short-wave radios at the five project schools and the NBTE. These schools, incidentally, were many hundreds of miles apart, making this sort of communication extremely difficult, if not impossible, with anything less than the most sophisticated equipment. Interestingly enough, although the radio system was to ensure reliable communications among all the project sites, there were no radios installed at the PIU office. This omission was rectified ten months later when another purchase order was issued for an additional 166,135 *naira* (about $16,000). An inspection of the installations revealed some very poor quality radios with inadequate antennas that never worked properly and were seldom used during the life of the project:

> Communications between sites and with PIU vary from poor to non-existent. . . . Because telephone communication between PIU and the sites is virtually impossible a short wave radio system was installed. It has only occasionally worked at all and never effectively. More than anything else this lack of communications has affected organization and control of the project. Only lack of funds for minor civil works has had a greater impact. At the very least an effective radio communication system with proper support (lacking from the supplier of this project) must be available for any future project.[3]

So, another million plus *naira* vanished on the needless procurement of overpriced junk that had no bearing on the success of the project. Between the two expenditures, about $116,000 was liberated from the project account. The actual value of the goods received was estimated to be less than $10,000. An overpricing of roughly one thousand percent. Not bad for one transaction!

LIVING WELL

Then there was the furnishing of two apartments, an activity that I found impossible to reconcile with the project objectives but which nevertheless consumed a considerable amount of project funds. Early in the project, the PIU issued a contract in the amount of 433,123 *naira* (about $50,000 at that time) to provide furniture, install carpeting, and do carpentry work at two locations on Victoria Island in Lagos. Victoria Island is a high-rent district with wealthy Nigerian and expatriate residences and offices of international firms and donor agencies. Victoria Island had absolutely nothing to do with the implementation of the project, but this did not stop the PIU from furnishing two "rented" apartments for unknown individuals.

Other red flags that aroused my suspicion were the five pages of invoices itemizing furniture, carpeting, curtains, linens, freezers, kitchen stoves, and other household items—and the fact that the PIU refused to identify the recipients of this largesse. My attempts to visit these locations to confirm the existence of the items were stonewalled by the PIU officials, who somehow could never find the keys to the apartments. Were these apartments for some senior government officials who may or may not have had any involvement with the project? Were the prices competitive? Were the goods delivered as invoiced? The Bank would never know the answers to these questions, nor would it care. And so, another $50,000 disappeared from the project accounts.

STAYING COOL

Other scams fabricated by the PIU involved items that it allegedly ordered for the technical schools but that had not been requested by the school administrators. High on the list were air conditioners, and the red flags were abundant. One disturbing fact was that two different suppliers in Lagos were awarded contracts on the same date to provide the same twenty-four air conditioners to the same schools at the same unit prices. No manufacturer or model numbers were provided in either contract to permit cost comparisons or inventory control. The most expensive units of this size available in the local marketplace cost less than half the price paid by the PIU. And last, but not least, these units could not be located at the project sites. How could I have possibly suspected that these contracts were just a small part of a series of scams perpetrated by the project officials? As shown in Figure 8–1, they had issued a steady stream of highly questionable purchase orders in 1990 alone, totaling roughly $535,000 of World Bank money that had been transferred over from the special account.

Figure 8–1. Fraudulent Procurement from the Project Account

SCHEDULE OF FIXED ASSETS.

PROJECT ACCOUNT.

Attachment 1
page 1 of 2

Appendix IIIA

S/No	Date of PV	Name of Supplier	Items Supplied	Location	Purchase Order No	Amount N
1.	23/3/90	M/S Espo Nig Coy.	PABX Equipment	PIU Lagos	WC 974/P.1914/1	398,119
2.	29/3/90	M/S Ara Tejumade Ltd and M/S Bowale Int. Coy.	Airconditioners	A/Ekiti, Mubi, Bida, Afikpo	WC 974/P.1781-2/1	504,000
	29/3/90	M/S Ara Tehumade Int Ltd	Refrigerators	A/Ekiti, Mubi Bida, Afikpo.	W.C. 974/P.1781/1	96,000
	"	M/S Bic office System/ M/S Bolanle Enterprises M/S J. Lidjas Stores.	Sharp Copiers	Bida, Afikpo, A/Ekiti, Mubi.	WC 974/P1780/1	627,800
	"	M/S Bic Office System	Filling Cabinets	"	"	120,000
	"	M/S Bowale Int. Coy	Deep Freezers	"	WC 974/P.1782/1	36,000
	"	M/S BOlanle Ent.	Gas Cookers	"	WC 974/P.1779/1	84,000
	"	M/S Bowale Int. Coy	Deep Freezers	"		36,000
	31/10/90	M/S Aurora Interiors	Furniture	V/Island Lagos	DTR 989/P.791/12	433,123
	7/9/90	M/S Dadson Nig Ltd	Power Generating Sets	Unwana-Afikpo	WC 974/P.4001/1	721,780
	6/9/90	M/S Malig Assoc.Nig.Ltd	Shredding Machines	PIU Lagos	FME/S/869/C.472/90	250,000
	21/9/90	M/S Spider Int. Ltd/ M/S J. Lidjas Stores.	Duplicating Machines	"	FME/S/869/C.479/90	110,000
	1/11/90	M/S Awoyemi Nig.Ltd	Tranceivers	Mubi, Bida, Afikpo, Kaduna, Ado-Ekiti & Yaba.	WC.974/P4009/1	946,969.97
	21/9/90	M/S Hamak Nig Ltd	Computers	PIU Lagos	FME/S/869/C474/90	135,000
					Total	N4,482,231.97

Average exchange rate for 1990 period is N8.3750 = $1.00

$535,192

AND THEN THERE'S THE INTEREST ACCOUNT

> IBRD interest or IDA service charges accrue from the date funds are advanced into the SA. To offset these charges, borrowers may make arrangements to earn interest on the unwithdrawn balance of the SA. Borrowers need not report the use of interest earnings to the Bank, but they should be encouraged to establish appropriate regulations for the use of these funds and to include an examination of compliance with these regulations as part of the annual audit of the SA.[4]

From April 1989 through November 1992, the special account earned $237,312 in interest. As allowed by the Bank, the PIU established a separate account for these earnings, but any intention to use these funds for the project, or any other legitimate purpose, appeared to end there. As noted previously, the longer the special account remained idle, the more interest the PIU was able to earn. And the fact that these funds were now outside the mainstream of the project's financial-management activities made them an easy target for further embezzlement by the PIU officials.

The project became effective on March 17, 1989, and the Bank's initial transfer of $2.0 million was made into the special account a month later. From that point on, interest earned in the special account was transferred into the project interest account. But despite the fact that counterpart funds were urgently needed to get the project up to speed, it wasn't until May of the following year that $5,071 was withdrawn for an airline ticket in the name of a ministry official. The destination and purpose of the trip were never specified, nor were any supporting documents submitted.

Two months later another withdrawal, of $15,037, was made by the project director for "incidental expenses" on a one-week trip to Washington. The director was the same person who, among many other things, had "urgently" requested the shredding machines for the PIU office; now he needed $15,000 for a one-week stay in Washington. This was in addition to his government travel allowance and his airfare ticket, which was purchased from the project account. Not bad for one week in Washington. Again, no supporting documentation was provided to account for these funds, nor were any unused funds returned to the project.

With money coming in faster than it was going out, within four months the increasing balance proved too tempting for the PIU officials to resist. And so, a $140,000 transfer was made to the PIU account. This account was another testament to the PIU's ability to move funds around, for it was totally off the Bank's radar screen and was apparently unknown by any government officials other than the project director, the project accountant, and the director of finance at the Ministry of Education. As there were no other records to substantiate the status of this fourth project account, I could only assume that it was treated as the private account of these individuals. Interestingly, the entry for this withdrawal only states that it was a transfer from the Central Bank of Nigeria to the Central Bank of Nigeria with a penciled notation that it was for the PIU account. There was no further explanation of the purpose of the transfer. Kiss another $140,000 goodbye.

So how did all this affect the project? Two accounts would have been sufficient to manage the funds provided by the Bank and those provided by the government; the special account for the foreign exchange provided by the Bank, and the project account for the counterpart funds provided by the government. The special account could have been used for hard currency payments, and the project account for local currency payments. It would have been neat, simple, and reasonably transparent. Interest earnings could have been retained in the special account or could have been transferred to the project account as part of the government's counterpart contributions. But by having the additional interest account and the PIU account, the PIU officials were able to divert funds as they saw fit.

And so, while the project schools struggled without funds to upgrade their facilities in preparation for the new workshop equipment, the PIU officials helped themselves to every dollar and *naira* they could get their hands on. Numerous costly junkets overseas on every sort of pretext. Letters of credit that were useless. Excessive stipends for overseas training. The mad rush to produce fraudulent contracts when asked to return unused funds. Extreme overpricing of goods and services. Shredding machines, telephones, short-wave radios, refrigerators, air conditioners, and household furniture. And let's not forget those eighteen cups of tea!

And what did all this cost? The previous examples I've cited were just a small fraction of the roughly $1.1 million that I'd found embezzled through these various scams (see Figure 8–2).

AND IT DOESN'T END THERE

Needless to say, the manipulation of the various project accounts in the Technical Education Project was not an isolated case in our Nigeria portfolio, as can be seen from the following:

There has been mismanagement of the Special Account. When funds ($2m) were transferred from the Special Account to the Project Account in March 1993 some of them were used to make investments in local finance houses. In all, N8m.

Figure 8-2. Embezzlement from the Interest Account

DATE	DEPOSITOR/BENEFICIARY	PURPOSE OF PAYMENT	INCOME	EXPENDITURE	BALANCE AVAILABLE
		BALANCE BROUGHT FORWARD	-	-	₦ 120,908.07
18/6/90	Interest Earned on Special Account	C R Transaction	₦9,653.68	-	₦ 130,561.75
10/7/90	Mr. T. O. Osolukoya	Incidental expenses in Washington during Primary Education Project Negotiation	-	₦ 15,037.50 *To be accounted*	₦ 115,524.25
27/7/90	Interest Earned on Special Account	Interest earned with effect from 1/6 – 29/6/90	₦9,070.30	-	₦ 124,594.55
16/8/90	Interest on Special Account	C R Transaction	₦9,906.25	-	₦ 134,500.80
27/9/90	Interest on Special Account	Interest earned with effect from August, 1990	₦9,458.34	-	₦ 143,959.14
10/12/90	Interest on Special Account	Interest on World Bank Technical Education Investment with CITI N.Y. for October, 1990	₦9,734.37	-	₦ 153,693.51
8/11/90	Central Bank of Nigeria	Transfer to Central Bank of Nigeria	TO P/W A/C -	*Rate ₦.e576* $140,000.00	₦ 13,693.51
		JANUARY 1991			
10/1/91	Nigeria International Bank	Transfer from Domiciliary Account to Project Naira Account	-	₦ 1,219.51	₦ 12,474.00
11/1/91	Nigeria International Bank	Credit to C/A	₦7,950.54	-	₦ 20,424.54
31/1/91	Nigeria International Bank	Transfer	-	₦ 18,146.11	₦ 2,278.43
15/2/91	Interest on Special Account	Interest earned for the month of January, 1991	₦7,129.29	-	₦ 9,407.72
15/2/91	Mr. T. O. Osolukoya & one other	Cash withdrawn	-	₦ 5,160.00	₦ 4,247.72
11/4/91	Interest on Special Account	C R Transaction	₦6,059.89	-	₦ 10,307.61

₦ 68,961. – ₦179,562.–

($307,600 at N26=$1, the exchange rate prevailing at the time),
was invested, of which N6.3 million ($242,300) has not been
returned to the project, and as the finance houses involved
have collapsed,[5] it is doubtful whether the monies can be re-
couped. This is the conclusion reached in the 1994 audit report. The source of these monies used in the investments was
never revealed to the Bank; it was assumed that the monies
had come from counterpart funds. The audit reports for 1993
and 1994, conducted by Price Waterhouse, while mentioning
that the investments were made, were silent on the source of
the funds and did not alert us to potential mismanagement
of the Special Account. The investigations started by the mission have revealed that an internal PAFA [public administration financial audit] review of the investments in November
1993 recommended staff suspensions and that charges be
brought against the staff involved. These reports have only
just been shared with the Bank. *None of the actions recommended
were taken.*[6] (emphasis added)

Given what we have already seen, it isn't hard to imagine that
this was not the only instance of mismanagement of the special

account in the National Population Project, nor in other projects in the Nigeria portfolio, as witness the following:

Our examination of the Special Account performance in Nigeria reveals disturbing data. At the end of May 1993 there were 88 Special Accounts under 34 operations with a total outstanding balance of $127.5 million. Of these 88 accounts, only 18 had been replenished in a timely fashion, namely, within the previous month; 33 had been replenished within two to six months; and 37 more than six months or not at all. (Accounts which are inactive for more than six months are officially designated as "delinquent" and are subject to recall.) By our internal rating system (the first group is rated at 100%, the second at 50%, and the third at 0%), Special Account utilization is currently at an unacceptable rate of 39%. The picture is even gloomier when we see that among the last group of 37, eight accounts were last active in CY [calendar year] 1991, six in CY 1990, and one in CY 1988.[7]

This was part of a lengthy letter to the Ministry of Finance that attempted to cajole the ministry into better management of the various project accounts. It was a joke! The Nigerians had been managing these accounts for years and knew full well what they were doing. They had left special account funds idle while they earned interest that could be diverted to less supervised accounts. They had created false documents to cover the embezzlement of funds. They had engaged in bid-rigging, extorted kickbacks from suppliers, and procured unnecessary goods and services for the sole purpose of facilitating these activities. This had been going on for years and would continue to go on, despite the halfhearted efforts of the Bank to maintain some semblance of probity in its dealings with the government. We could talk all we wanted; we could send letters; we could hold meetings with high-ranking officials; we could conduct financial management, procurement, and disbursement workshops; and we could stand on our heads. But our "partners," the government officials with whom we were dealing, had no intention of ending this wonderful arrangement by which they were enriching themselves. And the Bank had no intention of ending its relationship with these thieves.

NIGERIA IS NOT ALONE

Now, I may have created the impression that all the Bank's special-account problems are centered in its Nigeria portfolio, but that is not the case. While Nigeria is certainly a leading contender for the title of most corrupt country in Africa, it cannot claim to be unique in that regard. Even in such Bank-favored countries as Uganda, one can find similar examples of the legerdemain practiced with the special accounts:

> We would like to bring to your attention that almost all (90%) of the items checked for documentary evidence showed serious deficiencies in the documentation required for payments made using SOEs. One particular item, PV 14971 pertaining to the expenditure of Ush 52,750,000 [approximately $52,000 at the then-current exchange rate] for burglar-proofing is particularly disturbing. There does not seem to be any evidence that competitive bidding procedures were followed, evidence that work has been done, or of the Bank's prior no objection for this work. These findings would seem to indicate weaknesses in the basic financial and accounting systems of the project which need to be immediately addressed.[8]

What a revelation! This finding of obvious fraud "would seem to indicate weaknesses in the basic financial and accounting systems of the project." These people aren't thieves; the money has just disappeared due to systemic weaknesses! This was just one transaction paid through the special account, but what about the 90 percent? Can we assume that this was just an anomaly in an otherwise transparently managed project? Not really, for in this single example we see all the telltale indicators of pervasive corruption. No evidence of competitive bidding. No evidence of the work being done. No evidence that the use of project funds for "burglar-proofing" had been agreed to by the Bank. And all covered up by grossly deficient record keeping:

> The subsidiary Special Account in local currency has not been reconciled and attempts by the clerk responsible revealed

significant differences between the Bank Statements and the project's accounting records. This alone is sufficiently serious a weakness as to undermine all other accounting controls. Shortcomings in basic accounting procedures and internal controls seriously undermine sound management of project resources.[9]

Most disheartening about all this is the Bank's feeble attempt to deal with the issue. Like a firm but caring parent admonishing a wayward child, the Bank's letter to the Extension Directorate followed its concerns about the burglar-proofing payment with this:

> Immediate measures should be taken to determine the extent of the problem so that the necessary steps to correct them can be taken. As you know, if your office is unable to provide the appropriate documentation for payments using the SOE method, the GOU [Government of Uganda] could be asked to refund the Bank by depositing the corresponding amounts paid into the Special Account of the project.
>
> We have requested the Resident Mission to discuss this matter with you and assist you in developing a course of action which could lead to a satisfactory resolution of this problem. We suggest that you obtain a copy of the Disbursement Handbook where the SOE method is described in detail, and samples of appropriate SOE forms are provided.[10]

Who are they kidding? No different than the Nigerians, these Ugandan bureaucrats knew exactly what they were doing. They had been doing it for years and knew full well what was required on Bank-funded projects. And, like the Nigerians, they had attended all sorts of costly overseas workshops, seminars, and courses on the subject. But all that had nothing to do with their own agendas. So instead of immediately declaring misprocurement and requesting the return of stolen funds, the Bank suggests to the culprits that they should take "immediate measures to determine the extent of the problem." And if they can't produce, or should I say create, the appropriate documents, then the Bank "could" ask for the funds to be returned. Oh, and by the way, we suggest that you obtain a copy of the Bank's *Disbursement Handbook* to help you resolve this issue. Yes, Johnny, you have been a bad boy, and to encourage you to correct your ways, you cannot watch TV tonight!

And there are other examples. We shall see in later chapters that the embezzlement of the various project account funds was, and still is, being carried out on all Bank-funded projects while management continues to dance around the issue. Always hesitant to deal firmly and consistently with corrupt governments, and always hesitant to remain faithful to its fiduciary responsibilities. And yet, occasionally, there would be those moments of internal enlightenment when the extent of the problem would be recognized:

> The risk exposure of the Africa Investment portfolio to ineligible use of project funds and resources is high with respect to SOE procedures. The other major risk concerning the portfolio relates to the end use of project funds by borrowers. 23% (US$425 million) of the Africa region disbursements during FY96 for investment operations were made under the SOE procedure. With adjustment operations, disbursements using the SOE procedures increased to 40% of the region's disbursements. Current plans for raising the level of the SOE threshold limit will further increase this risk factor unless measures are taken to improve project financial management and the Bank's capacity to supervise the financial management of projects.
>
> The main issues concerning SOE procedures:
>
> i. *lack of accountability for prices and end use.* Project disbursements using the SOE procedure are technically subjected to post-review procurement procedures but in fact, they tend to escape all forms of control. TTLs [task team leaders] do not spend the necessary time to review SOE documentation, LOAAF [the Africa Region Disbursements Unit] staff only perform sporadic tests and external auditors tend to verify compliance of amounts paid against invoices, but do not ascertain whether proper procedures have been followed with regards to procurement procedures and end use of funds;

ii. *deficient project accounting.* A majority of Bank funded projects do not have accounting systems that adequately link cost accounts with budgets to ensure transparent utilization of Bank funds;

iii. *slow disbursements.* Poor project accounting and ineligible use of the Special Account advances tend to slow down projects disbursements. Borrowers have difficulties to justify the use of advances in Special Accounts which then become idle for long periods of time. The Bank will ultimately suspend the use of the SA after it has been idle for a period exceeding six months and will not resume disbursements until the borrower has adequately justified all expenditures.[11]

This sounds strangely like the 1976 internal audit report mentioned earlier. Here we were twenty years later and nothing had really changed. SOEs were still not adequately documented, and the Bank was still "not fulfilling its obligation to ensure that the proceeds of loans and credits were being used only for the purpose for which the loan or credit was provided." The only real difference was that SOEs accounted for 9 percent of disbursements back in 1976, and 40 percent in 1996. Could it possibly be that the Bank's management has a difficult time learning from experience?

But let us go a little farther and try to read between the lines of this latest assessment. In reality, "lack of accountability for prices and end use" is merely a polite way of saying that prices paid for goods and services are higher than market value and that we have no way of knowing if goods and services invoiced were actually delivered. In reality, we have dysfunctional budgetary and accounting systems that conceal, rather than reveal, the use of Bank funds. In reality, we have funds specifically provided to advance project implementation being parked in idle accounts so that they can earn interest that can be diverted into private pockets. In reality, the Bank doesn't always suspend the special account when it has been idle for more than six months:

I thought you may find useful the attached information. There are 163 special accounts for a total of $263 million in the Region that have been inactive for over twelve months (about half of the inactive balances are three countries: Tanzania, Somalia and Nigeria).[12]

The financial-management risk internal memo quoted above goes on to identify the principal causes contributing to these "SOE issues." Claiming that there aren't enough Bank staff with financial management skills, that task managers rely heavily upon audit reports that are often unreliable and overdue, and that the Bank's data base for managing project audit information is unreliable, the memo recommends a number of superficial remedies to be implemented within the Bank. The memo also states that "limited importance is attached by borrowers to good project financial management."

Could this be true? Don't all the appraisal reports indicate that the borrowers are committed to sound project management? Hasn't the Bank funded all sorts of consulting contracts to install proper accounting systems at the project and ministerial levels? Hasn't the Bank funded the recruitment of all sorts of technical assistance to set up, manage, and train the locals in financial-management procedures. Hasn't the Bank funded thousands of overseas fellowships for financial-management training? Hasn't the Bank insisted as a condition of project effectiveness that properly certified local accountants be placed in charge of project accounts? And hasn't this been going on for the past several decades? Could there possibly be something we may have missed?

This was no small matter, as there were 822 special accounts at that time with a total of $620 million outstanding in the Bank's Africa Region portfolio.[13] More than half a billion dollars, and no one dared mention even the remotest possibility that corruption might somehow be connected with this issue. By all means, let's install new computerized accounting systems, let's train more accountants, let's press for timely audits, and let's discuss the problem with our borrowers. But let's never, ever suggest that none of this will work without honest people in charge or that the root cause of the problem may be the rampant manipulation and embezzlement of project funds by a significant number of our client's representatives.

But did the Bank's management, in 1996, learn anything from this? Did it make any effort to correct what was obviously an untenable situation with regard to protecting its fiduciary responsibility? It is difficult to conclude that it has, for nine years later in 2004, the Bank was releasing roughly 60 percent of its disbursements (excluding adjustment lending) through special accounts and SOEs. Half again as much as in 1996, and roughly six times more than in 1976. And what does this mean in dollars? According to the Bank's 2004 annual report,[14] disbursements for project lending that year amounted to $11.0 billion, of which roughly $6.6 billion was paid out through SOEs. Over six billion dollars placed in the hands of corrupt government officials with no effective oversight by the Bank, and we are asked to believe that it will be used with probity! We are asked to believe that the Bank is doing all it can to ensure that its funds are used for the purposes intended! So much for Article III, Section 5(b) of the Bank's Articles of Agreement!

NOTES

1. Technical Education Project, Loan Agreement, Art. III, section 3.01 (d).

2. Steve Berkman, "Report on Project Financial Management and Accounting Practices," September 1993.

3. Project Progress Summary by the on-site British Council consultant, February 2, 1992, para. 2.1.

4. Special Accounts, GP 12.20, June 1994, para. 10.

5. *Author's note:* This was another factor that I encountered on several occasions in our Nigeria portfolio, and I sometimes had the suspicion that some commercial banks were established for the sole purpose of pulling off scams of one sort or another. There were numerous instances where project funds found their way into these institutions only to have the money disappear when the banks suddenly became insolvent.

6. Nigeria National Population Project, back-to-office report, August 25, 1995, para. 2 (c).

7. Letter from the Bank's director of the Western Africa Department to the director of the Multilateral Institutions Department of the Ministry of Finance, June 30, 1993.

8. Letter from the Bank's Agriculture and Environment Operations Division to the director of the Extension Directorate, January 19, 1996, concerning the Uganda Agriculture Extension Project.

9. Bank staff back-to-office report, January 15, 1996.

10. Ibid., paras. 2, 3.

11. Internal memo on an assessment of financial-management risk in the Africa Region portfolio, October 14, 1996. This is quoted from an initial draft that may have been revised in its final form.

12. Cover memo to the Africa Region's directors and vice president, November 11, 1993.

13. Loan Department report, July 8, 1995.

14. Letter of Transmittal, Operational Summary, FY04.

9

• • • • • • •

"C" Is for Corruption

The longer I worked at the Bank, the more difficult it was to be optimistic about our projects in Africa. I hadn't worked on one project during those twelve years that did not reek of corruption. And while many colleagues shared my frustration at the futility of our efforts to keep things on track, others seemed to be oblivious to it all. Some front-line managers seemed to be equally frustrated but never appeared able to convince senior management of the severity of the problem. It was the elephant in the room that no one wanted to discuss.

In one final effort to convince management of the pervasiveness of corruption within our portfolio, I began going through my files to put together a report that would present my observations over the past years. I had documented many instances of Bank funds being stolen and thought that perhaps a written account of these events might convince "somebody upstairs" that this was in fact a serious problem. By March 1995, I had completed the first draft, describing the different forms of fraud and embezzlement I had encountered in the field—every form of financial chicanery known to man, and all perpetrated within the myriad rules, regulations, and safeguards established by the Bank precisely to prevent such abuses.[1]

The message I'd hoped to convey was that we were avoiding dealing with, or even acknowledging, the most serious issue facing the Bank's portfolio, and it was time to do something about it. The timing was fortuitous, for change was in the wind with the appointment of James Wolfensohn as the Bank's president. At last, here was someone who intuitively understood the nature of the beast and appeared determined to do something about it. And while I would soon be leaving the Bank, I could take some comfort in the knowledge that the issue would not die quietly.

Although my report never got beyond the first draft, I was asked to co-chair an informal committee, the Financial Management Action Group, assigned to look into corruption issues in the Africa Region. But with only volunteer help and no budget, it was merely a facade to demonstrate to Wolfensohn that regional management was addressing the problem. Despite these handicaps, we were able to draw some attention to the special-account problem by reviewing a single project in Ghana—a project rated highly successful yet also rife with fraud, as we will see shortly.

THE ROAD LESS TRAVELED

The National Feeder Roads Rehabilitation and Maintenance Project was funded by an IDA credit of $55.0 million and became effective in 1992. Additional co-financing from other donors[2] and GoG [the Government of Ghana] brought the total project cost to $106 million. The objective of the project was to improve rural transportation through the rehabilitation and maintenance of feeder roads. This, in turn, would benefit the rural population by permitting better access to local towns and markets. Roughly $52.0 million in IDA funds were allocated for road repair and re-graveling. The IDA credit also funded $3.0 million for an institutional support program for the Department of Feeder Roads (DFR) within the Ministry of Roads and Highways (MRH) and other road agencies that had, in various ways, been the beneficiaries of six previous IDA-funded projects totaling $290 million between 1974 and 1992.

DIGGING FOR ANSWERS

Before leaving Washington to visit the project, I reviewed four withdrawal applications for replenishment of the special account. The applications were supported by SOEs totaling $3.7 million against seventy-four civil works contracts. I also obtained the project audit reports for the two previous fiscal years. And so, by my second day in the field, I had become familiar with the PMU contract files and began reviewing randomly selected contracts. With the project in its third year, the PMU had already awarded 170 civil works contracts. About 150 were awarded on the basis of local competitive bidding (LCB) below the $500,000 threshold established for prior review by the Bank. The remaining twenty contracts were priced above $500,000 and were awarded on the basis of international competitive bidding (ICB).

Prior review requires the Bank to issue a "no objection" to the contract, and if that is not forthcoming, the Bank would usually refuse to pay for that contract from the proceeds of the loan or credit. In this case, because of the repetitive nature of the work, a model contract had been approved by the Bank in advance so that all one had to do was fill in the blanks, sign it, and it was done— on the surface a logical and efficient approach to ensure consistency and efficiency. But there was no guarantee that it would also assure cost-effective procurement and transparency.

Approximately $45.5 million of the IDA credit had been allocated for civil works contracts, and of this amount, $38.5 million (85 percent) was to be awarded through ICB, while $7.0 million (15 percent) was reserved for LCB. Eighteen months after project start-up, this ratio was amended to $20.5 million (45 percent) for ICB and $25.0 million (55 percent) for LCB. Two years after that, it was amended again to $12.0 million for ICB (26 percent) and $33.5 million (74 percent) for LCB. So, beginning with a civil works program of which 85 percent would have required more intense Bank oversight, halfway through the project this had been reduced to 26 percent. More important, those contracts awarded under the Bank's radar rose from 15 percent to 74 percent. Again, while this would appear to be an efficient way to move things along by reducing the Bank's oversight of the contract-award process, it also posed a greater risk for bid-rigging, overpricing, and other forms of fraud.

This business of amending loan agreements was a tactic I would observe in later years when I returned to work with the Bank's Fraud Investigation Unit. Loan agreements would be presented to the board with clearly defined safeguards to minimize the misuse of project funds. Once the project was approved and under implementation, those safeguards would often be greatly diminished by subsequent amendments to the loan conditions. This is when the "feeding frenzy" would begin, as we shall see in the following examples.

FROM ROADS TO HOUSES

In reviewing a $520,000 ICB contract awarded to a local company, I came across the following clause:

> (13.4.2) 4.2 *Permanent Resident Engineer's Accomodation* [sic]
> The Contractor shall provide a permanent living accommodation for the Resident Engineer at a town and location to be approved by the Engineer. The building is of a minimum floor area of 95 square meters (See Appendix 2 Drawing No.1). The building shall be furnished and equipped as per details in Schedule IV.[3]

Schedule IV showed an impressive list of household items including beds, sheets, pillowcases, toilet brushes, tables, chairs, a tea set, frying pans, napkins, and numerous other items. Being a model contract form, all that was required to make this clause effective was to price it out in the bill of quantities, which in this case was $20,000 for the structure and $6,000 for the household items.[4] This caught my attention because I had seen no indication in the project appraisal report or the credit agreement that DFR staff housing was considered essential to meet project objectives or that IDA had agreed to fund such activities.

Another clause in the model contract called for the contractor to provide a permanent district office. This was also priced out at $20,000 with furnishings for an additional $4,000. But it doesn't end there! The contract also contained clauses for the contractor to provide "temporary" living quarters for DFR staff priced out at $10,000 plus another $5,000 for "temporary" furniture. But we're not done yet, for another clause called for the provision of a "temporary" field office, and while the office itself was not priced out and therefore not provided, "temporary" furniture for it was priced in at $26,000. From this we get a total of $91,000 for a bunch of stuff that was nowhere mentioned in the staff appraisal report or credit agreement. And I was able to physically verify *none* of it in the field.

Nowhere did any of the project documents point to a need for housing, offices, furniture, bed sheets, or toilet brushes, and yet, here they were, with just these items alone consuming over 17 percent of the contract price (see Figure 9–1). And this did not include numerous other red flags found in the contract. What did all this have to do with fixing the roads?

Figure 9–1. Furniture Embedded in Road Contract

DFR records indicated that this same contractor had also been awarded three LCB contracts totaling over $600,000 for the rehabilitation of an additional forty-two kilometers of roads. Review of these contracts raised more red flags: repeated provisions for temporary living accommodations, temporary office space, and temporary furniture. One contract contained provision for a temporary office and furniture at a cost of approximately $18,000. As it was not too far from Accra, I was able to visit the work site. The temporary office occupied half of a small, rundown hut with the sun shining through the roof, holes in the wall where the windows had once been, two broken desks, and a wooden bench. That was it! The Bank financed it all for $18,000 over six months, with no indication of who received the $3,000 a month "rent" for this hovel.

Other contracts contained similar charges for housing, office rentals, and furniture that were hard to reconcile with the civil works called for in the credit agreement. Adding to my concerns was the fact that there was no reliable documentation to show where the houses were located, who was living in them, or if they existed at all. The cost of nine houses and three offices embedded in the few contracts I reviewed came to $300,000, and I had no way of confirming whether that was all of it. It seemed to me that, with the automatic inclusion of the permanent housing clause in the model contract form, and with 170 contracts already awarded, there was a good possibility of more houses out there. With 22 percent of my sampling containing embedded housing, it was not hard to conclude that the same percentage might very well apply to the entire lot. If so, that would mean roughly thirty-seven houses were paid for with Bank funds at an estimated cost of $740,000. Was that really the case, or was my sampling just an anomaly? We will never know for sure, because the matter was never pursued further by the Bank or the government. But let us move on to other scams.

A TOYOTA FOR EVERYONE

During project appraisal it had been determined that a certain number of passenger vehicles, pickups, and motorcycles would have to be obtained to ensure the successful implementation of the project. Based upon this assessment, the Bank agreed to fund eleven four-wheel-drive vehicles, twenty pickups, and seventy-two motorcycles. These vehicles were procured through the ICB process at a total cost of $583,000, as per the credit agreement. But there was more chicanery afoot as the project officials quickly devised ways to obtain a number of vehicles that somehow seemed to vanish below the Bank's and the Government's radar.

> The contractor shall provide the following diesel powered air-conditioned vehicles for the use of the Engineer and his staff: One cross-country 4–wheel drive, Toyota Landcruiser [sic] 5–door station wagon or similar, complete with air-conditioning, diesel. One double-cabin pick-up, 4–wheel drive, diesel. In addition the Contractor shall supply spare parts and equipment to the amount of US$1,000 or equivalent (in other currency) per vehicle.
>
> The Contractor shall be responsible for and pay the cost of supplying, taxing for use on public roads, comprehensively insuring, servicing, repairing, maintaining, and running the said vehicles, including drivers, fuel, and lubricants.
>
> On the completion of the Works, the vehicle will be handed over to the Department of Feeder Roads in satisfactory condition and shall remain their property.[5]

Conveniently, the model contract contained the above clauses for the provision of vehicles by the contractor. And, as with the clauses pertaining to housing and office facilities, all that was needed to activate them was to include them in the bill of quantities. Needless to say, the PMU was generous in its application of this clause:

1. One contract included four vehicles at a cost of $48,000 although the model contract called for only two vehicles. In addition, the project was charged $43,200 to operate and maintain those vehicles over the 15-month duration of the contract.
2. Another contract included two vehicles at a cost of $40,000, with an additional $7,500 for operation and maintenance. The same company, the same model contract, the same vehicles, yet the vehicles cost $12,000 each in the first contract, and $20,000 each in the second.

3. An LCB contract included one vehicle at a cost of $33,000, although the model contract called for two vehicles; while only one was provided, the contract contained operating costs for two vehicles at $2,400 (see Figure 9–2).

Among the few contracts I reviewed, the PMU had procured thirty-three additional vehicles embedded within the civil works. At a total cost of roughly $550,000 this was about equal to the amount the Bank had agreed to finance for vehicles originally, and which had already been obtained through transparent ICB procurement. And this figure does not include an estimated $175,000

Figure 9–2. Bill of Quantities Showing Embedded Vehicles

STRESCON/DEPT OF FEEDER ROADS	NATIONAL FEEDER ROADS REHABILITATION AND MAINTENANCE PROJECT (NFRRMP) ZONE 1 – PHASE 1				Page 2 of 12
BILL 1		LOT 15			
CESSM CODE	DESCRIPTION	UNIT	QTY	RATE ¢	AMOUNT ¢
	Brought Forward			—	11,000,000
	Services for the Engineer's Staff				
A221.1	Provide transport vehicles for RE, and hand over to employer on completion of works (to be used by DFR for future maintenance operations)	Veh.	1		30,000,000
A221.2	*Percentage Adjustment etc* Maintain and operate 2No RE's vehicles, including drivers and fuel	% Veh/Mth	10 12	200,000	3,000,000 2,400,000
A221.3	Progress photographs, one set of negatives, two colour and one colour slide	sets	30	4000	120,000
	Specific Equipment for Engineer's Staff				
A231.1	Provide RE,s temporary office equipment including all furnishing as per schedule II	Sum			3,850,000
A231.2	Maintain RE's office equipment and furnishing as specified	Mth	6	50,000	300,000
A233.1	Provide as specified surveying equipment for RE's staff as per Schedule VI	Sum			2,000,000
A233.2	Maintain survey equipment	Mth	6	30,000	180,000
	Attendance Upon Engineer's Staff				
A242	Provide 1 chainman and 1 labourer for RE	Man/Mth	N/A		
A243	Provide 2 laboratory Assistants for RE	Man/Mth	12	120,000	1,440,000
	Carried Forward				54,290,000

that was charged for the operation and maintenance of those same vehicles. Thus, with the contract sampling being only a small fraction of all the contracts awarded up to that point, and with the project about halfway through implementation, one can only guess how many more vehicles had been, or would be, procured in this manner. Was this sampling just another anomaly? Would the Bank ever know just how many vehicles it had financed? Would anyone really care?

There were several other things that troubled me also. In the first place, the Bank was always quite clear about establishing disbursement categories. The procurement of civil works was normally disbursed through category one; the procurement of goods through category two; and consulting services under category three. In this way the Bank could verify that the financing of the various components of the project had been managed according to the loan or credit agreement. Hiding the procurement of goods within civil works contracts was considered a no-no and would, on the face of it, result in a declaration of misprocurement by the Bank. So, just from a procedural standpoint, it was hard to fathom why this had escaped notice by the auditors and the Bank.

Second, one had to ask why they procured another thirty-three vehicles if it had originally been determined that the project should fund only thirty-one vehicles? Were more vehicles procured through the contracts I was unable to review? And would more be procured during the second half of the project? If the original assessment of vehicle needs had been wrong, or if the DFR could demonstrate a legitimate need for more, I had no doubt that the Bank would have agreed to reallocate funds to purchase them through ICB procedures within category two. Something obviously did not smell right.

And, there were still other concerns. Why should the same civil works contractor be asked to provide four vehicles to the DFR for the rehabilitation of sixty kilometers of roads, and two more vehicles for another fifteen kilometers? Why did prices vary from $12,000 to $33,000 for identical vehicles as defined in the model contract? How could this random and capricious method of procurement ensure standardization of the vehicle fleet? And why wasn't the procurement of these additional vehicles based upon a clearly defined plan that was approved by the ministry and the Bank?

But there was an even bigger question in all this. What was happening to these vehicles when the contracts ended? According to the model contract, vehicles procured by the contractor were to be "turned over" to the DFR at the end of the contract. But with no clearly specified procedures regarding the transfer of ownership, the final disposition of the vehicles appeared to be a clouded issue, and by all appearances, it was intended to be that way from the beginning. My first suspicion that something was not quite right came from the auditor's reports:

(41.1) We observed that the underlisted vehicles were acquired with project funds for the use by some of the Consultants attached to the project.

1 Toyota Saloon Car	$17,213
8 Mitsubishi Pick-Ups	$86,133
1 8–Seater Station Wagon	$69,629
1 Nissan Sunny	$12,199
	$185,174

(41.2) These vehicles being of a capital nature were to remain the properties of DFR after the Consultants have completed their assignments.

(43.1) We recommend that future requirements of motor vehicles and other fixed assets needed for the effective implementation of the Project should be made in the name of DFR and allocated to the consultants who may require them

(43.3) They are all to be marked with the name of DFR or any other inscription for easy identification.[6]

The plot thickens! I was already concerned about the vehicles embedded in the civil works contracts, and now I found they were doing the same thing with consulting contracts. In addition to the vehicles properly procured under ICB through category two, we now had vehicles procured under category one for civil works, and vehicles procured under category three for consulting services. It was also noted that the vehicles procured outside of category two had not been marked as belonging to the DFR, as is standard for all government vehicles. And that wasn't all, for further on in the report, the auditors stated:

> It came to our notice that six (6) Four Wheel Drive Mitsubishi pick-ups were acquired for two of the Consultants on application No. J/14 and J/25 for a total amount of Yen 11,797,277 (USD 113,542).[7]

And again:

> We noted that six (6) Isuzu Pick-Ups with the cost of USD 108,970 were acquired under the PPF for the use by the Consultants in August 1991.[8]

So now we find that the DFR and the PMU had played the same game with the Japanese grant funds and the project preparation facility: vehicles embedded within consulting contracts, not recorded as fixed assets, and not otherwise identified as belonging to the government. There was apparently no end to the DFR's insatiable appetite for vehicles.

In their report for the following fiscal year the auditors noted repeat performances by the DFR and the PMU:

> We observed that two (2) Toyota Hilux Pick-Ups were purchased for Owa Consults at a cost of USD 52,878. These vehicles being of a capital nature were to be the property of DFR after the consultants have completed their assignments. We are of the opinion that the vehicles should be treated as fixed assets of DFR and recorded in the books as such. We also recommend that all future purchases of vehicles for consultants should first be received by DFR and entered into their fixed assets records before releasing them to the beneficiaries. This would serve as a means of control on the vehicles as well as easy identification of them.[9]

And again with the Japanese grant:

> During the year one Nissan Saloon Car was acquired for the Computer Specialist at DFR at a cost of USD 13,794 or YEN 1,357,842 on 20th October 1994. We suggest that all vehicles

acquired from the funds of T.F. 05 2430–0 GH JAPANESE GRANT (NFRRMP) since inception of the Project which are to remain the property of DFR be classified as fixed assets.[10]

And again with the contractors:

The following vehicles [five vehicles at a total cost of approximately $98,000], which were purchased for DFR by the contractors mentioned below were to enable the local supervising consultants [to] monitor the LCB Phase I projects. The contractors were, however, reimbursed by DFR as these vehicles were to remain the property of the DFR. We have transferred the cost of these vehicles, for Balance Sheet purposes, from the cost of civil works to fixed assets account and would request that the Project's records be amended accordingly. DFR should update their records and institute adequate control over these vehicles.[11]

So now, we have a new twist. The contractors include vehicles in their civil works contracts (category one) to provide vehicles for consultants (category three), who will return them to the contractors, who will then turn them over to the DFR. One could not accuse the DFR and the PMU of not being creative!

And there was a final twist to this tale, for further investigation into the status of the DFR vehicle fleet revealed that of 145 vehicles funded by the Bank and other donors through various aid projects, only 84 were properly registered to the government. The remainder, 61 to be exact, were nowhere to be found in the government's inventory records. It is interesting that those vehicles purchased through category two under ICB and in accordance with the credit agreement were all properly registered as government vehicles, while those embedded within civil works and consulting contracts were not. I wonder how that happened?

ALL IS NOT WHAT IT SEEMS

So what are we to make of the use of this $55 million IDA credit? From just a small sampling of the accounts there were nine houses, three offices, and thirty-three vehicles worth a total of $850,000 embedded within the civil works contracts. And there was an additional $275,000 for pots and pans, furniture, temporary offices, and vehicle maintenance. The houses and offices were never officially recorded or entered in the government's inventory. The property addresses were never provided, nor were the occupants of the houses identified. Vehicles were also embedded in consulting contracts funded by the IDA, the Japanese grant, and the PPF, and none was ever entered in the government's inventory. These items alone, in just a handful of contracts out of the 170 that had been awarded up to that point, came to over a million dollars. None of this was ever mentioned in the staff appraisal report, the credit agreement, or any subsequent project planning.

Could it be that by some strange coincidence I had randomly selected a group of problem contracts that did not represent the majority of contracts awarded by the PMU? Or, could it be that these irregularities just represented the tip of the iceberg? Sadly, logic pointed to the latter, for this contract chicanery was too systematic to conclude otherwise. And the fact that Bank oversight was greatly reduced through the shifting of ICB to LCB procurement, as noted earlier, only made it easier to carry out these scams.

And what about the project as a whole? The implementation completion report on the project indicated a somewhat conflicting assessment of its final outcome. Highly positive on the surface, the report stated:

> The achievement of project objectives, as set out in the Staff Appraisal Report, is considered *substantial.* The road rehabilitation and maintenance program was carried out largely in accordance with SAR forecasts.[12]

It then went on to present very impressive ERR figures, going as high as 200 percent for some road sections. But buried later in the report were some revealing comments that cast doubts on these claims of success:

> Evaluation had, however, to rely on secondary data which may have been inaccurate and tended to give unrealistically high figures of benefits. This allowed for the justification of high cost investments. . . . However, to prevent over-investment, some simple cutoff such as, for example, minimum

50 ADT [average daily traffic] and maximum US$6,000/km is suggested (some roads with 20 VPD [vehicles per day] and unit cost of US$25,000 per km were being undertaken).[13]

So, on the one hand, we are told of truly fantastic economic rates of return, while on the other hand, these figures "may have been inaccurate."[14] And then we learn that the DFR was awarding contracts costing $25,000 per kilometer on some roads that only had a traffic volume of twenty vehicles per day. How significant is this? If one wanted to play with numbers, we could calculate that at $6,000 per kilometer and fifty VPD, we would have a cost per kilometer per vehicle of $120. At $25,000 per kilometer and twenty VPD, the cost jumps to $1,250 per kilometer per vehicle. It is not hard to see that the latter figure is roughly ten times that suggested as the cut-off investment rate. And although these investments might have produced meaningful results for the rural poor, albeit at inflated rates, it turns out that this too was questionable:

The second objective "improving mobility and economic opportunity for the rural poor" was also *achieved*. The socio-economic impact studies indicated marked increase in the number of taxis and small vehicles on all rehabilitated roads, most noticeable being the number of round trips being made by commercial transport operators. *It needs, however, to be pointed out that the average daily traffic on the rehabilitated roads remains very low* [emphasis added]. For example, in Study Region 1 (Ashanti, Brong-Ahafo, Greater Accra, and Volta) 15 out of 21 road links have less than 30 vehicles a day. The use of intermediate and non-motorized means of transport has also remained low even when the terrain is conducive to its use. This points to the need to gain a better understanding of the factors which influence the demand and supply of transport services in Ghana. For example, it might be that there is little need to travel or it might be that IMT [intermediate means of transport] and vehicle ownership is unduly restricted.[15]

Once again we have contradictions that test our common sense. If the objective of improving the mobility and economic opportunity for the rural poor was achieved through the rehabilitation of the roads, how is it that the "average daily traffic . . . remains very low"? How could there be an increase in the number of taxis and small vehicles without a parallel increase in the daily traffic? What purpose is served by a road that has no traffic? These perplexing questions remind one of the old medical conundrum: The operation was a success, but the patient died. Well, in this case, we're just not sure the patient will live.

POSTSCRIPT FROM GHANA

Several years later, following discussions with a confidential source familiar with the project, I received a note in which he provided his own assessments of the contract management issues I had reported on. In it, he claimed:

i. Unit prices in the road construction sector were inflated by as much as 35% due to the structure of the bidding and contract award process. The desire of the donor agencies to promote "empowerment" and "decentralization" worked against any critical scrutiny of the actual workings of the procurement process.
ii. Misfeasance or malfeasance at the project award and project execution level was, in terms of money diverted, entirely dwarfed by the "arrears" problem, which had been throttled down significantly by end-2000, but then, following the change in government, doubled during 2001. The level of arrears is an indicator of the level of corruption in public life through the transport sector.

Perhaps I was not alone in my concerns after all, and his assessment of price inflations as high as 35 percent certainly appeared to be consistent with what I had seen during my brief mission. The second statement was an unknown topic to me, as I had never heard of the "arrears problem," and yet it seemed to be of much greater significance than the scams I had uncovered on the project. Apparently, the government made a practice of awarding civil works contracts in sums that far exceeded its annual budgets. As a study conducted by the Netherlands Economic Institute noted:

There had been substantial budget overruns, which had re-sulted in large arrears accruing to contractors. Budgets were exceeded by some 65 percent in 1994 and 1995 and arrears were estimated at US$75 million.[16]

Well, what we learn here is that road-works contracts exceeded the annual budgets by about 65 percent over a two-year period. And arrears for that period came to $75 million. Now, it is not unusual for budgets to be exceeded, but how could this happen so consistently and to such an extent? These are, after all, well-educated and highly trained government officials. The Bank and other donors had seen to that in project after project, through thou-sands of fellowship grants and the ever-present technical assis-tance. So how could these bureaucrats continue to award contracts when they did not have the funds to pay for them? They were not stupid, and they certainly had to know that overextending the government's financial commitments could not possibly work. At least not for the public good.

Now comes the interesting part. It appears that government policy allowed contractors to charge interest if payments were delayed. A reasonable and fair arrangement under normal condi-tions, but highly questionable when it is intentionally conducted on a systematic basis, as evident from the following:

In 1996 a substantial amount of money was paid to the con-tractors, however, the causes behind the arrears were not solved, enabling new arrears to emerge. A precise insight in the level of arrears on a year-to-year basis is lacking. How-ever, the combined arrears at May 2000 are estimated at US$68.76 million.[17]

And,

The basic cause of the accumulated debt for major contracts has been the commitments to undertake large-scale projects without adequate budget coverage. The problem has been aggravated by delays in payment that increased the bill with interest.[18]

This would appear to be more than just careless or incompetent contract management. So one has to ask why government officials would intentionally place the government in the untenable position of having to pay out huge interest charges? Apart from the obvious opportunity for kickbacks from contract awards, one has to assume that there was an additional scam afoot. All we have to do is award a contract to a complicit contractor who can then implement the civil works for as long as he receives his scheduled payments. When the payments stop, the works will stop, and from then on, the contract will accrue interest until payment is received at some time in the future. And so, at the end of the day, the contractor will have completed works valued at (x) but will receive $(x+y)$ as final compensation, with (y) continually increasing as the payments for (x) are delayed. Who could resist such an opportunity?

Yes, the extent of corruption in Ghana's public sector was common knowledge among all Ghanaians and the entire donor community. But this knowledge was too damaging to the symbiotic relationships among all the parties involved to be reported openly. No, it would not do for the government and its officials, or for the consultants, contractors, and suppliers who feed at the trough with them. Nor would it do for the Bank to expose the fact that it prefers to ignore this aspect of the development process. It is one thing to report how many culverts were installed, but quite another to report how much money was stolen from the project. Did corruption consume 10 percent of the project funds? If so, that would amount to roughly $10 million. Did corruption consume 35 percent of the funds, as alleged by one of my contacts? If so, that would amount to roughly $35 million. In either case, we will never know the complete facts in this matter, because no one is really interested in finding out. So much for making life better for the poor!

NOTES

1. Steve Berkman, "Corruption and Its Impact on the Management of Bank Funded Projects in the Africa Region," draft, March 14, 1995.

2. USAID, DANIDA, OPEC, and a Japanese grant.

3. DFR model contract, pp. 7–8, para. 4.2.

4. Using the approximate *cedi* exchange rate of 1,000 to 1 against the dollar at that time.

5. DFR, model contract, para. 13.7.

6. Pertinent comments in the auditors' management report for 1993 section 41.0, covering disbursements under category three, and section 43.0, covering the auditors' recommendations.

7. Ibid., section C, para. 56.0, concerning the audit of the Japanese grant. Requiring six vehicles for two consultants goes beyond credibility and demonstrates the project officials' total lack of fear of being caught in their scam.

8. Ibid., Section D, concerning the audit of the PPF [project preparation facility], an advance by the IDA to assist in project preparation, para. 72.0.

9. The auditors' management report for 1994, section A, paras. 48–51, concerning vehicles purchased for consultants.

10. Ibid., section B, paras. 68–69.

11. Ibid., section A, paras. 35–38, concerning vehicles purchased by contractors.

12. ICR, section B, para. 2.

13. Ibid., p. 12, para. 36.

14. I later learned from a reliable source that many of the ERR numbers had been "cooked," but that was not unusual in such matters.

15. ICR, p. 3, para. 8.

16. Netherlands Economic Institute, "Ghana: Joint Evaluation of the Road Sub-Sector Programme 1996–2000," section 5.3.

17. Ibid.

18. Ibid.

10

* * * * * * *

As the Train
Left the Station

November 1995. With my retirement just weeks away, management showed no interest in pursuing the special-account issues identified by our little group or the findings of my mission to Ghana. And although I sensed this lack of interest would continue after I left, there were stirrings throughout the Bank that would prove me wrong. The train had finally left the station, with staff and managers wondering whether they should get on board or not. While many of us were encouraged that the corruption issue was finally being discussed openly, others were struggling to determine how this would affect their careers and were adamantly against opening this threatening can of worms.

The vehemence with which these latter individuals defended the Bank's past track record was, to me, astounding. Their arguments in favor of the status quo defied all logic as they tried to explain away the wholesale plundering of Bank funds. Were they defending the Bank, or were they really trying to cover up their own dereliction of duty? Were they afraid open investigations might lead to questions about their individual roles in all this, or were they so focused on protecting their careers that they just didn't care at all about corruption? Whatever the reason, the intensity of their arguments seemed totally at odds with reality. And so, while many were pleased that they could now speak freely about the corruption issue, others remained in complete denial over the extent of the problem.

Yes, the train had left the station, and the frequency of meetings on corruption, memos on corruption, surveys on corruption, and pronouncements about corruption was increasing at a rate I never would have imagined. For many, it was a long-awaited moment as staff began to articulate openly their years of frustration at the shameful position management had put the Bank in. A survey of Bank task managers on the topic reached the following general conclusions:

> Raising the topic of corruption has tapped into deep and strongly held beliefs among the Bank's task managers. Corruption is generally felt to be commonplace in the developing world, in some cases, so deeply rooted and so widespread as to have become an integral part of government.
>
> In a disturbing number of cases, task managers claim personal knowledge—or strong suspicion—of instances where the Bank's projects have been tainted by corruption. This is an institutional exposure that must be addressed. Even when there is no evidence that Bank projects themselves are tainted directly, there is a consensus that corruption renders the implementation of these projects more costly and time consuming, and lessens their development impact.
>
> The Bank has not done enough to combat corruption, either in its analytical work, which suffers from excess timidity on the subject, or in its formal policy dialogue with governments, where the subject is almost always avoided as too sensitive. Experience in LAC [Latin America and Caribbean Region]—the exceptional region in this regard—indicates that this reticence is misplaced.[1]

As interest in the corruption issue gained momentum, and as it became obvious that Wolfensohn would continue to make it a high priority, different groups within the Bank began to carve out their own little areas of anti-corruption turf. All of a sudden, anti-corruption experts were popping up everywhere as the various policy and operational groups sought to demonstrate to their new president that they were on the leading edge of this newly revealed issue. After more than four decades of self-proclaimed leadership in economic development, who would have suspected that corruption had a negative impact upon our work? And after lending more than half a trillion dollars, who would have suspected that so many of our borrowers' representatives were nothing more than thieves in public office? As the intellectual leaders of the donor community, how could we have missed this?

But better late than never. We will deal with this problem that has just come to our attention. We will study it, we will research it, and we will analyze it until we know all there is to know about it. We will convene conferences on the subject. We will write reports, papers, and dissertations. We will teach our staff how to recognize corruption. And we will teach corrupt officials how to be less corrupt. But best of all, we will provide loans and grants to these corrupt governments so that they may fight corruption.

While this was all well and good, it still did not address the extent to which billions of dollars of Bank funds had disappeared into private pockets and offshore bank accounts. And so the Bank's Economic Development Institute (EDI),[2] its Poverty Reduction and Economic Management Network (PREM), its Operations Policy and Strategy Group (OPS), and the regional vice presidencies all began to produce an endless stream of documents proclaiming the new wisdom. EDI touted its Governance Program, designed to build "national integrity systems" to fight corruption,[3] while more catchy phrases were created to describe how we were going to bring honest government to these third-world kleptocracies. PREM produced a report that pontificated on all sorts of irrelevant abstractions about corruption and containing numerous "nuggets of wisdom" such as the following:

> The Bank recognizes that corruption is a complex and sensitive topic and that staff will need careful guidance on how to approach it in the country dialogue, in the lending program, and in economic and sector work.[4]

Yes, corruption is very complex, and that's the reason it has taken us so long to realize it has been a problem. But it really is very simple. Corrupt public officials collude with private firms and individuals in order to defraud their governments. One can conjure up all sorts of economic, social, and cultural theories as to why this occurs, but it is really all about greedy and dishonest individuals betraying their positions in government for their own enrichment. As for being a sensitive topic, how do you tell a thief he is a thief when his continued existence is related to the advancement of your own career? But wait, perhaps we can have our cake and eat it too:

> [The Bank can] build knowledge by dedicating more resources to understanding the dynamics of corruption and how some countries have reduced it, disseminating such knowledge, and applying such learning actively in its work.[5]

That's it! We will study the dynamics of corruption. Once again, management succumbs to its preference for contemplation over action. Once again it chooses to make simple things complex. Why can't it see the problem for what it really is? Corrupt individuals create phony documents to cover up the diversion of funds from government accounts to private accounts. Corrupt individuals order overpriced goods and services and pocket the difference. Corrupt individuals approve payments for goods and services not delivered and share the looted funds with accomplices on the outside. Corrupt individuals create shell companies that are awarded phantom contracts paid against fraudulent invoices. And the list goes on. Those, my friends, are the dynamics of corruption, and the reason for it all is pure and simple greed. The rest is just a lot of intellectual self-gratification for the economists.

In PREM's sixty-nine page report about corruption, nowhere does it mention the criminal aspects of all this. Whether at gunpoint or by deception, if someone steals from the private sector, it is considered a crime. There is an investigation, prosecution, punishment for the guilty, and attempts to recover that which was stolen. Yet when the theft is committed against a government, or more precisely, the general population, none of the above seems to apply. Why do we not discuss a government's obligation to pursue the culprits or recover stolen funds? Why aren't these things highlighted in Bank research to this day?

While EDI and PREM were doing their thing, OPS was producing operational memorandums to provide staff with guidelines for dealing with fraud on Bank-funded projects. At the same time, the regional vice presidents were busy demonstrating to Wolfensohn that they too were quite concerned about corruption. And while it was a mess that they had knowingly facilitated during their rise to office, they never touched upon that aspect of the issue as they carried the anti-corruption banner forward. Nevertheless, change was in the winds, and credit must go to Wolfensohn, who was taking the Bank in a direction it had never previously wanted to go, as witness the following:

> For your information, it appears the President wants to develop a significant program to counteract corruption in developing countries, a mandate that was reinforced by the recent G7 summit in Lyons. It appears that the management will support a 3 year action plan that will provide a comprehensive approach to the issue. If the VPs agree, a Bankwide working group will be set up and regional assessments/programs prepared. The plan is to be ready before the annual meetings. I presume we will be hearing more about this in the weeks to come.[6]

There was no turning back, and like it or not, management would have to deal with this new obstacle to the unbridled lending of the past. Background notes prepared for a meeting of the vice presidents, scheduled for July 17, 1996, provided further insights as to the difficulty management was having in coming to grips with these watershed events:

> Thus far the Bank has participated little in the international debate. While its actions across a broad front, we believe, contribute positively to the control of corruption, it has pursued them mostly for other reasons, such as improved economic performance. It has traditionally been cautious in addressing corruption directly, mindful of borrower sensitivity, the lack of data, and the variability of country and regional experience. One consequence has been a perception outside the institution that the Bank has yet to grasp the importance of the issue, exert intellectual leadership, and adjust its lending to new realities. Within the Bank, however, there is a concern to review existing approaches, building on them where necessary. Initiatives are already being taken to strengthen the control of corruption in Bank projects.[7]

How gently we approach the subject. We can't say with certainty, but we "believe" we contribute positively to the control of corruption. We have been cautious in addressing corruption directly, because we've not wanted to offend the sensitivities of our borrowers. And although we've studied economic development to death, we don't have any data about corruption, so please excuse us for not having done anything about it in the past. Yes, like it or not, management would have to bite the bullet and proceed along the path Wolfensohn was taking.

And so it was that the Bank finally, after decades of denial, began to move toward open recognition of the devastating impact that corruption was having on our portfolio. But it was a very painful process for many, especially for those who, over the years, had advanced their careers by ignoring the issue. Yet it was still very difficult for the Bank to discuss the substance of the corruption issue openly, as witness its *Annual Report 1997*, which contained only passing mention of the topic. With 250 pages covering every minute detail of the Bank's work that year, there were only five references to corruption. Four were a single sentence or less, and there was a single paragraph:

> The Bank is helping clients battle corrupt practices through project design and supervision and helping them improve the efficiency and transparency of procurement under Bank financed projects. This effort has been complemented by greater attention to improving the audit and monitoring functions under Bank financed projects. The procurement disbursement and audit team in the New Delhi office, for example, was strengthened to provide in-country expertise to assist implementing agencies in all aspects of procurement, disbursement, and audit. Similar steps are being taken in the Bangladesh and Pakistan field offices. (p. 64)

Why, one has to ask, was there no report on the events of the year that were shaking up the very core of the Bank's lending culture? Why was there no mention of the PREM report about combating corruption? Why was there no mention of the results of the staff survey on corruption in Bank projects? Why was there no mention of the senior-management meetings and the details of Wolfensohn's vision for addressing the problem? Although the Bank was now in its third year of anti-corruption introspection, and its president had publicly stated his resolve to pursue the issue, the denial factor was still quite evident within the ranks of management. This was eloquently stated by a former colleague in his response to a request for information concerning his division's efforts to address corruption:

> If we have failed or not been doing anything, that does not emerge. If there has been a ludicrously inadequate strategic analysis of the problem, that does not emerge. In the case in point, the corruption issue, I am quite convinced that we have failed across the board to persuade our borrowers to implement a strategy of transparency and accountability in key areas. But no individual staff member at my level can say with complete assurance, or report that as a fact. I also suspect that we have an inadequate institutional diagnosis of the causes of corruption within our borrower countries, but again that can only be a personal unconfirmed impression, and it is not the sort of thing that individual staff at our level can see clearly. *In other words, our normal system of enquiry seems designed to flatter our institution and create a flow of good news. It is not designed to confront us with hard questions, and release the critical faculties of the operational staff in general.*[8] (emphasis added)

Equally telling of the frustration experienced by staff in the trenches are the following excerpts from a Staff Association report submitted to the President in early 1998:

> Long before management released the new policy statement (in September 1997) confirming its intention to fight more aggressively corruption in the public sector affecting Bank projects, the Poverty Reduction Working Group of the S.A. had heard confidential stories on corruption from supervision missions. Nowhere is misappropriation of Bank investments by corrupt civil servants more shocking than when the funds were intended for the poorest segments of the population. Nowhere is misappropriation of funds more alarming than when NGOs certify that such misappropriation would not be possible without the Bank staff complicity. According to NGO testimonies there are two kinds of complicity: the passive one where Bank staff do not want to see,

investigate, record nor report the evidence and the active complicity where misappropriation of funds is done with the approval or the assistance of Bank staff. A number of national managers of poverty reduction projects have resisted closer scrutiny by Bank staff on supervision missions who have received no support from their own line managers. . . .

Some NGOs have commented bitterly that . . . of Bank funded projects . . . the poor see no more than the dust caused by the passage of Toyotas. Newly recruited Bank staff discover also to their surprise that ignoring evidence of corruption has been standard for many years in the Bank. How could they not look at some managers with disillusion and cynicism? Is this not at the root of some of the dissatisfaction reflected in staff surveys? Some consultants have commented that they would have lost their consultancies a long time ago if they had disclosed what they have observed on this issue. Even a U.S. Ph.D. student confessed that he could not report certain facts for fear of not being any longer in a position to finish his doctoral dissertation in the country where the Bank was funding his research. Reporting is presently not encouraged.[9]

Needless to say, the full report contained numerous other insights into the failure of Bank management to address the issue effectively. While not wanting to present the entire document here, the following two sentences sum up the issue well:

Stealing from Bank funds is the rule, not the exception. (para. 4)

Although there has been recently some indication that the Bank is wanting to fight corruption, many managers are unwilling to do so. (para. 5)

Thus spoke the Bank's staff association, and I can assure you that these were not just the ramblings of a few disgruntled staff, for there were many who had voiced similar feelings both verbally and in writing over the years. Yet by the time these things filtered up through management, they were rendered null and void by the self-congratulatory "good news" approved for publication by those same managers. Yes, the train had left the station, but it has yet to arrive at its destination.

NOTES

1. "On Corruption: A Survey of Bank Task Managers," an undated draft prepared sometime between late 1995 and mid-1996, p. 2.

2. Later renamed the World Bank Institute.

3. *World Bank Annual Report 1997*, p. 5.

4. PREM, "Helping Countries Combat Corruption: The Role of the World Bank," September 1997, p. 4.

5. Ibid., p. 7.

6. Internal memo to a regional procurement advisor, July 14, 1996.

7. "World Bank and Corruption—Operational Issues," July 11, 1996, para. 2.

8. Internal memo, July 15, 1996.

9. *Proposal to Increase Effectiveness of Some Poverty Reduction Targeted Projects,* staff association report, undated, "Annex: Bitterness, Disillusion, and Possible Solutions."

11

· · · · · · ·

A New Regime

Within a year of Wolfensohn's arrival, it was clear that he would not be intimidated by the career bureaucrats within the Bank. Many of the vice presidents, department directors, and senior advisors had been quite adept at controlling and manipulating the information fed to previous Bank presidents. To compound the problem, the Bank's legal department had, over the years, insisted that corruption was a political issue outside the Bank's purview. But Wolfensohn appeared to be having none of that, and it was interesting to see the discomfort with which some managers were struggling to comply with the disturbing requests for information coming from above.

On July 23, 1996, the Bank's senior management held an informal meeting with the board of directors to discuss a paper on corruption that had been presented to the board several weeks earlier. Among other things, management's background notes submitted for discussion had this to say:

> While the Bank has always sought to minimize the misuse of funds within the projects it finances, it has never had an explicit "strategy" to control corruption. But the Bank has recognized for many years that corruption is an integral issue of governance, and has sought to help governments control it, both directly and indirectly. This has occurred in the context of Bank actions in three broad areas: economic policy reform, institutional reform, and the control of corruption

within Bank financed projects. In addition, surveys and research directed primarily at other problems are yielding insights into corruption, as a by-product. Combined, these areas
of action constitute the Bank's present "strategy" to control
corruption.[1]

One could sense the difficulties they were having trying to reconcile the old culture with the new. Was it accurate to say the Bank
had always sought to minimize the misuse of funds? Not really,
for while the framework for transparent procurement was there,
it was never seriously enforced. And while it was true that the
Bank never had an explicit strategy to control corruption, the note
conveniently omitted to explain why this critical issue had been
ignored for so long. Is one really to believe that the Bank had recognized corruption as integral with governance? If so, one has to
ask why it allowed corruption to fester for so many decades before taking the kinds of actions now being proposed? Meanwhile,
the talk of reforms, surveys, and research merely becomes more
of the same obfuscation the Bank's management has been apply-
ing to every problem it has encountered over the years. Study it,
but don't get too close to it. Nevertheless, this was still progress,
and events would soon unfold that would finally propel the issue
to the forefront.

DIRTY LAUNDRY

Although I was completely convinced that corruption permeated
our lending program, never once did it occur to me that some
Bank staff might also be corrupt. It just didn't enter my mind. I
had worked with so many honest and dedicated colleagues over
the years that the thought of any of them embezzling funds from
our lending operations was unthinkable. Bank staff colluding with
government officials to approve contract awards? Never! Extort
kickbacks from suppliers? Never! Embezzle money from trust
funds? Never!

It is my understanding that Wolfensohn, from the beginning,
had intuitively concluded that no institution with over ten thousand employees dispensing billions of dollars each year could be
entirely free of corrupt individuals. During the first year of his

tenure, in response to allegations concerning a corrupt staff member, he sought the services of an outside professional fraud investigator to look into the matter. This was a significant departure from Bank responses to such allegations in the past, which, if not ignored, were quietly dealt with internally. And so began a new chapter in the Bank's struggle against the demon of corruption.

> The World Bank has hired outside auditors to investigate expenditures from its annual $25 billion fund for development projects after an internal examination uncovered "alarming information" about possible kickbacks and embezzlement, according to bank officials.
>
> One phase of the investigation, according to (James D.) Wolfensohn's statement, has led to a civil lawsuit in federal district court against a former bank official, Fritz Rodriguez. The lawsuit seeks to recover "tens of thousands" of dollars in alleged kickbacks that the bank believes Rodriguez took from a contractor on a water utility project in Algeria. The bank alleges in court papers that the contractor was a former neighbor and close friend of Rodriguez and that the work was never satisfactorily completed. . . .
>
> According to the bank's complaint, in early 1995 Rodriguez was assigned to manage a project that would computerize billing for Algeria's water utility. He obtained two bids, one from a well-known French company, and another from Managed Information Systems [MIS] of Chevy Chase.
>
> In its bid, MIS said it had four fully staffed corporate departments and planned to join forces with the French company in a joint venture to complete the work. The bank contends these statements were false.
>
> David Pearson was MIS's only full-time employee. Pearson and Rodriguez had been neighbors in Potomac for approximately 10 years in the 1970s and 1980s, and MIS had for a time employed Rodriguez's daughter, the bank alleges.
>
> It contends that Rodriguez did not disclose this information to his supervisor and awarded the $434,000 contract to MIS.
>
> The bank alleges that MIS used part-time subcontractors and that most of the work was performed on Pearson's home computer.[2]

While the above are only a few excerpts from the *Washington Post*'s front-page article, this was just the kind of scam I had seen perpetrated by our borrowers' representatives, and it was disheartening to realize that in addition to the Bank's bureaucratic mismanagement, we also had some thieves among us. How many will undoubtedly never be known, but I do believe in the integrity of the great majority of Bank staff and that these rotten apples are but a tiny minority within the Bank. Nevertheless, they are there, and it was clear that Wolfensohn intended to continue seeking them out.

This was merely the beginning of a period of internal turmoil, for at least some of us were now reduced to appearing just like the thieves we were lending to. The impact this had upon the rest was impossible to measure. It was, without question, an unimaginable insult to those who had struggled to overcome all the obstacles placed in their paths as they tried to perform their jobs professionally. Meanwhile, with much of the focus on the corruption of a few Bank staff, the real issue of corrupt public officials within the Bank's client countries was not getting the attention it deserved. But, still and all, this was progress.

FROM TALK TO ACTION

As unwelcome as it was, the revelation of a few corrupt individuals within the Bank contributed greatly to the creation of an internal-fraud investigation unit. But it was still difficult for management to admit that much larger sums were disappearing each day at the hands of our borrowers' representatives. And while a few hundred thousand dollars stolen by Bank staff was receiving front-page headlines, the millions stolen by third-world government officials seemed to go unnoticed. But at least the Bank would now have a mechanism to go after the thieves. In May 1998 a staff announcement stated:

> The World Bank Group is strongly committed to helping our members eliminate corruption. This means we must address vigorously any instances of possible fraud or corruption involving our own staff. Prompt action must be taken

whenever it is clear that staff may have abused their position for financial gain or misused Bank Group funds or other public funds for private gain. To ensure a thorough, prompt, and responsible investigation in all such instances, and to advise on whether specific cases merit possible criminal or civil action, an Oversight Committee on Fraud or Corruption Involving Bank Staff is hereby established.

The Committee will oversee significant fraud or corruption investigations conducted by the Internal Audit Department, Office of Professional Ethics, or any outside investigator appointed by the Bank Group, and for any matter involving fraud or corruption referred to it by the President. The Committee will also decide, in case of any uncertainty, whether an investigation should be conducted by the Internal Audit Department or by the Office of Professional Ethics. The Internal Audit Department and the Office of Professional Ethics will keep the Committee fully informed of all cases of significant fraud or corruption as they arise.[3]

At long last management was obliged to recognize that fraud and corruption were significant enough to warrant the creation of an investigative function within the Bank. Two months later Wolfensohn made the following announcement:

I have set up a special team from the Internal Audit Department in collaboration with the Office of Professional Ethics, alerted our Legal Department, engaged two outside specialists in fraud matters who are now working with us, retained a special team from PricewaterhouseCoopers skilled in exploring such issues, and have alerted our auditors, Deloitte Touche, to my concerns.[4]

For the Bank, these were earthshaking events. Never before had there been such admissions that the integrity of the Bank's staff and its clients might be somewhat less than perfect. Never before had the Bank moved to address these revelations with such firmness. With these announcements the Internal Audit Department Investigation Unit (IADIU) was born. Finally, after decades of doing everything it could to avoid the issue, the Bank was ready to investigate the corruption of our borrowers. The ugly truth that fraud had been part of the Bank's lending program for decades was at last being mainstreamed into the Bank's lexicon.

In May of that year I returned to the Bank to work with the new unit. Initially organized with a half dozen individuals, the unit was quickly joined by an investigative team from PricewaterhouseCoopers. And while this first effort involved the usual growing pains of any new undertaking, the level of commitment throughout the group was high, and it was refreshing for me to again work in an environment that put more emphasis on substance than appearances—an emphasis that had been singularly lacking during my previous years in the operations group.

Previously, allegations of corruption were handled on an ad hoc basis. Most of the time it was the task managers, procurement specialists, and disbursement officers who would receive specific complaints regarding bidding irregularities, improper contract awards, and payment problems. These issues would seldom be reported beyond the immediate project-managing division, while corrective action, if any was taken, would be handled bureaucratically. The Bank might not give its "no objection" to a rigged contract award, or it might require that the bidding process be repeated, or it might cancel funding for the relevant component of the project. But these were all actions that avoided confrontation with our clients and did nothing to deter them from future corrupt acts.

But with the establishment of the IADIU, a fraud hotline, and other reporting mechanisms, things began to change. Individuals both within and outside the Bank now felt less constrained about reporting fraudulent acts. The number of incoming complaints increased exponentially as word spread of our existence. In addition, there were the "walk-ins" by Bank staff with allegations of fraud on projects they had managed. In these latter cases it soon became clear that staff members had been suppressing their frustrations for many years over the waste, inefficiency, and corruption that permeated our lending program. On several occasions I was taken aside by colleagues who told me of corrupt acts they had witnessed ten to fifteen years earlier, and it was obvious from their demeanor that they had kept this information bottled up for a painfully long time.[5]

And so the floodgates were opened as staff shed their apprehensions about coming forward with what they knew, and within a short time, our new unit was receiving more allegations of wrong-doing than it could possibly investigate. While this was encouraging, it also created problems in prioritizing our work. Inevitably, a number of these complaints were frivolous at best and would require triage to enable us to focus on more important cases. In one six-month period alone we received 430 complaints that had to be prioritized within our limited resources. From the frivolous to the serious, these allegations consumed precious time as each one had to be reviewed to determine if further action was necessary.

But while sifting out the frivolous complaints was relatively easy, the serious ones required a much harder look to determine how to proceed. Was the complaint about a Bank staff member? How much money was involved? Did the fraud involve high government officials? Did the complainant provide credible evidence? These were all important questions to be assessed before assigning a priority to the case. And while these general criteria were applied effectively in most cases, there were times when perverse agendas within the Bank could intrude upon the process. This, of course, would throw a monkey wrench into things and prevent the unit from dealing effectively with the most serious cases.

Among the more difficult obstacles was the intrusion of Bank politics into the process. This could take different forms depending upon the nature of the allegations and the level of management concerned. Was the subject of a pending investigation so sensitive that it would cause a serious public relations problem for the Bank? Did it involve highly placed persons within the Bank or the client government? Would it expose gross mismanagement within the Bank? Would it reveal that the Bank had knowingly approved loans to government mafias? These were just some of the factors that could hinder an investigation if it became evident that it was leading to such exposure.

In the early days of the IADIU's existence, the unit seemed able to direct its resources effectively towards the most important cases. But as the volume of complaints increased, and as different groups within the Bank sought to insert themselves into the process, things became more complicated. As noted earlier, the exposure of corruption within Bank operations caused traumatic moments for some managers as they tried to decide which side of the issue to take. Many came on board eagerly, while others obviously wanted the issue to fade away. And within this latter group were those who did their utmost to stonewall our investigations.

Yet, despite these obstacles, there was hope. It was clear that things would never be the same regarding the Bank's approach to the corruption issue. No longer could management sweep corruption under the carpet. No longer could it ignore the blatant theft of Bank funds by corrupt individuals. Yes, there were still many problems to resolve and still much resistance to overcome, but with the arrival of Wolfensohn and a new regime, the light was finally shining into the dark corners of the Bank's lending operations.

NOTES

1. "Background Note on Fraud and Corruption from the Vice President and Secretary to the Executive Directors," July 11, 1996, para. 4.

2. Lorraine Adams, "World Bank Hires Auditors to Probe Its Own Spending," *Washington Post,* July 16, 1998. © 1998, The Washington Post. Reprinted with Permission.

3. Shengman Zhang (managing director), announcement, May 12, 1998.

4. James D. Wolfensohn, announcement, July 15, 1998.

5. One such allegation concerned a loan made to the Philippine government during the Marcos regime in which several hundred million dollars were embezzled from a rural development project. Not surprising, given the corrupt reputation enjoyed by that regime. But unfortunately it was so far in the past that, given our already huge case load, we were unable to pursue the matter further.

12

• • • • • • •

The Potemkin Village

The creation of the investigation unit was such a traumatic departure from the Bank's past handling of corruption issues that it was
hard to imagine it as a permanent fixture within the institution.
And while those who were pleased to see this new turn of events
were encouraged, others who were not so pleased appeared to be
anxiously waiting for this latest fad to run its course and disappear. But with each disclosure of the theft of Bank funds, the case
for having such a unit within the Bank became stronger. Like it or
not, with each passing month it was increasingly evident that the
unit was here to stay.

Yet it was not a smooth transition as the bureaucracy began to
intervene in subtle ways. First, there were the usual reorganizations (which occurred four times during my four years with the
unit). Starting out as the Internal Audit Department Investigations
Unit (IADIU) under the auditor general, we were soon reorganized as the Anti-Corruption and Fraud Investigation Unit
(ACFIU) reporting to the secretariat of the oversight committee.
Within a year this became the Corruption and Fraud Investigation Unit (CFIU), encompassing a number of internal management
changes within the unit. Then, with great fanfare, the Department
of Institutional Integrity (INT) was created in early 2001, and we
became the Investigations Unit (INTIU) within that department.
It was indeed a watershed event.

But as always, good things do not come without a price, and
while I was excited about the progress that had been made, I was

also wary of what appeared to be the gradual intrusion of the Bank's culture into our midst. Apart from the reorganizations, we had moved our offices five times during that same four-year period. Each reorganization cost us valuable time away from our work as we held countless meetings to discuss the game of musical chairs. Each office move meant more lost time as we met to discuss who would get which office, packed our files, had our computers moved, then unpacked our files, and had our computers reinstalled. Meanwhile, we worked out of boxes for weeks at a time while the game played out. None of this improved our ability to carry out our work. Nevertheless, we now had the INT, and that was good. Still, we were not immune to the bureaucratic machinations of management, and we were still understaffed with a caseload that required two to three times more investigators than we actually had.

But the reorganizations and office moves were merely minor manifestations of the bureaucracy's envelopment of the INT. The freedom that we had in conducting our investigations was circumscribed bit by bit during each reorganization, and while one can understand the need to prevent abuse of the process by an overzealous investigator, it often seemed that abuse of the process by overzealous management was a much greater threat to our operations. Each time around, it seemed that more approval was required from more managers during the course of an investigation. Increasingly, we had to abide by guidelines and limitations imposed by management when dealing with the borrower's representatives. More and more we had to explain ourselves and justify our findings to individuals who were unable to comprehend the investigative process, lacked the moral compass to see the criminal aspects of the corruption issue, and lacked the courage to deal with it decisively. More and more we had to consider possible repercussions for the Bank if highly placed individuals were involved, or if relations with a client might be affected. Yes, we want you to investigate the theft of Bank funds, but let's be careful that we don't rock the boat too much! You may catch all the little guys you want, but please don't go too far up the food chain!

And so, after more than four decades, the Bank finally found integrity and institutionalized it. For years the Bank's rampant lending culture had dispensed far too many loans to governments run by thieves. Thieves who would steal whenever they had the opportunity, and nothing was more opportune than a World Bank loan. Obsessed with moving money to further our own careers, we had somehow forgotten our fiduciary responsibilities and just plain old-fashioned logic as we approved loan after loan, enriching the corrupt while ensuring that the poor would remain in poverty.

My cynicism aside, the creation of the INT was something I would have never predicted in 1995 when I first retired. It was, without question, a major milestone in many ways and was unimaginable prior to Wolfensohn's arrival at the Bank. Although initially there was considerable opposition from some Bank staff and management, this slowly gave way to reluctant acceptance as investigative findings continued to show the depth and pervasiveness of corruption within the Bank's portfolio. Those who truly cared about the Bank and its mission were encouraged by this event. But there was always the risk that improvements would be marginalized by the bureaucracy, becoming a "Potemkin village," creating the image that management was fighting corruption while doing little to stop the loss of funds from its portfolio. The Bank was still afraid to confront the corrupt government officials it dealt with. Still afraid to report how much is stolen each year. Still afraid to exercise due diligence. Still afraid to do anything that might slow the pace of lending.

But why did it take so long to get to this juncture? Did management know the depth of the corruption problem yet lack the courage to act upon it? Or did it not have a clue? The recent highly publicized recognition of corruption as a critical obstacle to development has been a dilemma for management, perhaps more for the questions it raises than the questions it answers. For if corruption was, and is, such a serious impediment to development, why did the Bank's management not admit to it and address it sooner? Bank management was, by its own admission, on the "cutting edge" of development economics. They were, by their own admission, the ones to whom the whole world looked for leadership in development matters. If that was true, and Bank managers were the leaders they claimed to be, how, in all good conscience, could they have looked the other way for all those years while many of their esteemed clients looted every last penny of Bank funds they could get their hands on? And if they knew they were dealing with corrupt government officials, why did they continue to provide those same officials with such wonderful opportunities to be more corrupt?

Conversely, if they really hadn't a clue as to what their corrupt friends were doing, perhaps one might conclude that they weren't as bright as they claimed to be. And herein lies their dilemma. After all those decades of lending hundreds of billions of dollars to corrupt governments, did they or did they not know what was going on? If they did know, then why didn't they do something about it? If they did not know, then how could they justify their claims of leadership in the development arena, and how could they justify their stewardship of the funds entrusted to them? Perhaps these questions will never be answered fully, but knowing that the issue had been raised repeatedly over the years by concerned Bank staff and others, without any substantive follow up by management, it is hard not to conclude that Bank managers knew full well what was going on and intentionally chose to ignore the issue for the sake of their careers and God knows what other agendas.

Although it provides a telling insight into the culture of the institution, management's past disregard for the criminal aspects of corruption and its willingness to ignore its fiduciary responsibilities is somewhat of a moot point. The Bank has finally admitted to the world that corruption exists and has made numerous public pronouncements about its commitment to fighting it. It has supported a plethora of intellectual exercises on the issue. It has created hotlines and other avenues for reporting the theft of Bank funds. It has created and supported a fraud investigation unit to pursue allegations of corruption. It has established a system for debarring firms and individuals found guilty of fraudulent acts against the Bank and Bank-funded operations. And while these are all good things, the Bank has yet to wean itself from its culture of lending—a culture that only feeds the beast of corruption while denying the poor a chance for a better life.

So while the creation of the INT was commendable, one has to ask if the Bank is addressing the problem adequately and effectively? Is the Bank doing all it possibly can to protect its portfolio, or is it merely doing just enough to keep the critics at bay? More important, is the Bank's management addressing the issue because it genuinely believes in the cause, or is it going through the motions because the rest of the world will no longer allow it to keep its collective head in the sand? Most likely, the truth lies somewhere in between.

While the Bank continues to publicize its commitment to fighting corruption, much of that publicity tends to be more intellectual fanfare than substance. A 2005 visit to the Bank's website underscored this point. Buried among glowing success stories of Bank projects and esoteric topics on every subject in the world of economic development, we finally locate the anti-corruption pages and see the following introduction:

> The Bank has identified corruption as the single greatest obstacle to economic and social development. It undermines development by distorting the rule of law and weakening the institutional foundation on which economic growth depends.
>
> The harmful effects of corruption are especially severe on the poor, who are hardest hit by economic decline, are most reliant on the provision of public services, and are least capable of paying the extra costs associated with bribery, fraud, and the misappropriation of economic privileges.
>
> Corruption sabotages policies and programs that aim to reduce poverty, so attacking corruption is critical to the achievement of the Bank's overarching mission of poverty reduction. We believe that an effective anti-corruption strategy builds on five key elements:
>
> 1. Increasing Political Accountability
> 2. Strengthening Civil Society Participation
> 3. Creating a Competitive Private Sector
> 4. Institutional Restraints on Power
> 5. Improving Public Sector Management
>
> To reduce the corrosive impact of corruption in a sustainable way, it is important to go beyond the symptoms to tackle the causes of corruption. Since 1996, the World Bank has supported more than 600 anti-corruption programs and governance initiatives developed by its member countries.[1]

At last, after decades of missing the point, we have finally identified corruption as "the single greatest obstacle to economic and social development." At last, after many hundreds of projects designed to strengthen corrupt and dysfunctional government institutions, we have learned that corruption "weakens the institutional foundation on which economic growth depends." At last, after thousands of studies dissecting every minute aspect of poverty, we have realized that corruption is "especially severe on the poor." These revelations are certainly long overdue, but better late than never. Yet if corruption is the greatest obstacle to the Bank's mission, why isn't it right up there on page one of the Bank's website where it can be seen immediately? If it is so critical to the Bank's mandate, why is it buried beneath so many innocuous topics that are obviously of lesser importance, if important at all?

And what of the professed anti-corruption strategy with its five key elements? Do they really tell us anything of substance? Do they propose anything with teeth in it? Described by phrases that tell us nothing, will any of these key elements be effective as long as corrupt government officials are allowed to get away with their crimes? What good is any of this if we don't also address the criminal aspects of the whole business? What good is it to prattle on about "political accountability" and "creating a competitive private sector" while the criminals are allowed to continue their corrupt activities with impunity? And what good is it to support "more than 600 anti-corruption programs and governance initiatives" if Bank funds continue to be stolen at every turn? Some times, I might add, through those very same anti-corruption programs and government initiatives.

Perhaps a more telling point about the Bank's ambivalence in publicizing the fight against corruption is its treatment, or rather lack of treatment, of corruption in its annual reports. The *World Bank Annual Report 1997* devoted only a few sentences and a single brief paragraph to the subject. Five years later, despite growing awareness of the impact of corruption on development, one is hard put to find any reference to this "greatest obstacle" to reducing poverty. And while the *World Bank Annual Report 2002*'s index will lead us to "clean air initiative," "environmental sustainability," "knowledge sharing," and "poverty reduction," to name just a few, the subject that is, by the Bank's own admission, among the most critical factors in the whole business, is missing. One hundred and sixty seven pages of glowing praise for the Bank's leadership in economic development, and not one paragraph about corruption! How could "the greatest obstacle" to alleviating poverty somehow have escaped notice in the preparation of this widely circulated and widely read World Bank report? How strange that an issue so central to the Bank's mission could somehow be forgotten, while any number of less important topics received top billing.

Again, the Bank's dilemma, again the bureaucracy at work, for while there is no turning back to the "good old days," it is not in management's interests to be overly aggressive about this corruption issue. Yes, the Bank is doing more about publicizing the issue than it has in the past, but this is not necessarily saying much, when its efforts in the past were zero. In this regard the Bank has barely scratched the surface, and it must do much more. It must shift priorities from the usual intellectual pablum it disseminates and focus on the real issues of protecting its portfolio from the corrupt individuals it often finds itself dealing with. It is not enough for the Bank to disseminate these academic treatises that do little, if anything, to stop the theft of its funds. It is not enough to talk about good governance and political accountability, while conveniently omitting to discuss the losses suffered on Bank-funded operations due to corruption. It is not enough to pretend we are sincere in uncovering every act of fraud committed against Bank funds, while doing everything behind the scenes to impede the process.

So why not include a full chapter on allegations received, investigations carried out, firms debarred, stolen funds recovered, identification of the government agencies and projects involved, and anything else that would demonstrate the Bank's commitment? Just as management does on all the other topics it considers important to economic development and the alleviation of poverty. This kind of transparent and comprehensive reporting would have a positive impact and would go a long way toward improving the Bank's credibility in its fight against corruption.[2]

Although the Bank has been inconsistent and frequently inadequate in reporting on the corruption issue, it has done somewhat better in other areas. The establishment of a hotline and other dedicated sites for reporting fraud and related crimes against Bank funds has been instrumental in encouraging more people to come forward with information about corrupt acts. The creation of the fraud investigation unit and the evolution of the INT, although encumbered by the bureaucratic agendas noted previously, has been a long overdue watershed event for the Bank. It is now easier to report instances of fraud and corruption to the Bank, and there is a mechanism for investigating such allegations. There are also mechanisms for the debarment of firms and individuals found guilty of fraud, and relations with the investigation units of other donor agencies have been established. Precedents have been established regarding the referral of case findings to national law-enforcement agencies for the prosecution of guilty parties. It now appears that those who previously stole from Bank-funded operations with impunity must now consider at least a minimal risk of being exposed. All of this adds to the Bank's credibility regarding its commitment to the fight against corruption. But is this sufficient?

Obviously, with billions of dollars at risk, one can only conclude that much more must be done to stop the theft of funds from the Bank's portfolio. But is the Bank willing to back up its anti-corruption rhetoric with concrete action? Is its management willing to push beyond what it has done so far? Will management finally accept that Bank funds are being robbed at every turn, and that these losses are much larger than it has previously been willing to admit? Such steps will require a tremendous amount of soul searching, something that management has heretofore been incapable of doing. And it will require decisions that are heretical to any good bureaucrat.

Given the sheer volume of annual disbursements, such steps will require at least a doubling, but more likely a tripling, of the present resources, both budgetary and human, allocated to the INT. They will require the recruitment of more professional investigators, increased interaction with government enforcement agencies and judicial systems, a formal framework for the recovery of stolen funds, a comprehensive reporting system that will include the identification of government officials when they have been found guilty of corrupt acts,[3] and full reporting of the amounts stolen.

The Bank claims international leadership in the realm of knowledge management, data collection, and economic analysis. And it claims to employ the world's experts in these fields. It thus follows that if the Bank can report on the most minute details of poverty or "sustainable development," it surely can do the same for corruption. It is incomprehensible that an institution such as the World Bank cannot account for the losses within its portfolio. Losses that may conservatively run to several billion dollars each year. And while there have been numerous disputes between the Bank and its critics about how much has been stolen from its lending program, the fact is that the Bank doesn't know and refuses to find out. A sad commentary for an institution that claims to be at the cutting edge of economic management!

Last, but not least, there is the ultimate Bank solution to all third-world problems. We will lend money. This "solution" applied to corruption defies all logic, for in many cases it is akin to letting the fox guard the chickens. A government may be corrupt in the extreme, yet all it has to do is inform the Bank's management that it wishes to fight corruption, and the money will flow. It will flow right into the hands of the corrupt officials who have made the government corrupt in the first place. And this frequently occurs under the guise of promoting "good governance," the Bank's catch-all justification for making loans to countries that have endured decades of bad government. Or, if "good governance" is not quite appropriate, we can always use "economic management" as an excuse to make a loan or two. And how egregious is this? According to *World Bank Annual Report 2002*, $3.9 billion was loaned for "public sector governance" and $536 million was loaned for "economic management" during that year alone.[4]

Now obviously, not all that money went into the wrong hands, nor was all of it lost to the kinds of scams I have described previously. But, using a loan of $730 million for "public-sector governance" made to Argentina as an example, one has to wonder just how much of this money will be used in accordance with Article III of the Bank's Articles of Agreement, and how much will be stolen?[5] In the same year a $500 million IDA credit for "governance" was provided to the Democratic Republic of the Congo. With a long history of one corrupt government after another, and a ranking near the bottom (133 of 145) on TI's Corruption Index 2004, how can the Bank's management conclude that the risks associated with this credit are acceptable? What guarantee is there that the current thieves in office will not help themselves to this little pot of World Bank gold?

In addition to the 2002 Argentine and Congo "governance" projects, we also have $355 million to Mexico, $351 million to

Russia, $350 million to India, and $100 million to the Philippines, all known for widespread corruption. Also in the same year, $500 million of IDA funds was provided to Pakistan for "economic management." This to a government that was rated 77 of 102 in 2002 in TI's Corruption Index and then downgraded to 129 of 145 two years later. While this may not be the most accurate way to assess the risks posed to the $500 million credit, it is interesting to note that within two years from the time the IDA credit was approved, Pakistan went from the twenty-fifth percentile on the TI Index to the eleventh percentile. In other words, after receiving $500 million from IDA, the government apparently became worse at economic management. Or perhaps it became better at corruption. So much for governance and economic management.

Of course, not all these funds will be stolen, and some will certainly be used for the purposes intended, whatever that may be. But it would be foolish to assume that the roughly $4.5 billion approved in 2002 for governance and economic management and loaned to governments known to be egregiously corrupt would be completely safe from theft. How much will be siphoned off through phony consultancies? How much will be spent for useless overpriced studies? How much will be used for overseas junkets by government bureaucrats? How much will be lost through procurement scams? How much will be paid to shell companies owned by government officials? And how much will wind up in private offshore accounts?

The Bank's management cannot possibly answer these questions, and worse, it has no desire to do so. But, even using a conservative figure of 10 percent lost to corruption, this would amount to $450 million; a more realistic estimate would undoubtedly come to two or three times that amount. Will these losses justify the promised but often unmeasurable improvements in governance and economic management? The end results have frequently proven to be questionable at best, while the losses to theft and corruption are never analyzed, discussed, or accounted for.

Finally, despite increasing evidence that lending for governance and economic management frequently carries enormous risks while producing questionable results, it appears that the Bank's obsession for approving loans and credits under whatever pretext has not diminished. An interesting example of this is a recent $73 million IDA credit for Haiti to support economic governance[6] and disaster recovery efforts that, according to the Bank's website announcement, was approved for the following reasons:

> The World Bank Group's Board of Directors today approved a package of $73 million in credits and grants for Haiti and endorsed a Transitional Support Strategy which projects up to $150 million in credit and grant commitments over a two year period. The package of loans approved today includes an Economic Governance Reform Operation of $61 million and an Emergency Recovery and Disaster Management Project of $12 million from the International Development Association, the Bank's concessional window. This assistance includes $36 million available as grants and $37 million as zero-interest credits.
>
> *"The chief goal of the Bank is to help the Government deliver urgently needed basic services to the Haitian people and strengthen the transparency and credibility of public institutions,"* said World Bank President James Wolfensohn. "Given the urgent need to support recovery efforts in the country, we plan to disburse $46 million of this assistance in the next couple of days." . . .
>
> The $61 million Economic Governance Reform Operation aims to restore credibility in Haiti's public institutions by increasing transparency and efficiency in the use of public resources and external assistance. In particular, the operation will support reforms in budget management and financial controls, strengthen the public sector's institutional capacity in human resources management and procurement, and an anti-corruption strategy. In addition the operation will promote economic governance reforms at the sectoral level, including to strengthen a road maintenance fund, key public enterprises and public-private partnerships to increase access to health and education services. Civil society organizations and representatives from the private sector will be involved in monitoring and evaluating Government reforms supported by the operation.[7]

Who can dispute that the Haitian people suffer as much, if not more, than any other people in the world? Who can dispute that each regime that has come to power in Haiti has been at least as corrupt as its predecessors? Who can dispute that generations of Haitians have been ruled by thugs posing as government officials? Who can dispute that Haitian politics have historically centered around the power to instill fear in the population while raping the treasury? And who can dispute that these truths are known by all? In TI's Corruption Index 2002, Haiti was ranked 89 of 102 countries, losing out to Uganda, Indonesia, Kenya, Nigeria, and a few others in its bid to be named the most corrupt country on the planet. It finally achieved this status two years later when it was ranked 145 of 145, a distinct honor to be sure.

Can the Bank's management truly believe that by dumping $61 million into the hands of Haitian officials, all this will change? Does it really believe that this money will "restore credibility in Haiti's institutions"? Did Haiti's public institutions ever have credibility in the first place? Do Bank officials really believe that putting $61 million in the hands of these thieves will "increase transparency and efficiency in the use of public resources"? How could they possibly believe these things when, up through 2001, the Bank had approved roughly $626 million in IDA credits to Haiti for all of these lofty objectives and more, with little if anything to show for it? They had thrown money at one Haitian regime after another with the same wildly optimistic promises that somehow never seemed to materialize. And nothing changes! The Haitian population remains mired in abject poverty, public institutions are totally dysfunctional, and the treasury is constantly looted by the governing elites, while the donors never tire of feeding their voracious appetites.

So where does all this leave the Bank in its search for integrity? Has it achieved all it can achieve in this regard? More important, has it convinced its borrowers that they too must embrace integrity? And how can progress on both fronts be measured? In the first instance, if we consider the actions the Bank has taken since Wolfensohn's arrival in 1995, it is clear that many things have been accomplished to establish a veneer of credibility on the Bank's efforts to combat corruption. But after the creation of the INT, these efforts seem to have reached a plateau. Meanwhile, the Bank has yet to make any concerted effort to recover stolen funds, a critical factor if management is serious about its fiduciary responsibilities.

On other fronts, the Bank's bureaucrats have taken over center stage with their research, studies, conferences, and publications on the topic of corruption, while management has pushed ahead with "new" lending products using the anti-corruption cachet. It has not done nearly enough in addressing the criminal aspects of corruption, while at the same time devoting far too much effort on inane intellectual discourse on the subject. The man and woman in the street intuitively know what corruption is and recognize the damage it does to society. They intuitively know that corrupt government officials are no different from common thieves. But sadly, the Bank's management does not seem to have these same intuitions and continues to dance in circles while avoiding the aggressive actions that are required to deal with this issue effectively.

As for convincing the Bank's borrowers that they too must embrace integrity, the efforts that have been made to encourage participation by various social groups within each country are commendable. Anti-corruption workshops, seminars, and conferences with government officials are commendable. Publications, research, and all the other intellectual exercises carried out in the name of corruption are also commendable. But these activities must be conducted with caution and must be properly balanced with the aggressive actions discussed previously. Too much talk and too little action changes nothing, and the Bank must never lose sight of the fact that in many cases those it is preaching to are the worst sinners. Sinners who are seldom, if ever, interested in changing their ways. Sinners who profess concerns about corruption while continuing their corrupt activities on a daily basis. Mafiosi attending church on Sunday while robbing the poor the rest of the week.

In this, it is clear to me that nothing, I repeat, *nothing*, will send a stronger message or do more to convince the world that the Bank is serious about the corruption issue than to pursue the corrupt individuals aggressively, both those inside and those outside its client governments who are stealing the funds it provides for economic development and the alleviation of poverty. Nothing will do more to convince corrupt individuals that they are in the wrong business than the knowledge that they are at much greater risk of being exposed, prosecuted, and punished when they steal Bank funds. Nothing will deter them more from their corrupt acts than the knowledge that they will lose their stolen gains if they are caught. Nothing will do more to convince corrupt governments to change their ways than the realization that they may be ostracized by the donor community and no longer be allowed to feed at the trough unless they clean up their act and begin to do a little more for their people and a little less for themselves.

The Bank's awakening to the corruption crisis has been a critical event in its history. It has, under pressure from Wolfensohn, and from the short-lived Wolfowitz presidency, at last openly come to grips with the issue and has taken the difficult steps needed to overcome the internal bureaucratic opposition to it. But although this is a tremendous step forward in many ways, the anti-corruption issue is now at risk of becoming just another topic to which much lip service is given but very little concrete action taken. The Bank's fight against corruption has become "bureaucratized." With much fanfare it has become a paper tiger, attempting to assure the public that it is at the forefront of the battle in the hope of assuaging its critics. And while it has taken the first difficult steps, in a difficult environment filled with conflicting agendas, it has yet to achieve any measurable reduction in the amount of funds stolen from the loans, credits, and grants that it dispenses each year to corrupt governments. Until the day arrives when such a reduction can be effectively demonstrated, the Bank will not be able to claim that it has done all that it can to address the corruption issue.

NOTES

1. World Bank website, "Overview of Anti-corruption," accessed January 15, 2005.

2. In recent years this issue has been ameliorated somewhat with an annual INT publication that nevertheless falls short of providing an in-depth report.

3. If the Bank can identify corrupt firms and individuals, it can certainly identify the corrupt government officials who are, in most instances, the driving force behind those fraudulent acts.

4. See *World Bank Annual Report 2002*, vol. 2, Appendix 11: Projects Approved for IBRD and IDA Assistance in Fiscal 2002 by Theme.

5. According to Transparency International's Corruption Index, Argentina was ranked 70 of 102 in 2002 and was downgraded to 108 of 145 in 2004 (TI website, accessed January 21, 2005). Based upon my own observations of widespread corruption found during several Argentine investigations, I estimate that at least $220 million (30 percent) of this loan will disappear through fraud and embezzlement.

6. A new twist on words, as we join *economic* with *governance,* making the whole business even more intellectually palatable in the minds of the Bank's economists.

7. "Haiti: World Bank Approves $73 Million for Economic Governance and Disaster Recovery Efforts in Haiti," news release #272, January 6, 2005. Available on the World Bank website.

13

• • • • • • •

Death by a Thousand Cuts

While management would readily admit that "some" money might be lost through "leakage" or "rent seeking," it was in complete denial regarding the wholesale plundering of Bank funds. Unfortunately, plundering is the order of the day for too many third-world government officials who oversee projects funded by the Bank. And there is strong evidence to support this claim, evidence that clearly shows that the Bank is losing millions of dollars each working day through fraudulent procurement transactions orchestrated by its clients. And while management will vehemently deny that such huge amounts are being stolen, some simple calculations can help us understand the extent of the problem.

The *World Bank Annual Report 2004* shows $11 billion disbursed for projects during that fiscal year.[1] Assuming just 10 percent lost to corruption, a figure no one has ever disputed, and dividing that amount ($1.1 billion) by 260 working days a year, we find that roughly $4.2 million may very well be vanishing each day into the pockets of corrupt government officials and their accomplices. Of course, 10 percent is an extremely conservative estimate of these losses. In reality, losses are more likely to vary between 15 percent and 40 percent, depending upon the government concerned. Thus between $6 million and $17 million are being stolen each day from the Bank's portfolio. And we have not even considered funds stolen from structural adjustment loans!

While the higher figures will bring loud cries of denial from management, there is no doubt in my mind that the problem is at least that large, if not larger than what I have described. Nothing will demonstrate this more aptly than the findings of an investigation carried out in West Africa in 1998–99, an investigation I call "Death by a Thousand Cuts" because of the pervasive fraud and embezzlement that bled the project dry with each passing day.

The matter concerned a project in The Gambia, a small West African country that had received roughly $243 million in IDA credits between 1970 and 2001[2] for a variety of projects and adjustment credits.[3] With a population of roughly 1.5 million and a per capita income of $330[4] The Gambia and its capital of Banjul was always a relatively stress free place for Bank staff to go about the business of appraising and supervising lending operations. Things were considerably less frenetic than Lagos or Abidjan, life moved at a slower pace, and the hotels and beaches at the mouth of the Gambia River provided a relaxing environment during off hours.

During my years in the Africa Region operations group I had worked on several Gambian projects in the highways, ports, energy, and water sectors and had become quite familiar with local conditions. Despite the fact that Gambian projects tended to be small in comparison with other lending operations, they often required as much effort to appraise and supervise as projects in the larger and more populous countries on the continent. So, while a $5 million highway project in The Gambia might require the same amount of effort for Bank staff as a $200 million transportation project in Nigeria, it offered much less reward on the road to a promotion.

But these concerns aside, it would be fair to say that this never seemed to detract from the commitment and dedication of my colleagues as we tried to keep "our" projects on track. And while dealing with government officials tended to be somewhat less frustrating than in other countries on the continent, it was just as difficult to achieve any substantive progress. Despite the smiles and friendly atmosphere, and despite mission after mission, things never seemed to move forward as planned. And there was always the undercurrent of corruption that, in one way or another, often prevented any meaningful achievement of project objectives, a condition that made The Gambia no different from Nigeria, Kenya, or the others.

THE ALLEGATIONS

In July 1998, IADIU received allegations concerning financial difficulties faced by some Gambian trainees on overseas fellowships. The fellowships were funded through a $12.3 million IDA credit for an agriculture services project (ASP) of which $3.9 million had been set aside for various agriculture training programs. While most of the funds were to be used for in-country training and outreach programs for the farmers, the credit agreement also made provisions for twenty-four overseas fellowships for selected government staff, and it was within this latter component that the first indications of systemic corruption arose.

Overseas training was a much sought after perquisite on Bank-funded projects because of the opportunities for abuse that typically resulted in egregious overcharging for tuition, travel, and stipends that could never be accounted for. But strangely, in this case, the initial allegations contradicted all previous experience, for we were informed that several ministry staff studying abroad in the United Kingdom had not been receiving their living allowances and were suffering considerable hardship.[5] This situation was totally at odds with the many fellowship programs I had encountered in the past.

STARVING STUDENTS

An initial review of withdrawal applications for the special account and the attached SOEs indicated that a large number of individuals were attending various overseas universities, with a majority in the UK and a smaller number in the United States. By creating a spreadsheet of the trainees, the host universities, and payments made, several facts soon became clear. First, despite an agreement to fund twenty-four fellowships from the IDA credit, the number of trainees sent overseas came to ninety-three, a fourfold increase over the credit agreement. This, among other things, meant that funds had been diverted from somewhere else to pay for the increased numbers of overseas trainees. Second, payments for tuition, travel, and living allowances were made in inconsistent and illogical patterns. And third, there were questionable variations in the amounts paid for similar line items. Taken together, these three facts raised questions about the overall financial management of the project and appeared to be significant enough to indicate something more serious than the initial allegations.

Among the individuals identified in the SOEs as having received payments for tuition, travel, and living allowances, seventy-six were studying in the UK at twenty different universities, while thirteen were attending nine different universities in the United States. This in itself was a bit troubling, as the widespread distribution of trainees appeared to be more a haphazard scramble to find acceptance at any university than a planned effort to seek appropriate training for each individual consistent with project objectives. Beginning with this information, each of the schools was contacted to obtain the status of the trainees and the costs of tuition and living allowances, in order to determine the validity of the payments made through the SOEs. But the more information we obtained, the more bizarre things became.

Indeed, there was compelling evidence that seven of the trainees had not received sufficient living allowances and were struggling to survive. Some faculty members had loaned them funds for food and housing, and in one case, a degree was being withheld until monies owed the university were paid. In total, roughly $101,000 had not been paid for the tuition and stipends of these seven individuals.

But in the course of unraveling the non-payments, it also appeared that excess funds totaling roughly $595,000 had been withdrawn under the names of fifty-four other trainees. To add to the confusion, it appeared that the proper amounts had been paid for the tuition and living expenses of the remaining thirty-two trainees in the program. In effect, we had fifty-four fellowships that had been overcharged, seven that had been undercharged, and thirty-two that had been charged the correct amounts. Of the fifty-four cases of excess payments, twenty-six involved amounts ranging from $10,000 to $40,000 each, while the remainder ranged from $2,000 to $10,000 each. The red flags began to wave, as witness to of the cases uncovered during the investigation.

Case 1: $40,000 unaccounted for. The trainee, an employee of the ministry, received a $20,000 scholarship grant from a U.S.

university to attend an eighteen-month agriculture research program. It was agreed that the project would fund an additional $20,000[6] for travel and living expenses so that the trainee could accept the scholarship. At the time of the investigation, SOEs from the special account indicated that $48,000 had been disbursed against this activity in the trainee's name. This was already $28,000 more than the agreed amount, while evidence provided by the university indicated that only $8,000 had actually been paid by the project. In other words, out of the $48,000 shown to have been disbursed from the special account, only $8,000 could be properly accounted for, leaving an unexplained discrepancy of $40,000 between the SOEs and university records. Further investigation revealed that the trainee would not receive a diploma until an outstanding balance of $12,000 for housing was paid to the university.[7] The project director was unable to provide a suitable explanation or supporting documentation for the missing $40,000.

Case 2: $40,000 unaccounted for. An employee of the Ministry was accepted at a US university for a ten-month master's degree program. According to the university, tuition and living allowances came to approximately $23,000, with airfare adding several thousand more to the costs. The trainee attended two semesters full-time and three semesters part-time thus staying in the United States for twenty-two months. In addition to receiving an $8,000 scholarship from the university, which should have been credited against the tuition paid from the project account, he was alleged to have been gainfully employed while attending these courses. A review of disbursement records indicated that approximately $66,000 had been withdrawn from the project accounts against actual costs of $26,000, leaving $40,000 unaccounted for.

These patterns of embezzlement through the fellowship program were repeated many times as I compared the SOEs against the actual costs provided by the universities. Whether it was for short courses, undergraduate studies, master's degrees, or doctorates, the tactics were always the same: inconsistent methods of payments, inconsistent prices for the same line items, excessive living allowances, and payments for extended time abroad. Reviewing the accounts was an exercise in confusion as we tried to unravel the Byzantine process by which funds were withdrawn.

ACCOUNTING 101

The first thing that appeared unusual was the inconsistent methods of payment for tuition and living allowances as disbursed by the project officials. Normally, the most efficient and transparent way to pay these fellowship costs would be to send the funds directly to the host university where they would be applied to an account established in the trainee's name, a standard practice at most institutions. The university could then withdraw tuition payments at the start of each semester. Living allowances would also be paid from this account, while the trainee would also be able to withdraw cash as needed for miscellaneous expenses. A straightforward, simple, and transparent accounting process that could be easily monitored.

In fact, the project officials did follow this process in the thirty-two cases previously mentioned in which the fellowship funds had been disbursed properly. In those cases a withdrawal application was prepared by the project unit for direct disbursement by IDA to the university. A single disbursement was made to the university covering those trainees in attendance. Each trainee was identified, as was the distribution of funds from the total amount shown on the application. The application was sent to Washington, and the money was sent to the university. Lo and behold! there were no accounting discrepancies among those fellowships that were paid through this process.

It is clear from these thirty-two cases that project officials knew how to process fellowship payments properly. So, why did they not use this same process for all the fellowships? Why had they processed fifty-four fellowship payments in ways that cost the project an additional $595,000 above actual expenses? Although puzzling, this was not a difficult feat, for as we have seen in earlier chapters, there is always that special account for all sorts of financial legerdemain. For this select group of fellowships, the confusing methods of payment only served to throw a cloud over any oversight by the government or the Bank.

Apart from the unexplained disappearance of the $595,000 was the appalling fact that those funds could not be used for training the farmers, the primary objective of the project—training that would show them how to make better use of fertilizer, how to practice better soil management, and how to use farm implements, among other things. Up to this point, of the $3.9 million allocated for training, roughly $3.0 million had already been disbursed and almost all of that went for overseas fellowships for civil servants. So much for training the farmers!

BUT IT DOESN'T END THERE

Beginning with the original allegations of the financial hardships encountered by a handful of trainees in the UK, our investigation had revealed much more serious problems concerning the financial management of the project. This fact was reinforced by a mid-term review (MTR) that had been carried out by the Bank and was supported further by our review of the fellowship program. The MTR, conducted ten months prior to the investigation, referred to a number of financial issues, including:

- The use of IDA resources for non-project activities.
- The provision of services to non-project entities without cost recovery.
- Over-expenditures in salaries, training, and incremental operation costs.
- The use of project funds for other purposes by the government.
- Excessive cost of vehicle operation and maintenance.

In effect, the review team found numerous examples of the flagrant diversion of funds from the project accounts and, while not using the word *fraud* or *corruption*, reported that the situation was "totally unacceptable and not in accordance with the IDA Credit Agreement." Two months later, a follow-up MTR report was submitted by the project task manager. This report referred to

- Weak financial management.
- Large numbers of personnel paid without IDA knowledge or approval.
- Ineligible expenditures made through SOEs.

- Unqualified audit reports that did not address unauthorized spending.[8]

But what does this mean in practical terms? As we continued examining the special account, more egregious abuses slowly became apparent. A spreadsheet constructed to establish disbursement patterns revealed an endless outflow of funds for numerous expenditures that appeared to have little to do with project objectives. Keeping in mind that this $12.3 million IDA credit was supposed to provide direct assistance to farmers while strengthening the delivery of services by the Ministry of Agriculture, it was disconcerting to find that huge sums had been expended on frivolous and ineligible procurement:

- Office furniture, $333,000.[9]
- Office supplies, $107,000.
- Office maintenance, $186,000.
- Office equipment, $298,000.
- Computers, $276,000.
- Project vehicles, $1,393,000 (including $430,000 for the purchase of 230 motorcycles).
- Fuel for project vehicles, $330,000.
- Maintenance of project vehicles, $336,000
- Project operating costs, $3,185,000.
- Salaries for project staff, $483,000.
- Building construction, $312,000.
- Fencing, $207,000.
- Air conditioners, $132,000.
- Household furnishings, $108,000.
- Refrigerators, $16,000.
- Books, $36,000.
- "Sundry payees," $103,000.
- Unidentified equipment, $104,000.

These kinds of project expenditures were all too familiar to me. And one has to wonder what all this had to do with helping the poor farmers. With a grand total of almost eight million dollars, this was not exactly chickenfeed; it was, in fact, slightly less than 65 percent of the entire IDA credit! In fairness, it should be noted that the project officials actually did spend $659,000 for agricultural research materials and farm products—a whopping 5 percent of the project budget. Yet even here questions arose concerning the transparency of those transactions. Not only did these disbursement patterns raise strong suspicions of systemic fraud and embezzlement, but coupled with the findings of the MTR report, it was hard not to conclude that the project was being raped at every turn. And as we shall see shortly, that is exactly what occurred.

A report of our findings thus far was prepared and submitted to management. Focusing upon the original allegations of trainee hardship and our subsequent findings of excessive payments on more than half of the fellowships, the IADIU recommended that the Bank's regional management conduct a detailed field review of the project accounts to corroborate our findings. Upon reviewing the evidence presented in the report, the country director requested that I undertake a mission to carry out this objective.

BACK TO BANJUL

Four months later I left on a two-week mission to continue the investigation in the field. My first week in the field was devoted entirely to the fellowship program and the missing funds. The SOEs were reviewed with the project accountant, and discussions were held with the project director. Interviews were held with a number of trainees who had returned to The Gambia. Meetings were held with travel agencies in Banjul to confirm airline tickets charged to the project.[10] All the data from the project files was compiled and compared with the data collected from the universities. With some minor exceptions, my findings of fraud and embezzlement were confirmed, and it was clear that the project had indeed lost over half a million dollars through these criminal acts.

With roughly one week left in the mission, I completed my review of the fellowship program and was free to pursue disbursements in the other categories that had increasingly attracted my attention as the investigation progressed. While I was limited by the remaining time available, the findings were as egregious as anything I had seen during my tenure at the Bank. Each transaction that was reviewed raised more questions than it answered. Each transaction revealed the extent to which the project officials defrauded and embezzled funds from the special account. Each transaction demonstrated the total lack of fear on the part of the perpetrators that they would be caught and punished for stealing IDA funds.

NOTES

1. Inside cover of the "Operational Summary."

2. According to the Bank's Integrated Controller's System, over this thirty-one-year period, only $14.4 million had been repaid as of December 2001.

3. The findings of this investigation also demonstrate how an allegation of a minor financial matter can lead to the discovery of much more serious issues of systemic corruption within a project.

4. Figures are from the U.S. State Department website. These numbers should be kept in mind when we discuss fraudulent transactions later.

5. This program was coordinated by the British Council handling logistics and assisting with the placement of trainees in various UK universities.

6. Dollar amounts in these two examples are rounded for convenience.

7. It is not known if the $12,000 was paid subsequent to the investigation, but if so, it would bring the total cost to the project to $60,000.

8. "Unqualified," indicating there were no adverse issues with the accounts.

9. Numbers are again rounded for convenience.

10. All the travel agencies used standard international procedures and quoted airfares considerably lower than most of the fares shown in the project accounts.

14

• • • • • • •

Alhaji the Car Dealer

In pursuing the other procurement transactions, it was only logical that I start with the first withdrawal applications and work my way through chronologically. I didn't have to search far, as the very first application contained some strange entries that would ultimately reveal the first scam of the project. As shown below, the application was for a direct payment of 50 percent of the cost for "motor vehicles." There was, of course, the usual provision for vehicles in the credit agreement, so this in itself was not disturbing. What was highly unusual, however, was that the payment was to be made to a local "trader" in Danish kroner to the Midland Bank in London. After it was received in Washington, the original application was changed to effect payment through Den Danske Bank in Copenhagen, to then be transferred to the Meridien International Bank in the Bahamas (see Figure 14–1).

It seemed rather strange that Industrial Land Trading Ltd. (ILT), a fictitious Gambian firm allegedly selling vehicles in Banjul for Danish kroner, would first want the payment sent to London but would then change the routing through Denmark to the Bahamas. To further complicate the matter, our disbursement officer revealed that the vendor had personally contacted her requesting the change in routing. This was also strange, as normal procedure would be for the project officials, not the vendors, to request such changes. How could the vendor, without the assistance of the project officials, even know who to contact at the Bank? And if he had discussed this with the project officials, why didn't they

Figure 14-1. First Payment to the Bank in the Bahamas

Attention: Disbursement Division

1. IBRD Loan No: _____
   or IDA Credit No: _2453-GM_
2. Cofinanciers Ref. No: ~~_____~~
   IBRD/IDA Ref.No: 05- ____ or 14- ~~~~
3. Application No: _2-N_

4. Please Pay   **DANISH KRONERS**   DKK 304,575
   (Currency name)   (Amount to be paid in figures)

We apply for this withdrawal from the account opened under the Loan or Development Credit Agreement, and hereby certify and agree as follows:

A. The undersigned has not previously withdrawn from the Account to meet these expenditures. The undersigned has not and does not intend to obtain funds for this purpose out of the proceeds of any other loan, credit, or grant;
B. The goods and services covered by this application have been or are being purchased in accordance with the terms of the Agreement;
C. The expenditures have been made or are being made only for goods or services from eligible sources;
D. For those items where reimbursement is being claimed on the basis of a Statement of Expenditures (SOE), all documentation authenticating these expenditures will be made available for review by auditors and World Bank missions upon request. These documents have been retained at the location shown on the individual SOE sheet;
E. In the event that all or part of the funds withdrawn from the Account pursuant to this application are returned to the World Bank, the undersigned hereby authorizes the World Bank to apply the current value of such funds as a credit to the Account or, if the amount is small, apply such funds to the borrower's next payment due for interest, commitment charges, service charges or principal.

DETAILS OF EXPENDITURE

(use summary sheets if additional space is required or if expenditures relate to more than one supplier, category, or sub-project)

5. NAME AND ADDRESS OF CONTRACTOR OR SUPPLIER
   (if different from payee)

6. PROCUREMENT DETAILS
   a) CONTRACT OR PURCHASE ORDER NUMBER AND DATE
   (or other reference to contract document)

   Contract Agreement with Supplier signed 31/3/94
   b) DATE OF PROCUREMENT NO-OBJECTION NOTICE
   (complete for contracts above prior review limit)

   27/3/94 (as attached)
   c) BRIEF DESCRIPTION OF GOODS, WORKS OR SERVICES

   MOTOR VEHICLES

   d) CURRENCY AND TOTAL AMOUNT OF CONTRACT

   DKK 609,150   (BPRL)

   e) TOTAL AMOUNT OF INVOICES COVERED BY THIS APPLICATION
   (net of retention and other deductions)

   (50%) DKK 304,575

7. WITHDRAWAL DETAILS
   a) CATEGORY OR SUB-PROJECT NO.
   2A (vehicles)

   b) PERCENTAGE OF EXPENDITURES TO BE FINANCED:
   BY THE WORLD BANK   100% DKK 304,575
   BY COFINANCIER (if any)   NIL

PAYMENT INSTRUCTIONS

8. NAME AND ADDRESS OF PAYEE'S BANK AND ACCOUNT NO.
   Account No. 35689765 with
   Midland Bank PLC   BIAO
   27-32 Poverty   MERIDIEN A BANK
   LONDON EC 2P BX   (GAMBIA) LTD.
                              BANJUL, THE GAMBIA
   SWIFT CODE: A/c # 115 CCC91 51

9. PAYEE NAME AND ADDRESS
   Industrial ▓▓▓▓▓▓ Company Limited
   31 New Perseverance Street, Banjul
   The Gambia,
   West Africa

10. If Payee's Bank is not located in the Country whose currency is claimed, enter the name and address of their bank's correspondent in the country whose currency is to be paid.
    Midland Bank   DEN DANISKE BANK
    P.O. Box 181   2-12 HOLMENS KANAL
    27-32 Poverty   DK-1092 COPENHAGEN K
    LONDON   DENMARK
                              FOR MERIDIEN INTL
    SWIFT CODE: BANK LIMITED
                              NASSAU, BAHAMAS

11. SPECIAL PAYMENT INSTRUCTIONS AND INVOICE REFERENCES
                              FOR A/C #
    Account No. 35689765 with   51029-4
    Midland Bank (London) is a
    Meridien Bank (Gambia Ltd) Account
    Number.

12. By   The Gambia Government   14. [signature]
    Name of Borrower   Signature(s) of Authorized Representative(s)

13.   5 April 1994   15. ▓▓▓▓▓▓▓ - Senior Loans Officer
      Date   Print Name(s) and Title(s) of Authorized Representative(s)

SUBMIT APPLICATION IN DUPLICATE TO ADDRESS SHOWN ABOVE

For World Bank Use Only   * Revised Banking instructions provided in.

contact the Bank if his request was indeed legitimate?[1] Two months later a second withdrawal application for the remaining 50 percent was received in Washington and instructions were again given to re-route the funds to the Bahamas. The two payments totaled approximately $95,700 (at the then-current exchange rate).

But even more curious than the payment process was the vendor's profile. There was no evidence that ILT was a legitimate business, or that it sold vehicles in Banjul, where several reputable firms maintained modern vehicle dealerships complete with sales and service facilities. It just did not make sense, and one had to ask why the project officials would accept ILT as a qualified vendor under any circumstances. With these questions in mind, I requested the project accountant to provide all the documents related to the contract award and began my search for the answers.

Although a public invitation to bid on four vehicles was apparently published in the local newspapers, the only bid I was shown was an ILT price quotation signed by Alhaji W.____, who was otherwise unidentified. The submission appeared to have been produced on a computer and was on plain stationery without any reference to the company he allegedly represented. This, I was informed, was ILT's winning bid,[2] and while I was told that it had won the contract award based upon its low price, there were no records available to indicate that competing bids had actually been received and reviewed by the tender board, as required by government regulations. And while the project unit asked for, and received, the Bank's "no objection" to procure the vehicles, it appeared that this approval was given on the mistaken assumption that the Bank's procurement guidelines had been followed.

The ILT bid quoted a price for four vehicles in Danish kroner and stated that the vehicles were in stock and ready for immediate delivery. A contract was subsequently signed between the Ministry of Agriculture and ILT. As noted above, the two withdrawal applications were processed, with the payments going to the Meridien International Bank in the Bahamas. To support these payments, the project accountant provided an undated ILT invoice for four vehicles, vehicles that were impossible to identify, because the invoice did not contain any corresponding serial numbers (see Figure 14–2).

Figure 14-2. Undated Invoice Omitting Manufacturer's Identification Numbers

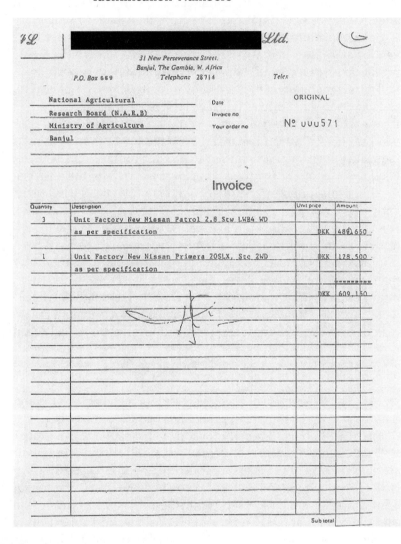

███████████ Ltd.

31 New Perseverance Street.
Banjul, The Gambia, W. Africa

P.O. Box 669   Telephone 28714   Telex

National Agricultural   Date   ORIGINAL
Research Board (N.A.R.B)   Invoice no
Ministry of Agriculture   Your order no   Nᵒ uuu571
Banjul

Invoice

Quantity	Description	Unit price	Amount
3	Unit Factory New Nissan Patrol 2.8 Stw LWB4 WD		
	as per specification	DKK	480.650
1	Unit Factory New Nissan Primera 20SLX, Stc 2WD	DKK	128.500
	as per specification		
			=========
		DKK	609.150
		Sub total	

With more than a few red flags waving, I went to the address shown on the ILT invoice, only to find that no such firm existed there. Situated in an area of small shops, none of the local vendors knew of a firm by that name, nor did they know of any vehicle dealers in the vicinity. I then went to the motor pool to inspect the vehicles and was told that three were out on assignment. I was then shown an older vehicle that could not be opened for inspection because the keys had allegedly been misplaced. It would have been a useless exercise anyway, as I had no serial numbers to confirm that it had been purchased from ILT. Unable to contact Alhaji W._____ or the person in charge of the motor pool, both of whom were strangely unavailable, I gathered whatever evidence I could obtain for later reporting.

In my final report I noted that the bills of lading and other documents that would show the point of origin of the vehicles, along with the chassis and engine serial numbers, were missing. Two and a half years later, following our submission of the investigation findings to management and the government, we received a response from the ministry concerning the missing documents. Well, not exactly, for all we received was a handwritten unsigned note containing four serial numbers. This information was forwarded to Nissan in Japan, and we were subsequently advised that the serial numbers in question were not the serial numbers of any Nissan vehicles.

What can one conclude from all this? The very first order of business, the very first transaction undertaken on the project, was to procure four vehicles from a firm that was not franchised to sell those vehicles, could not provide after-sales support, and could not be physically located at the address shown on the invoice. There was no evidence of competing bids, or of tender-board review, and although the project officials received the Bank's "no objection," it was clear that this was obtained through deception. There was no way to identify the vehicles, nor could it be shown that they had ever been manufactured by Nissan. In fact, there was no clear evidence that the vehicles existed at all. And this only raised more questions.

Could "Alhaji" have pulled off this scam without any help from the project officials? Who was he anyway, and why did he have the entire payment of $95,700 sent to a bank in the Bahamas? If he really did sell the vehicles to the project, how could he recover their cost and related local expenses if the entire amount was deposited in an offshore bank—a Bahamian bank, incidentally, that allegedly "collapsed" one year later due to allegations of gross fraud committed by its managing director? Could there be more to this story than we would ever find out? Most likely, these questions will never be answered, for in the end, "Alhaji," like the vehicles he allegedly sold, was nowhere to be found.

NOTES

1. It does not take much imagination to see how counterproductive it would be if each vendor on each project had direct access to the Bank's disbursement officers.

2. I was never able to confirm the authenticity of this document, which appeared suspiciously different from all the other documents that allegedly emanated from ILT. A marked difference in Alhaji's signatures on the tender and the contract added to my suspicion.

15

• • • • • • •

Bigger than Wal-Mart

Welcome to the world of one-stop shopping, where dedicated government officials can enrich themselves with World Bank money. To understand this better, let me introduce you to "B&T Enterprise Ltd."[1] Again, it was SOE statements that drew my attention to payments made to B&T. Payments authorized by the project officials through the special account totaled over $430,000 for a range of goods that defied common sense:

- Furniture
- Farm equipment
- Laboratory equipment
- Air conditioners
- Computers
- College textbooks
- Poultry supplies
- Fencing
- Cattle scales
- Audio-visual equipment
- Surveying equipment
- Freezers

My first thought on compiling this information was, Wow! These guys must be bigger than Wal-Mart. I have to see this place! And I did. But the reality was slightly less than I anticipated. B&T was no more than a tiny roadside stationery shop! Making one of my usual visits as an off-the-street customer, I attempted to buy various items similar to those on the invoices submitted by B&T. It was an exercise in futility, for with the exception of stationery, paper clips, and general office supplies, I was told they did not carry any of the items noted above, and that I would have to go elsewhere if I wished to purchase them. When asked about laboratory equipment that they allegedly sold to the project, the manager looked at me as if I was crazy. This stupid foreigner, couldn't he see what goods they had for sale? But how could this be? There were dozens of B&T invoices for these same items, and it was clear that the payments had been duly authorized by the project officials. How could we have paid for them if B&T didn't sell them? As the following examples show, it was all about fraud and corruption, and nothing about supporting the project or helping the farmers.

Figure 15–1.
B&T Invoiced over
$430,000 to the Project

THE HONEYMOON SUITE

Obviously essential to improving the lot of the farmers, it was apparently deemed necessary to procure furniture for one of the project officials: king-size beds, coffee stools, refrigerators, door mats, and all the other things needed to make a civil servant's life comfortable. Supporting documents were either missing or contained conflicting information for this $17,600 transaction, making it difficult to uncover just exactly what happened to the money and the furniture.[2]

Apart from the payment voucher, the only other supporting documents were a three-page invoice from B&T and a competing price quotation from another local trader that was less than the B&T invoice, yet was rejected. But accepting the higher quotation was not the only thing weird about this, for the time line was also amazingly brief. The rejected quotation was dated November 5, 1996; the B&T quotation, now submitted to me as an invoice, was dated November 6, and the payment voucher was dated November 7. That transaction time frame in Africa is about as likely as my walking on the moon. Furthermore, the project officials could not provide any records to confirm that the furniture had been entered into government inventory. And last but not least, visits to several local furniture shops revealed that similar items could be purchased for less than half the prices charged by B&T for the goods they allegedly delivered.

IT AIN'T CHICKENFEED

But the story does not end there, for among the other B&T transactions was a $12,700 invoice for chickenfeed! That's enough feed for a *lot* of chickens. These chickens allegedly belonged to the School of Agriculture at the Gambia College, another agency supported by the project. I say allegedly because I saw only a few dozen running around loose when I visited the place. And while there were any number of local feed suppliers selling the same products at roughly half the price, the project officials, in their obvious commitment to transparent procurement, chose to purchase these items from B&T's all-purpose stationery shop instead.

The supporting documents for this transaction were a purchase requisition, three price quotations, a purchase order for B&T, and a voucher authorizing payment. Notably missing again were documents to confirm that the goods had been delivered and placed in inventory, but that was the least of it, for further examination revealed bizarre price entries that were impossible to comprehend. It almost seemed as if the chickens themselves had prepared the paperwork, so again, please bear with me as we follow another example of Byzantine procurement.

The three price quotations showed different unit prices per bag of feed with B&T being the lowest, and this was the basis for the award. The purchase order for five hundred bags of feed costing $12,700[3] was issued, and on that very same day, B&T allegedly delivered the feed to the college, payment was authorized, *and* the money was deposited in B&T's account. All in one day. A testament to the efficiency of both parties and the possibility that I may yet walk on the moon. But again, the story does not end there.

Further examination of the documents revealed that the project officials, in their apparent haste to carry out the scam, had gotten their price entries all mixed up. Although the purchase order price and B&T's quote were identical at $12,700, the amount shown on the payment voucher was $11,430. This last figure was derived through some strange calculations involving the unit prices of a higher bid and a deduction of the government's 10 percent share of the transaction.[4] So, what we have here is a payment based upon the unit prices of a losing bidder that doesn't correspond to the price on the purchase order or the winning bidder's price quotation.

My intention here is not to show how brilliant I am with numbers, but rather to show how one might conclude that this whole business was a scam in which special account funds were transferred into B&T's account, after which the spoils would most likely be divided up among the conspirators who, in their frenzy to create the necessary documents, just couldn't get the numbers right. And there were two other facts that tended to support this conclusion: one, this payment was charged against "general operations" and not "agriculture products," as was done for similar transactions; and two, there was the question of the other "traders" who had submitted the two competing price quotations, for my attempts to find them at the addresses shown on their proforma invoices were futile.

So let's try to make some sense out of all this. B&T, a tiny shop selling stationery supplies, received numerous purchase orders worth over $430,000 from the project officials. These orders were supposedly awarded through competitive price quotations against other shops that were either equally *unqualified* to provide the goods requested or could not be located at the addresses given. Yet, despite having the lowest price quotations, B&T's prices were more than double the prices found on the open market for identical items. However, this did not seem to deter the project officials, who *had* to know the true value of the goods they were allegedly procuring from B&T. In addition to the overcharges, it was found that B&T could not provide a majority of the items identified on the invoices. In fact, when queried as to where such items could be obtained (agriculture textbooks, science lab equipment, and so forth), B&T hadn't a clue.

And then there was the matter of documentation to confirm that the goods invoiced had indeed been received and entered into inventory—documentation that the project officials were unable to produce. Finally, there are both mathematical and account entry errors that even the most junior clerk would have avoided. And this from the same individuals we had sent on overseas fellowships to become better accountants and financial managers. Where do we draw the line between incompetence and corruption? When do we quit calling this "weak financial management" and label it the fraud, embezzlement, and theft that it really is?

TRADERS FROM THE SOUK

Figure 15–2. This Shop Invoiced $166,000 to the Project

B&T was not the only favored supplier doing business with the project officials. Supporting documents for payments to a number of other "traders" showed similar patterns and red flags pointing to the fabrication of competing quotations, overpricing, and the provision of a range of goods far beyond the supplier's capacity. In the case of another small shop in the local market, over $166,000 was paid for furniture, office equipment, vehicle spares, and unidentified "research material," to name just a few of the items allegedly delivered. Additional payments were embedded within government fund transfers and other disbursement categories, making it difficult to ascertain exactly how much the shop had received in total. Competing bids were submitted under the names of shops that could not be located at the addresses on their invoices and appeared to have been fabricated for the sole purpose of establishing this shop as the lowest bidder. Nevertheless, despite being accepted by the project officials as having the lowest prices, the invoiced prices were more than double market prices for the same items. Meanwhile, delivery and stores receipts were unavailable to confirm that the goods procured had been entered into inventory. With some exceptions, these were the findings in all of the transactions I reviewed from the special account.

It was evident that the project officials had practiced wholesale fraud and embezzlement at every turn—from fabricated bids, careless calculations, overpricing, and lack of delivery receipts and inventory records, to deceptive line entries each time a withdrawal application was submitted to the Bank. The arrogance of the project officials and their total lack of fear of being caught were evident in the sheer volume of fraudulent transactions perpetrated each month during the life of the project, a volume that had reached $3.185 million, or 26 percent of the IDA credit by the time of our investigation.

So it went, day after day, a thousand dollars here, five thousand dollars there, a few thousand somewhere else, every scam slowly draining the project of the funds needed to ensure a successful outcome (see Figure 15–3). An outcome that hadn't a chance in hell of ever coming to pass. But who are these people, these traders from the souk? Why is so much being procured from those who, with no inventory, sell anything and everything at grossly inflated prices and who are unable to provide product support services, while legitimate suppliers are ignored? Why didn't the project officials group all similar items (office supplies and equipment, computers, farm equipment, etc.) into lots, requesting quotations from legitimate suppliers and awarding contracts on a transparent basis? And what roles do the "traders" play in all this? Are they crooked individuals who have figured out a way to deceive innocent and well-meaning government officials in order to steal IDA funds, or are they willing accomplices in well-orchestrated scams conceived by thieves disguised as civil servants? I would learn the answer to the last question firsthand during a subsequent interview with one of the "traders," who was surprisingly candid about the whole business, as we shall see in the next chapter.

NOTES

1. A fictitious name.
2. The local currency in *dalasis* at roughly 10 to 1 against the dollar.
3. The dollar equivalent for the *dalasi* figures on the documents.
4. Per the credit agreement, IDA was to pay 90 percent of the cost and the government 10 percent.

Figure 15-3. Monthly Payments to Traders

AGRICULTURAL SERVICES PROJECT (ASP)

THE WORLD BANK
4 Hem, KM Wulapu, IX 30UU.
APPLICATION FOR WITHDRAWAL.
STATEMENT OF EXPENSES (SOE)
CONTRACT DETAIL

Period 1/8/96 — 31/8/96   Application No: 78   Summary Sheet No: 2

Category or Sub-Project No. 28 (Equipment & Furniture)   IBRD Loan, IDA Credit or Cofinancer Ref No. 2453 GM

Name and Address of Contractor/Supplier	Contractor or Purchase Order No. and Date (or other ref.)	Brief Description of Goods, Works, Services	Currency and Total Amount of Contract	Total Amount of Invoice covered by Application (net of retention)	Elig %	Inv. Amount Eligible for Financing GMD	Amount Paid from Special Account USD	Remarks	Date of Payment
Insyle Trading Co	LPO 001820	Communication equipment	139,883.00	139,883.00	100	139,883.00	14,288.39		05/08/96
Insyle Trading Co	LPO 000284	Duplicating machine	30,000.00	30,000.00	100	30,000.00	3,064.35		05/08/96
Darusalam Enterprise	LPO 000257	weighing scales	3,400.00	3,400.00	100	3,400.00	347.65		05/08/96
Darusalam Enterprise	LPO 000755	weighing scales	3,400.00	3,400.00	100	3,400.00	347.65		05/08/96
Darusalam Enterprise	LPO 000754	weighing scales	3,400.00	3,400.00	100	3,400.00	347.65		05/08/96
Darusalam Enterprise	LPO 000756	weighing scales	4,250.00	4,250.00	100	4,250.00	434.56		05/08/96
Darusalam Enterprise	LPO 001841	Garden equipment	3,200.00	3,200.00	100	3,200.00	327.20		05/08/96
Darusalam Enterprise	LPO 001842	Garden equipment	3,850.00	3,850.00	100	3,850.00	393.66		05/08/96
Raslan Company	LPO 000787	Air conditioners - sharp	33,000.00	33,000.00	100	33,000.00	3370.79		05/08/96
Raslan Company	LPO 000786	Air conditioners - sharp	16,500.00	16,500.00	100	16,500.00	1,687.12		05/08/96
Raslan Company	LPO 000783	Air conditioners - sharp	33,000.00	33,000.00	100	33,000.00	3374.23		05/08/96
Raslan Company	LPO 000782	Air conditioners - sharp	33,000.00	33,000.00	100	33,000.00	3374.23		05/08/96
Saad M. Raslan Company	LPO 000760	Electrical equipment	12,240.00	12,240.00	100	12,240.00	1,250.26		05/08/96
Darusalam Enterprise	LPO 001838	Wheel barrows & spades	3,525.00	3,525.00	100	3,525.00	360.43		05/08/96
Darusalam Enterprise	LPO 001839	Wheel barrows & spades	4,000.00	4,000.00	100	4,000.00	409.00		05/08/96
Darusalam Enterprise	LPO 001840	Wheel barrows & spades	3,525.00	3,525.00	100	3,525.00	360.43		05/08/96
Beggen Agric works	LPO 001833	Dairy and livestock equip.	9,560.00	9,560.00	100	9,560.00	977.51		05/08/96
I.M. Secs	LPO 000985	Computer Printer	8,000.00	8,000.00	100	8,000.00	817.16		05/08/96
Bijaokcer Trading Enterprise	INV 000089	4 cupboards & 17 tables	149,586.56	149,586.56	100	149,586.56	15,295.15		05/08/96
Sakou S Njie Enterprise	LPO 000839	Computer equipment	17,500.00	17,500.00	100	17,500.00	1787.54		06/08/96
Lai Famoi & Sons Ltd	LPO 001833	Census tables	1,400.00	1,400.00	100	1,400.00	143.15		06/08/96
Kawoon Enterprise	LPO 001841	House furniture items	64,600.00	64,600.00	100	64,600.00	6605.32		06/08/96
Afri Trade Link	LPO 000842	Fire Extinguishers	14,600.00	14,600.00	100	14,600.00	1,491.32		06/08/96
lborics gen spare parts	LPO 000821	Farm Implements	26,160.00	26,160.00	100	26,160.00	2,672.11		20/08/96
lborics gen spare parts	LPO 000818	Farm Implements	24,300.00	24,300.00	100	24,300.00	2,482.12		20/08/96
lborics gen spare parts	LPO 000861	Farm Implements	23,870.00	23,870.00	100	23,870.00	2,438.20		20/08/96
lborics gen spare parts	LPO 000803	Farm Implements	23,870.00	23,870.00	100	23,870.00	2,438.20		20/08/96
lborics gen spare parts	LPO 000802	Farm Implements	23,870.00	23,870.00	100	23,870.00	2,438.20		20/08/96
lborics gen spare parts	LPO 000800	Farm Implements	23,870.00	23,870.00	100	23,870.00	2,438.20		20/08/96
lborics gen spare parts	LPO 000799	Farm Implements	23,870.00	23,870.00	100	23,870.00	2,438.20		20/08/96
lborics gen spare parts		Farm Implements	23,870.00	23,870.00	100	23,870.00			20/08/96

16

• • • • • • •

Lamin Tells All

Another name that kept popping up in the special account was "Kalley Trading Enterprise."[1] As with the other traders, the wide variety of goods supplied defied all logic as I reviewed a number of invoices for laboratory equipment, agriculture textbooks, poultry supplies, and irrigation equipment, to name just a few. Payments made from the special account to Kalley totaled approximately $137,000 and were supported by the same questionable documentation found in the cases discussed in Chapter 15. Entries also surfaced in the government counterpart funds account, bringing the total amount paid to Kalley to some higher figure that I was unable to determine due to missing documents and time limitations. Nevertheless, the few documents I was able to obtain were more than sufficient to conclude that Kalley was just one more accomplice in the daily scams perpetrated by the project officials.

In reviewing the SOEs, a $15,100 textbook order placed with Kalley for Gambia College caught my attention. But before we go any further, I must again beg your patience as we examine the minutia of this transaction, for as always, the devil is in the details. Details that require careful scrutiny yet are often overlooked during Bank supervision missions. And whether these supervision oversights are due to time constraints, other pressures, or to a lack of concern for the Bank's fiduciary responsibilities, the results are always the same. The project officials perpetrate their scams day in and day out with impunity, while the project dies from a lack of funds.

But let us return to the purchase of the textbooks. Again, I was provided with the usual requisition form, competing price quotations, a purchase order (see Figure 16–1), and a payment voucher (see Figure 16–2). Four book titles were requested on July 26, 1995, by the Gambia College. Three price quotations were submitted, with Kalley's being the lowest. A purchase order was issued to Kalley on September 18, and a payment voucher was issued the same day. Payment was made to Kalley one day later.

While on the surface all appeared to be in order, several nagging questions remained. For one thing, the books requested were most certainly not available on the local market and could only be ordered from specialized book suppliers overseas. This process was known to the college administrators but most certainly was not known by the traders from the souk. So why would the project officials seek bids for $15,000 worth of books from suppliers such as these? Why would they ever need 150 books costing $57 each?[2] Why was this payment routed through the government account and then replenished from the special account?

But even more puzzling was the phenomenal speed with which Kalley obtained the books and delivered them—on the same day he received the purchase order! The trader contacted a supplier in London, who shipped the books immediately, with the shipment arriving in Banjul and delivered to the college all in the same day! Clearly, Kalley could not have ordered the books from the supplier in London until the purchase order was written, and clearly, he could not have been paid until the books had been delivered to the college. Clearly, Kalley had performed a miraculous feat. And my walk on the moon seemed more and more likely.

Then there was the matter of the books themselves, for there were no records to confirm that they had been delivered and placed in inventory. To satisfy my curiosity, I visited the college and sought out the head librarian. After briefly discussing the management of the library, I showed her the list of books that had been provided with IDA funds.[3] She was, to put it mildly, amazed at the numbers and titles of books that were listed and claimed that she had never seen any of them. Opening up the library records, she confirmed that none of the titles I'd shown her had been received by the library.

Pursuing this further, I met with the head of the School of Agriculture and the principal of the college. Appearing a bit agitated

Figure 16–1. Purchase Order for Textbooks

MINISTRY OF AGRICULTURE

Agricultural Services Project (ASP)

LOCAL PURCHASE ORDER   Nr: 000172

To: ████████████ *Eeekeypdec.*

POB·1258

BANSUL·

Date: *18/9/95*

Please supply the undermentioned goods/services to this Project.

Authorised by: _____ Project Coordinator

Quantity	Description of Goods/Services	Unit Price	Amount D	B	Head/ Subhead
40	Books Agriculture in African Rural Communities (Crop & Soil)	470.00	18800.00		
150	Books Introduction to Tropical Agriculture	565.00	84750.00		Phong
40	Books Fruits & Vegetables Production in Africa	580.00	23200.00		Banlo
40	Books Goat & Sheep Production in The Tropics	615.00	24600.00		Eodles Sch &
					ASARC
	GC. 22BR.				

Nkasi-Type Press Tel 392512

TOTAL *157350.00*

Amount in words: *One Hundred and Fifty One dessis Three Hundred and Fifty decosis ans.*

The above goods/services have been duly received by me for and behalf of the Project.

Date: _____   Signed: _____ Receiving Officer

ORIGINAL

Please attach original copy (white) to your invoice & return to ASP for payment.

Figure 16–2. Payment Voucher for Textbooks

223625

(V)

/

MINISTRY OF AGRICULTURE

AGRICULTURAL SERVICES PROJECT (ASP)

PAYMENT VOUCHER

PV NO........

Project Cost Cetre: _Gambia College._ Special Account: _A L F_

Head: _SI_ Subhead: _90_ Item: _143 ._ Cheque Number: _563300 ._

Name of Payee : ▓▓▓▓▓▓ _Euchoypruse_ Amount : D _151350_ B _00_

PO Box 1258 . Date: _18 — 9 —_ 1995

DETAILS OF PAYMENTS	AMOUNT D	b
Being payment enrode to the above in respect of supplying books to Gambia College Sch of Agriculture as per IR 003771 of 26/9/95. Invoice 00240 of 10/8/95. LPO 00192 of 18/9. 000522 of 8/8/95. 00386 of 10/8/95 attach 151350 00		

AMOUNT IN WORDS:

One hundred and Fifty One Thousand Three hundred and Fifty dollars only.

TOTAL D _151350 00_

Received by: ▓▓▓▓▓

Prepared by: _(signature)_ 18/9.

Name: _Lamin_

Account Officer

Address: _P.o. Box 1258 Banjul ._

Passed by: _(signature)_

Financial Controller

Date _9/5/95 ._

Approved by _(signature)_

Project Coordinator

FOR PROJECT ACCOUNT OFFICE USE ONLY

COST ALLOCATION

CODE	ACCOUNT NAME	AMOUNT D	B
_AC 22.65._ _Books and Periodicals_		_151350_	_00_

DONOR	CODE	CAT	%	D	B	US DOLLARS
IDA						
IFAD						
GOTG						
	TOTAL					

that I had spoken to the librarian without their permission, they insisted that the books had been received and that the reason they were not at the library was because they had been "loaned out" to the students. Yet they could not provide a list of the students who allegedly received them. Nor could they explain why the number of books allegedly purchased far exceeded the number of students in the agriculture program. Nor could they explain why, after more than three years, the books were still not listed in the library inventory records. Further discussion became futile, as they continued to deny any wrongdoing. Sadly, I later learned that the librarian had been severely reprimanded for having spoken to me.

But the story doesn't end there. Two years later, in a much delayed response to our final investigation report, the government provided additional documents to show that the books had indeed been obtained from a supplier in the UK, and that they had indeed been loaned out to students. Again, on the surface, it appeared that the government had provided sufficient evidence to refute my earlier findings of fraud. But what are we to make of the disturbing details that we find in these additional documents?

To begin with, based upon the supplier's price quotation addressed to the college and dated March 14, 1994, it was clear that the college had contacted the supplier, not Kalley. What does this tell us? In the first place, if Kalley had procured these books from the UK supplier to be resold to the college, one would expect that the letter would have been addressed to him. And what about the fact that this letter was dated roughly seventeen months *before* the college ordered the books from Kalley? And the fact that the quantities of the four titles offered by the supplier were considerably less than the quantities in the Kalley transaction? And the fact that the prices for those same titles on the Kalley invoice were inflated so high as to defy belief? Such fraud makes a mockery of claims that corruption accounts for only 10 to 15 percent of Bank lending (see Figure 16–3).

And what of the list of books loaned to the students? First, we find that they were loaned out prior to the date of the Kalley transaction.[4] Then we find that the costs of these titles, as shown on the list of books loaned to students, closely match the costs quoted by the UK supplier (see Figures 16–4 and 16–5), thus exposing the Kalley business for the fraud that it is. And yet, despite these

Figure 16–3. Inflated Textbook Prices

Title	Supplier Price[5]	Kalley Price[6]	% Increase
Agriculture in African Rural Communities	$13.50	$47.00	348
Introduction to Tropical Agriculture	$4.70	$56.50	1200
Fruit and Vegetable Production in Africa	$19.50	$58.00	297
Goat and Sheep Production in the Tropics	$3.50	$61.50	1757

obvious discrepancies, we are asked to accept that all was transparent and proper in this $15,100 purchase of textbooks that were nowhere to be found. How dare we suspect otherwise?

A PARTNER FOR LAMIN

But let us return to the events of my mission. Having gathered all the information I could from the project officials, it was now time to pay a visit to Kalley Trading Enterprise to see if any sense could be made out of these transactions. Fortunately, the establishment actually existed at the address shown on the invoices, and upon arriving, there was "Lamin Kalley" himself, a young man in his mid-twenties, standing in the doorway of his small shop—a very small shop with nothing inside but a desk, two chairs, a telephone, and some empty shelves.

Beginning with my usual pretense of needing supplies for a new business I was setting up in Banjul, he became increasingly excited as I asked if he could sell me some of the scientific items and textbooks that were listed on his invoices. It was evident that he hadn't a clue about any of it. He didn't know what the items were, nor did he know where to obtain them.

But as we discussed these things, he began to shift the conversation to a new subject. Would I be interested in joining him in business? Well, that was a new one for me, and it took me an

Figure 16-4. Price Quotation from British Supplier

TITLE	PRICE	QTY	NET VALUE
1- The Tropical Agriculturist. Guy Rouanet (1987)	£6.88	40	£275.54 ✓
2- The Tropical Agriculturist. Gerard Sement (1988)	£6.88	40	£275.54 ✓
3- Success in vegetable Production D.H.J.Sydenham	£5.74	25	(Reprinting)
4- Success in Farming Dr. M.Upton (1985)	£5.74	25	£143.46 ✓
5- Fruit and Vegetable Production in Africa R.P.Rice,L.W.Rice&H.D.Tindall (1986)	£14.93	25	£374.25 ✓
6- Michel Jacquob&................. Translated by Paul Skinner (Upland Rice)	£ 6.88	40	£275.54 ✓
7- Agriculture in African Rural Communities (crops & soils) Land and Life	£ 10.34	40	£413.60 ✓
8- A.Youdeowei, F,O,C, Ezedinma, & O,C, Onazi (1986) Introduction to Tropical Agriculture.	£3.56	40	£142.40 ✓
9- C, Devender & G,E, McLeroy (1982) Goat and Sheep Production in the Tropics,	£2.59	40	£ 103.60 ✓
10- EVERETT Heath & Segun Olusanya, (1985) Anatomy & Physiology of Tropical Livestock	£2.07	25	£ 51.75 ✓
11-.................A. Edwards & Co Animal Nutrition.	£5.46	10	£ 54.62 ✓
12-W. J.A. Payne (1990) An Introduction to Animal Husbandry in the Tropics.	£4.60	10	£ 46.00 ✓
13-E.A. FitzPatrick (1986) n Introduction to Soil Science	£3.16	40	£126.40 ✓

Figure 16-5. Student Book Loan List

HDA III   IN-SERVICE STUDENTS

NAME	TEXTBOOKS	COST	TOTAL
Mawdo.S.K. Jiana	1. Agriculture in African rural communities.	D135.00	D697.00
	2. Anatomy & Physiology of Tropical Livestock	D 30.00	
	3. Pest & Diseases of Tropical crops.	D215.00	
	4. Introduction to Tropical Agric.	D 47.00	
	5. Animal Nutrition	D 75.00	
	6. Fruit & Vegetable Production	D195.00	
Amadou.K. Baldeh	1. Animal Nutrition	D 75.00	D752.00
	2. Fruit & Vegetable Production in Africa.	D195.00	697.00
	3. Anatomy & Physiology of Tropical Livestock	D 30.00	
	4. Pest & Disease of Tropical crops.	D215.00	
	5. Introduction to Tropical Agric.	D 47.00	
	6. Agriculture in African rural communities.	D135.00	
Alieu.A.N.Sanyang	1. Pests & Disease of Tropical Crops	D215.00	D410.00
	2. Fruit & Vegetable Production in Agrica.	D195.00	
Kebba Jammeh	1. Pest & Diseases of Tropical Crops	D215.00	D712.00
	2. Anatomy & Physiology of Tropical livestock	D 30.00	607.00
	3. Animal Nutrition	D 75.00	
	4. Introduction to Tropical Agric.	D 47.00	
	5. Fruit & Vegetable Production in Africa.	D195.00	
	6. An Introduction to Soil Science	D 45.00	
Lamin Fatajo	1. Economics of Tropical Agric.	D120.00	D962.00
	2. Fruit & Vegetable Production in Africa.	D195.00	
	3. Agriculture in African rural communities.	D135.00	
	4. Goat & Sheep Production in Africa.	D 35.00	
	5. Animal Nutrition	D 75.00	
	6. Pest & Diseases of Tropical Crops.	D215.00	
	7. Handbook on Animal Diseases in the Tropics.	D 50.00	
	8. Anatomy & Physiology of of Tropical livestock	D 30.00	
	9. Introduction to Animal Husbandry in the Tropics.	D 60.00	
	10. Introduction to Tropical Agriculture.	D 47.00	

Already paid for by ATF, Mithra. [signature] 8/10/94

instant to decide how to respond. Here was the deal: if I would help him obtain foreign goods from overseas sources, we could both make a handsome profit. I asked, "How would that work and what's in it for me?" Lamin assured me that it was all very simple, and that we could make a lot of money. He took some notebooks from the desk drawer and began to explain how it all worked.

It was, he said, common practice for local traders to have contacts within the government. The trader would either approach the government officials with offers to do business, or the officials would approach the trader. In either case the trader would be instructed by the officials to submit three competing bids with his own being the lowest. The two competing bids could be obtained from other cooperating traders, or he could fabricate them himself. Prices would always be inflated well above fair market value and were usually dictated by the government officials.

Kalley then gave an example of how it works in the sale of stationery to his contacts in government.[7] Under the arrangements just described, he would buy stationery in large packets (five hundred sheets), and then break them down into packets of fifty each. These would be sold at prices marked up by roughly 700 percent. The government officials would create purchase orders for pack-

Figure 16–6. Kalley Invoiced over $137,000 to the Project

ets of paper without specifying the number of sheets per packet and would normally receive a 20 percent kickback against the invoice amount. Other government officials involved in the transaction (tender-board members, accountants, stores clerks, etc.) would receive lesser kickbacks of 5 to 10 percent. The total amount of the kickbacks would vary depending upon how many government officials were involved in processing the transaction. But despite the various kickbacks, Kalley assured me that there was still considerable profit to be made. I was also assured that one could do "any" kind of business with the government. As an interesting sidebar, he also informed me that he'd gotten his start in the trading business from his former employer, B&T Enterprise. It's a small world after all!

Expressing interest in Kalley's offer of a partnership, I gradually shifted the conversation to Gambia College and the textbook order. He was a bit surprised at my mention of the college, and although hesitant at first, he soon began to explain his business dealings with them. Referring to the book order, I asked him where he would obtain them, how he would import them into the country, who his overseas contacts were, and how much they would cost. He was at a total loss to answer my questions. In fact, he claimed to have no knowledge of the order and invoice for which, according to the special account records, he had been paid the *dalasi* equivalent of $15,100 dollars!

Becoming a bit uneasy as we continued to discuss the matter, Kalley explained how he conducted business with the college. He claimed that things were handled indirectly through a contact at the college and that he had no idea about the exact nature of the orders that were placed in his name. He would be told to provide blank invoices from time to time, and the contact would take care of the rest. He stated that he would then receive checks made out to his business—checks that would be deposited into his account, converted to cash, and then passed back to his contact. In return for this service, Kalley received a commission, a commission for which he had to do nothing more than provide blank invoices and a bank account to receive the payments. It was a business opportunity difficult to refuse, and I told him I would think about his offer of a partnership and get back to him after I'd returned to the United States. I confess that I lied.

NOTES

1. Again, the names are fictitious.
2. See the second item in Figure 16–1: "Introduction to Tropical Agriculture."
3. I also had several other invoices for books that had allegedly been purchased from other local suppliers.
4. Per the students' dated signature on the list.
5. Converted to U.S. dollars using the same pound Sterling to dollar rate used by the project officials.
6. Converted to U.S. dollars for comparison.
7. At this point in our conversation, he revealed that stationery and other consumable office supplies were the only products he sold.

17

• • • • • • •

In the Eye of the Beholder

I called the Gambian project investigation Death by a Thousand Cuts to emphasize the destructive nature of corruption as I've observed it on every Bank-funded project I'd ever worked on. The previous chapters have described just a few of the endless scams found on this project alone. Further examples would merely bore you with page after page of fabricated documents, inflated prices, and lack of evidence to prove the delivery of the goods allegedly procured, the same basic scam in each case except that the suppliers, the goods, and their quantities would be different. These same scams were repeated month after month by the same group of complicit suppliers working in concert with the project officials.

As an example, a brief review of a monthly SOE summary sheet for the equipment and furniture disbursement category found repeated orders for identical items from the same suppliers. And while many of the individual payments were too small to attract attention, at the end of the month the total was significant enough at $144,000. Do this throughout the year, and the numbers become even more significant. But if these expenditures for furniture and equipment were needed to achieve project objectives, why weren't they procured two years earlier at the beginning of the project? Why did they need to be procured month after month from suppliers who quoted prices many times higher than true market value? Were these goods delivered at all, and if so, where did they go? And most important, what did this have to do with helping the farmers improve their productivity?

The sheer number of these scams guaranteed that no one, not the Bank, not the government, not the auditors, would ever take the time to investigate this systematic plundering of the project accounts. In one month alone, one trader from the souk received payments totaling $21,800 for carpeting, curtains, furniture, refrigerators, air conditioners, overhead projectors, automobile tires, office supplies, and—would you believe—eight boxes of tea bags for sixty-eight dollars? The same kind of business was awarded to B&T, Kalley, and others month after month, in a feeding frenzy of corruption that defied belief.

With the remaining week of my mission devoted to the non-training-related procurement fraud, there was precious little time to investigate each and every transaction nor to pursue individual transactions as thoroughly as I would have liked. But nevertheless, there were more than enough obvious cases of fraud to indicate rampant corruption within the project. Well aware that my previous exposure to corruption during my days with the Africa Region made me more suspicious than most, I did not want this past experience to bias my findings. If what I had found was more the result of incompetence, negligence, or misguided management, then it would be reported as such. For this reason, on my final day in the field, I scheduled a meeting with the permanent secretary of the ministry[1] and the financial controller for the project to review my findings with them and to correct any mistakes or misunderstandings on my part. The ensuing discussions were interesting, to say the least.

And what were my findings? Although not always 100 percent conclusive due to missing documentation, missing government officials, and suppliers who could not be located, it was clearly evident that a lot of money had been lost due to gross financial mismanagement at best and/or systemic corruption at worst. Rampant abuse of the overseas-training component indicated a complete disregard for the conditions established in the credit agreement, a total lack of fiduciary responsibility, and a pattern of financial management that appeared to have little to do with achieving project objectives. With numbers of trainees far in excess of what was originally specified in the credit agreement, and roughly half a million dollars in excess stipend payments over those confirmed by the host universities, the British Council, and USAID, what else could one conclude?

The project officials had demonstrated that they knew how to process fellowship payments properly and transparently when it suited them. But they also demonstrated that they were fully capable of manipulating the system for their own personal benefit whenever the opportunity presented itself. And it appeared that such opportunities presented themselves frequently. While vehemently denying that there had been any mishandling of the fellowship funds, they provided no logical explanations regarding the excess stipends and the bizarre differences in the payment processing from one fellowship to another.

And even within their denials there were contradictions. At one point I was informed by the financial controller that he was "instructed to pay per diems to people outside the project," although he would not say exactly who those people were; nor could he provide any written evidence to support his claim. He also admitted that the fellowship program had been "overbloated" but claimed this was due to pressure from department directors and staff, as if that were sufficient justification for the whole business. And so, with half a million dollars given out like free candy and only a few feeble excuses to justify the facts, they asked me to understand the difficulties they had faced in managing the fellowship funds and stated they would be grateful if I would report that they had done the best they could under the circumstances.

Our discussion then shifted to the fraudulent procurement of goods and services. As I described the pervasive pattern of ineligible expenditures, fabricated bid documents, overpricing, unqualified vendors, lack of evidence confirming the delivery of goods, and instances of deception in advising the Bank of certain transactions, I was greeted with stony silence. Upset that anyone would question how they had spent IDA funds, they again presented me with feeble excuses in their attempt to convince me that I had misinterpreted many of the things I had found.

It was, I was told, standard practice for government agencies to purchase goods from these "trading enterprises." And the trading enterprises charged excessive prices because the government was always late in honoring its payment obligations. Inventory records were not always kept up to date due to staff negligence. Accounting entries were not always made properly due to poorly trained clerks. And so it went. Yes, mistakes had been made, but everything had been as transparent as possible. It was, they assured me, all just a misunderstanding.

Perhaps they were right, as there were a number of things that were truly puzzling. I couldn't understand why they would procure goods and services from unqualified suppliers with no inventory to sell, and who, when interviewed, had not the slightest clue about what they had allegedly sold to the project officials. I couldn't understand why these phony suppliers needed to charge obscenely high prices to compensate for lengthy payment delays when the project records indicated that the payments had been made immediately in most cases and even prior to delivery in some. I couldn't understand why goods procured from these phantom suppliers couldn't be found at the places where they had allegedly been delivered. I couldn't understand the endless procurement of air conditioners, household furniture, and all the other things previously discussed. I couldn't understand the movement of funds back and forth between the special account and the counterpart fund account. And they couldn't understand why I didn't understand. We were obviously looking at things from completely different perspectives.

But slowly, as we talked, there were some tacit admissions that perhaps the IDA funds had not been as well managed as they could have been. Of course, poor management is not corruption, so we must be careful how we interpret all this. When queried about comments in the mid-term review pertaining to the apparent use of project funds by other agencies within the government, the controller confirmed that this had indeed happened. Claiming that he was under "intense pressure" from higher officials, he stated that between 20 and 25 percent of project funds had been "taken" by other agencies. Now, if true, it would mean that roughly $2.5 to $3.0 million had been siphoned out of the project accounts for unknown purposes, an amount not easily ignored.

Intrigued that he was able to quantify the amount in general terms, I asked whether he had any records to substantiate this claim. A bit startled at my question, and obviously bewildered that I would not just take his word for it, he informed me that there were no records of this. I then asked how project funds could be used by a non-project agency without any accounting for the transfers? If, for example, every dollar of IDA funds was supported by a purchase order, delivery receipt, and payment voucher, and charged against a specific disbursement category within the project, then how could that dollar also have been "taken" by another agency? How, I asked, could the documents show the money was used for the project when it was used for something else? And this only led to more questions.

Who exactly were the officials from the other agencies that had "taken" these funds? Which agencies were we talking about? If, for example, an invoice from B&T Enterprise was used as a cover for the diversion of funds to another agency, then how did the payment to B&T benefit that agency? Or, looking at it another way, if the goods purchased for the project actually went to another agency, then how could the payment voucher claim that the goods had been received by the project? No matter how one looked at this business, it was clear that the documents used to support the withdrawal of IDA funds were fraudulently fabricated to create the illusion that those funds had been used entirely for the project.

Despite their continued insistence that project funds had been managed as well as possible under the circumstances, I expressed my concern that their own explanations for the missing 20 to 25 percent of the IDA credit only tended to confirm my findings. There was, after all, by their own account, between $2.5 and $3.0 million missing without any record to show where it had gone. It was hard not to conclude that they had created fraudulent documentation to cover up the disappearance of those funds, and I asked them to provide me with any evidence to the contrary.

They sat silently for a few moments, and then in apparent resignation the controller stated, "Yes, there was fraud on the project, but ours is not the worst." He followed this by saying, "If you look at other projects, you will find even more." But this final admission was of little value, as it revealed what I had already found, without giving me any more information of substance. And so, at the end of our meeting, there was little to add or subtract from my findings, and I informed my hosts that my mission report would state the facts as I had found them. A bit subdued at this point, the permanent secretary requested that the report reflect the general conditions within the country[2] and hoped that it would not be too critical of the government. His final words: "The government would like to close this chapter and would like to pay more attention to the future, and not dwell on the past." And there was no doubt in my mind that it would like nothing better!

NOTES

1. I had requested to meet with the minister, who had been the project director prior to his appointment. Although most of my findings were related to fraud that had occurred on his watch, I was informed that he was unable to attend.

2. Although not stated specifically, I took this to mean the general corruption throughout the government.

18

•••••••

And the Dance Begins

By the time I returned from The Gambia in July 1999, one year had elapsed since we'd received the original allegations concerning the fellowship program. But although the investigation itself was over, it was only the beginning of a protracted process that never seemed to reach closure as everyone tried to dance around the issue. A dance that provided the appearance of action without dealing with the findings for what they were: the organized theft of IDA funds by Gambian officials.

After numerous delays due to my work on other cases and the internal review process, my mission report was finally completed in late January 2000. Concluding that approximately $523,000[1] had been overcharged for the fellowship program, the report noted that this represented about 13 percent of the IDA funds allocated for training. The gross abuses involving local procurement were also reported, as was the alleged disappearance of 20 to 25 percent of the project funds by "other government agencies."

The report also noted inadequate supervision by the Bank due to excessive staff rotation, inadequate attention to the financial management of the project, and insufficient resources for supervision. Contributing factors, to be sure, but no excuse for the Bank's negligence in ignoring the rampant corruption that prevailed within the project—corruption so rampant that with only nine days on the ground in The Gambia I had obtained compelling evidence to indicate the theft of roughly $1.3 million between the fellowship scams and the local procurement scams perpetrated by the project officials and their accomplices from the souk. Pointing to the Bank's need to tighten up its supervision of local procurement with a number of specific actions, the report also recommended that the Bank require the government to conduct a further investigation of the project to account for, and recover, all misappropriated funds.

Meetings to review the report were held with the country director and his staff, and a letter was sent to the government in March 2000 advising it of "the appearance of mishandled funds" on the fellowship program. Three months later the Bank received a letter from the Department of State for Agriculture (DOSA)—formerly the Ministry of Agriculture—that merely reiterated information previously submitted by the project officials without clarifying any of the issues raised by the investigation. Eight months after that, in February 2001, the full investigation report was sent to the government. Pending proof to the contrary, the government was advised that the Bank would be "obliged" to declare those expenditures ineligible, in which case the Bank would be "required" to request the return of $1,276,000, undoubtedly causing great concern in The Gambia. I was pleased at this point that we were at last talking about the recovery of stolen funds, at least from the government, if not from the thieves themselves.

Three years after the investigation began, and two years since my mission, in July 2001 the government finally submitted a report of its own investigation into the matter. On the surface, this was encouraging, for it appeared that the government had made some attempt to look into things. But closer examination revealed that the report was more window dressing than substance. The report selectively dealt with some issues while ignoring many of the more egregious scams found during my mission. It also provided some interesting insights as to how corruption is viewed among the Bank's clients. With regard to the overpayments in the fellowship program, their report stated:

> Our study of the documents revealed that not more than five individuals received more money than the required amount for their training. Out of the ninety-three students we examined, only fifteen received excess payments ranging from $852 to $21,500 each for stipend and settlement allowances. The total overpayment amounts to about $64,000 instead of $450,000[2] contained in the second ACFIU report.[3]

This was a far cry from my own findings, in which excess payments had been charged against the names of fifty-four individuals; there were numerous omissions, contradictions, and errors in the case-by-case assessments presented by the government's team. The statement above is just one example of this. With the claim that "not more than five individuals received more money than required" followed by the claim that "only fifteen received excess payments," one is hard put to understand these conflicting numbers and the difference in semantics between "more money" and "excess payments." Was this just another example of Gambian logic, or were they really serious? And while the general tenor of the report tended to downplay the whole business as just some minor accounting issues, it also contained a number of telling statements that confirmed my mission's findings:

> There was no predetermined rate of stipend for the fellowship(s). Consequently, the project coordinating Unit (PSU) came up with stipend rates which in a number of cases were higher than those quoted by the University. (p. 9)

The team then went on to say that the higher amounts paid were necessary in order to ensure that the students did not face any hardships while overseas. Of course that's all it was! They didn't want the students to suffer, and the fact that this was done for some and not for others was irrelevant. So while they claimed that only a few students received excess payments, we are also informed that in a "number of cases" the stipend rates paid out were higher than required by the universities. What are we to conclude from these conflicting statements? Didn't this merely confirm my original findings that a majority of the trainees received more money than they actually needed? Then, to justify it all, they reminded us:

> It should also be noted that the rate was used consistently and IDA did not raise any objection even though most withdrawal applications clearly show the amount of stipend payable to trainees. (p. 9)

So, it was all the Bank's fault for not catching them in the first place! As for the overpriced airline tickets, the absence of proper airline receipts, improper payment procedures, excess numbers of trainees sent overseas, and the other fellowship issues noted in my report, these were either downplayed with feeble excuses or ignored completely. The report's conclusion:

> There was no evidence whatsoever that there was any collusion between PSU and the trainees to fraudulently misappropriate Project funds. (p. 5)

And with this exonerating statement, we were asked to reduce the fellowship overpayments to be returned to IDA from $450,000 to $64,000. How could I have been so far off the mark with my findings?

The government's report became even more interesting with regard to the local procurement scams. While basically confirming many of my findings, its final conclusions were ambivalent and laced with feeble excuses. While not using the word *fraud* specifically, but alluding to it in roundabout ways, the report noted that it had indeed occurred, as witness the following statements of their findings:

Collusion between Suppliers in the Submission of Invoices
We found evidence that in certain cases single suppliers were submitting three invoices which defeated the whole purpose of prudent shopping as contained in the DCA [development credit agreement].

Prices in Excess of Normal Market Prices
We found evidence that in some instances the prices were above normal market prices. This is largely due to the fact that some of the suppliers admitted not carrying stock as a result of which they added a margin on the normal market prices to make a profit.

Collusion between Project Staff and Suppliers to Overcharge Project Accounts
We found no conclusive evidence of collusion between suppliers and Project Staff to overcharge Project accounts. However given the fact that single suppliers were repeatedly submitting three invoices at prices higher than normal market prices

for all range of goods and services without any attempt by the Procurement unit to arrest this practice might indicate collusion or negligence on their part.

Lack of Delivery of Goods
We found evidence that some goods ordered for the Gambia College are still not delivered and some items delivered by suppliers were not the items ordered by the Project.

Supplying of goods and services beyond market niche
We found evidence that this was true. However the justification given by the suppliers was that they are registered with the Department of State for Finance and Economic Affairs as general merchants that qualified them to supply anything required.

Piecemeal Purchases
We found evidence that this was largely true for PSU. However in the case of NARB/NARI [National Agriculture Research Board/National Agriculture Research Institute] this was not absolutely correct.

Bank Supervision
We found a general lack of adequate supervision by the various Task Managers as Financial Management and the adherence by PSU to stipulated guidelines as contained in the Development Credit Agreement, Staff Appraisal report for the procurement of goods and services. Which in our opinion contributed immensely to the problems identified in the ACFIU report. (p. 6)

Without once mentioning fraud, embezzlement, bid-rigging, kickbacks, theft, or corruption, this "hard-hitting assessment" was followed by four recommendations that could not even be considered a mild slap on the wrist for the perpetrators:

1. We recommend that IDA reconsider its demand that the Gambia Government refund $1.276 million since the amount of excess payments of about $64,000 representing 1.6% of the training component is not significant.

However if IDA insist on recovering this amount, then GOTG [the government of The Gambia] should in turn recover the amount concern(ed) from the trainees.

2. Since the cardinal objective of the project was to "generate increases Agricultural productivity and sustained growth . . . [and] promotion of self-reliance and farmer empowerment, the task force recommends that the World Bank drops the sales condition as contained in the No-Objection Notice of March 8, 1994 on the farm chemicals distributed to farmers for seed storage."[4]

3. The Gambia Government should recover the amounts relating to the procurements of undelivered goods to the Gambia College.

4. During our review of the procurement allegation, we found that most of the malpractices involved Government registered suppliers who do not carry any stock, do not even have a permanent business premises and lack(s) the technical and Financial competence to supply the items contracted to them. Consequently the Gambia Government should consider regulating the procedure of registering Government vendors to avoid the above problems. (p. 8)

And there you have it! The whole business was just an unfortunate misunderstanding, so let's put this all behind us and move on. We found $64,000 for you, and we're willing to recover it from the trainees, but is it really necessary to go after the remaining $1.212 million that was stolen from the project?

Is it possible there were more scams lurking in the project accounts that escaped notice? Is that it? What about the 20 to 25 percent of the project funds that had allegedly been used by other government agencies and for which there was no corroborating documentation? This alone would have amounted to between roughly $2.5 and $3.0 million and had been openly reported during the Bank's mid-term review and admitted by the financial controller during our investigation. Yet the government's report was strangely quiet about this whole matter. How convenient that we would overlook this little financial indiscretion.

It was reassuring to me that, whether it realized it or not, the government's team had basically confirmed our overall findings of rampant corruption on the project. And although it had either glossed over or ignored many issues in its belated response to our investigation, we still had to continue with our polite little dance with the government. During the three-year duration of the investigation, I'd had to interact with two country department directors and three task managers in the Bank's typical revolving-door management of the project. Despite this, all had been highly supportive of the investigation; now, with the end almost in sight, this support seemed to be fading away.

In between other caseload assignments, I reviewed the government's report point by point and prepared an analysis of its findings. At the end of the day, there was little to support any major revisions of our own findings, and I informed management of this. There was no question that large sums had been stolen from the project accounts and that the $1.276 million should be returned to the IDA. Even at that, they were getting off easy, as there were a lot of other potentially fraudulent transactions that we hadn't investigated.

Over the following months I met with the country department team and its director to establish the Bank's final position on the matter. Meanwhile, other agendas were looming on the horizon. Management had been holding back on further lending to the sector pending resolution of the investigation, but pressure was building on both sides to resume as soon as possible. Our lending targets for The Gambia were falling behind, and the government officials were running out of money to steal. But while I had hoped that this pressure might coerce the government into taking further action against the perpetrators and recover some of the stolen funds, it was not playing out that way. Instead, with all the meetings and communications back and forth, and with management's waning willingness to take firm action, it was evident that the momentum was slipping away with each passing month. Time was definitely on the government's side, and it was obvious that it had no intention of prosecuting the perpetrators or recovering any stolen funds. It was beginning to look as if the entire business was going to slide off everyone's radar screen.

Prior to my second departure from the Bank in February 2002, I made several attempts to rekindle the Bank's efforts to recover the stolen funds. It was now two years and seven months since we'd obtained clear evidence of the fraud perpetrated against the project. We had identified a pattern of systemic corruption that was not only prevalent on this project but was most likely the modus operandi in all our other projects in the country. We had identified the government officials who had authorized, aided, and abetted endless numbers of fraudulent transactions. We had identified a number of outside accomplices and the business names under which they had been paid from the project accounts. We had obtained statements from some individuals confirming our findings. And we had provided considerable documentary evidence to justify the return of $1.276 million to the IDA. But apparently, this was not enough, and I could read the writing on the wall. Nothing was going to come of the investigation. No one would be held accountable for these crimes. The stolen money would not be returned. We would continue to lend to our corrupt clients. Our projects in The Gambia would continue to be plundered. And the Bank would continue to proclaim its commitment to the fight against corruption.

In the early part of 2005, seven years after we'd received the initial allegations concerning the starving students, I received word from a reliable source that nothing further had come of the investigation. All the memos, reports, and evidence are buried somewhere in the Bank's files, out of sight and out of mind. The stolen funds have never been returned to the Bank, and it is a sure bet that the plundering of IDA funds is as pervasive as ever, while the government officials continue to conduct business as usual.

NOTES

1. Revised downward from the original finding of $595,000 as a result of corrections made during the mission.

2. At the request of the country director, I had deleted a number of minor overpayments from our findings, thus reducing the earlier $523,000 figure to $450,000.

3. "DOSA's Response to the World Bank Report on ASP," vol. 1, World Bank internal document. The page references in the text are to this document.

4. This refers to another scam regarding the purchase of pesticides at grossly inflated prices and for which there was no record of delivery or placement in inventory.

19

· · · · · · ·

The Fifty-Year Dilemma

In the late 1990s, during the Bank's fiftieth anniversary, critics mounted a campaign calling for an end to its existence. Protesting in the streets during the Bank's annual meetings, they blared through bullhorns and waved banners proclaiming "Fifty Years Is Enough." With ample coverage by the press, they cited oppressive debts foisted on the poor as a result of loans made to corrupt governments. They cited damages to the environment and the displacement of indigenous populations as a result of ill-conceived projects. They cited adjustment lending and a host of other Bank-funded failures. While some of these complaints had some validity, others were founded upon rumors and half-truths. But what exactly is the Bank's track record over the past several decades? Is the Bank really as bad as its critics claim? Is it the glowing success that its management claims? Or is the truth really somewhere in between? Is fifty years really enough? Should the Bank continue on its present path? Or is it time for serious changes in the way the Bank is managed and the way it does business?

As is so often the case with complex issues, there are no easy answers. The Bank's management and its critics have taken opposite positions on the relevance of the institution. Management feels it is beyond reproach, while the critics want to throw the baby out with the bath water. Neither side is correct. For although the Bank has failed its mission in many ways, it has also accomplished a number of good things. The real questions to be asked here are whether the Bank's good deeds outweigh its failures, and whether those good deeds have been worth the money and effort expended to accomplish them.

I believe the answer to both questions is no. My conclusion is that the Bank's failures far outweigh its successes when measured against objective criteria and that even when successful, the price of those successes has been exorbitant. Mindless squandering of donor funds has placed an unbearable debt burden upon present and future generations of the Third World. But despite that, I do not believe that the Bank should be shut down. Neither should it continue along its present path.

Let's consider what should be done to return this great institution to its mission of alleviating poverty. The World Bank has an enormous reservoir of talent and expertise and has much to offer the world's poor. It has tremendous influence within the donor community and among its borrowers. And it has the potential to be so much more effective than it has been to date. But its management has used neither the Bank's talent nor its influence effectively. As stated earlier, it has become home to an inwardly focused bureaucracy that is more concerned with its own survival than with achieving results on the ground. If, and this is a big if, the Bank is to continue justifying its existence, if it is finally to become the leading institution it claims to be, then it must return to basics and address the problems of development directly. It must stop contemplating its navel and replace talk with action. It must become more open, honest, and forthright in assessing risks and reporting on its lending operations. And above all, it must drastically change its culture of lending, a culture that only serves to enrich the corrupt elites of dysfunctional governments. These things can, and must, be done.

LITTLE THINGS OF GREAT SIGNIFICANCE

Quite clearly, nothing is simple in the world of economic development. The issues created by lending to corrupt and dysfunctional governments, and the misguided efforts of the Bank's management to deal with this reality are only one part of the big picture. Complex and interrelated political and commercial interests, both national and international, are obviously key factors in all of this. In addition, when we add natural calamities and civil wars into the equation, it is not difficult to conclude that development is perhaps as much a game of chance as it is a calculated undertaking.

It is not my intention to suggest solutions for every aspect of the Bank's mission, for it is equally clear that the Bank cannot be held responsible for each and every development failure that its loans and credits have financed. But, and I believe this to be important, there are some basic actions that the Bank's management could take that would strengthen its ability to produce more substantive outcomes than we have seen up to now. Things that require greater focus on fiduciary responsibility, genuine accountability, and other aspects of portfolio management. Things that require a shift from management's obsession with intellectual self-gratification to an obsession with getting measurable results of substance. Results that actually bring benefits to the poor rather than enriching the government elites that rule them.

The examples of corruption I have presented in the previous chapters can be repeated many times over. Scams perpetrated in myriad ways, but with always the same objective: to steal as much money from Bank-funded lending operations as possible. Variations of crimes that merely reflect the relative extent of corruption among the Bank's borrowers, the sophistication of the scams perpetrated by government officials and their accomplices, and the degree to which all this is accepted by the donor community. From Ghana to Argentina, from Nigeria to Haiti, from the Philippines to Cote d'Ivoire, from Indonesia to Tanzania, it all comes down to the same thing. National treasuries are plundered by dysfunctional government hierarchies whose primary concern is to remain in power so they may continue to enrich themselves. And so much the better when those treasuries are filled with foreign aid grants or World Bank loans, money that is truly "manna from heaven" for corrupt government officials.

But while there are no quick or easy solutions to addressing the corruption issue, it is clear that the donor community in general, and the World Bank in particular, could, if the will existed, do so much more in this regard. For the Bank's policies of profligate lending only encourage corrupt government officials to continue looting their national treasuries under the guise of economic development. And to exacerbate the problem, this illegal diversion of Bank funds further perverts the development process by rendering remaining aid resources ineffective, leaving unfulfilled all those wonderful promises made by management when it presents its glowing appraisal reports for board approval.

I hope that you are by now convinced that the self-praise that continually emanates from the Bank may not be quite as accurate as management would have you believe. And while there are those who will, without doubt, attempt to discredit what I have observed during my sixteen years with the institution, what I have presented in the preceding pages is what I have witnessed firsthand. I am firmly convinced that the extent to which corruption has permeated the Bank's symbiotic relationship with its clients has diminished its accomplishments far more than its management dares to admit.

Corruption is, in my humble opinion, one of the most serious issues facing the Third World, the donor community, and the Bank, undermining the very essence of economic development and the opportunity for a better life for the world's poor. And yet, despite the increasing lip service given to the corruption problem over the past decade, it continues to grow, diverting aid monies provided by the donor community, while fostering continued economic enslavement of the poor. It enriches the government elites of the Third World while creating employment for an army of international civil servants, consultants, suppliers, and contractors. Billions of dollars are poured down a rat hole with very little to show for it. Unbridled lending in the guise of alleviating poverty. And while only a fool would think that the cancer of corruption can be eliminated completely, ways must be found to reduce the economic devastation caused by these criminal activities. A difficult task to be sure, but not insurmountable.

And so, what are we to make of all this? Can the Bank do more than it has done so far in its vaunted fight against corruption? Should it do more? Does it have the authority to do more? Most important, will the bureaucracy and its management culture allow it to do more? I believe the first three questions could be answered in the affirmative if the Bank's shareholders were to insist that management adhere to the objective of truly fighting corruption. The last question may not be so easy to answer, however, for it is not clear that management has the courage or the desire to take the necessary actions, no matter how much pressure is applied by the shareholders. Actions that require resolve, focus, and professional honesty in protecting the Bank's interests, and above all, the interests of the poor souls struggling to survive under the corrupt regimes that govern them. Actions that, until now, have fallen far short of the scope and intensity needed to accomplish substantive results. Actions that may be too painful for the Bank's management to contemplate, much less carry out.

GETTING BACK ON TRACK

How, then, can these things be accomplished? Obviously, there are no quick answers, nor can any proposed solutions be guaranteed to work 100 percent, but there are nevertheless a number of things that I firmly believe could move the Bank along the desired path. Some of them involve major changes in the Bank's bureaucracy, its focus on certain priorities, and some of its basic precepts for development lending. Changes that involve both a reduction in staff levels and a more sensible distribution of staff skills. Changes that involve less intellectual self-gratification and more emphasis on results in the field. Changes that call for a shift away from the untenable concept that all development problems can be solved with loans and credits to dysfunctional governments. Changes that involve practical matters concerning portfolio management, accountability, and fiduciary responsibility. Characteristics that have been appallingly absent over the past few decades.

To bring these changes about there must be clear recognition of certain basic management failures that lie at the heart of the Bank's poor track record. Not in any order of priority, they include:

On Corruption: The Bank's management refuses to admit that corruption severely affects its portfolio and has yet to show sufficient commitment to deal with it effectively. Despite all the hoopla about its anti-corruption activities over the past decade, it has yet to make any substantive progress in dealing with this issue as it relates to the lending program. Meanwhile, corruption continues unabated, with billions of dollars being stolen each year. Can management truly say that the amount of money being stolen from the Bank's portfolio is less now than it was ten years ago? I think not.

On Fiduciary Responsibility: The Bank's management has shown little desire actively to address issues of fiduciary responsibility. The Bank exists to provide funding for development, constantly telling the world of all the safeguards it has put in place, constantly telling the world it is committed to addressing the corruption issue, but never effectively exercising due diligence over its portfolio, thus facilitating the very thing it claims to be fighting. The money keeps going out the door, and no one has a clue as to what really happens to it. Meanwhile, the poor remain mired in poverty.

On Knowledge Management: The Bank's management has demonstrated repeatedly that it would rather study an issue than act on it. It is unable to control the rampant growth of irrelevant institutional activities that suit the agendas of the bureaucracy at the expense of the Bank's stated mission of alleviating poverty. Too much talk and contemplation, and too great a gap between promises and results. The Bank talks, and the money walks.

On the Veracity of Reports: The disconnect between what Bank management reports and conditions on the ground provides a smoke screen that shields Bank managers from any accountability for their actions. The disingenuous manipulation of information concerning the Bank's portfolio creates the illusion that all is well, when it is not. Truth, honesty, accountability, and professional integrity are gradually filtered out as information rises up through the bureaucracy so that only glowing self-praise reaches the shareholders and the public. Despite myriad failures, I know of no instance where management has admitted unequivocally that it screwed up. And in those instances where problems have been discussed, the information is so vague that one has no idea what exactly it was that went wrong or who was responsible. It is time to stop the lies and deception.

On the Pressure to Lend: Well known by all, the Bank's lending culture continues to put loan approval at the forefront of its priorities. Guided by the principle that if the Bank doesn't lend, it will cease to exist, projects are designed and loans are approved without careful consideration of the risks involved. Ignored in the rush to get money out the door, the Bank disregards the lack of borrower commitment, past implementation failures, governmental dysfunction, and the scourge of corruption as it paints rosy scenarios around proposed lending operations that are too often doomed to failure from the start. This avoidance of critical risk analysis has resulted in many more failures than management is willing to admit and has served the Bank and its shareholders poorly while creating huge third-world debt without the concomitant benefits that were promised at the inception of those loans.

Without doubt, some will dismiss what I've described above as "minor management issues" that have little bearing on the "big picture" and that the real solutions lie in improving governance and economic management. But governance and economic management are nebulous concepts that are difficult to measure, and I submit that such improvements cannot take place without addressing the overriding constraints posed by corrupt and dysfunctional governments. It is the underlying failure of management to recognize and act upon this that has led the Bank into the dilemma it now faces—the dilemma of having to create bigger smoke screens to cover up the mounting failures of economic development in the Third World. Nothing exemplifies this more than a recent statement by Paul Wolfowitz shortly after his appointment to the presidency: "Poverty has doubled in Africa over the last decade and half its population is below the poverty line, which is less than a dollar a day."[1] And this from an institution that had provided roughly $38.0 billion to Africa during the previous decade, of which $8.3 billion was for "governance" and "economic management."[2] What are we to make of that?

In sum, the prevailing culture of "see no evil, hear no evil, speak no evil" serves to protect Bank managers from being held accountable. And so, with their heads in the sand, they continue to pretend that they are on the cutting edge of all things and that all is well in their world. Hubris suits them well.

NOTES

1. Paul Wolfowitz, "Remarks by President Wolfowitz at the Society's December 2005 Luncheon," *1818 Newsletter*, no. 89 (Fall 2006), p. 3. The 1818 Society is a group of Bank retirees.

2. *World Bank Annual Report 2002*, vol. 2, Appendix 8 (February 20, 2001).

20

• • • • • • •

The Cost of Corruption

According to the Bank's management, its portfolio losses to corruption are minimal. Government officials may loot their own treasuries, but they definitely aren't looting the funds we've loaned them. Yes, they may be corrupt, but they can't get away with it on "our" projects, because we have procurement guidelines. They can't get away with it because we've insisted that their accounting systems comply with international standards. They can't get away with it because project accounts are audited annually. And they can't get away with it because we supervise project implementation. No problem.

But there *is* a problem, and we must ask ourselves why it has been so difficult for management to come to terms with it. Why are Bank managers constantly seeking to minimize the issue with all sorts of intellectual diversions that lead us in circles without effectively dealing with it? What are they afraid of?

If the Bank accepts the cancer of corruption as a serious development issue, then it follows that management should have an overriding interest in curbing it as much as possible. And while much noise has been made about good governance and economic management as critical factors in addressing the issue, other equally important factors have received little more than lip service. It was only with the arrival of James Wolfensohn in 1995 that the Bank finally announced that corruption was indeed an issue that severely affected economic development. And it was only through Wolfensohn's stubborn insistence that corruption became mainstreamed in the Bank's lexicon. But many within the bureaucracy had to be dragged kicking and screaming to the table, and to this day there are those within the institution who oppose any serious efforts to deter the theft of Bank funds.

Why, for example, has management been so averse to investigating the amount of money that has been stolen from its lending portfolio? Is there any logical reason why it would not want to know this? Bank managers will readily admit that *some* money *may* have been stolen by their clients but show no desire to quantify how much has actually been ripped off. They eagerly study all sorts of economic trivia and prepare all sorts of economic reports but become suddenly quiet when asked to provide data on the true dollar losses due to corruption. Why are they so afraid to quantify these numbers? Why don't they want to know how much is being stolen from the Bank? Why don't they want their shareholders and the public to know? Such information would certainly help manage the Bank's portfolio more effectively and would also be essential to reinforcing the Bank's fiduciary credibility.

Off the record, even those managers most supportive of the status quo will admit to losses of around 10 percent, but they will never correlate that percentage to actual disbursements that often hover around $20.0 billion annually.[1] Translated into dollars, that comes to about $2.0 billion stolen each year, a figure that somehow never seems to penetrate their consciousness. And it might be more, for as I have tried to demonstrate in previous chapters, our corrupt clients have no self-imposed limits when it comes to how much they are willing to steal.

So let us begin with the assumption that at least $2.0 billion is being stolen from the Bank's portfolio each year. With a more realistic assumption of 20 to 30 percent being lost through corruption, this figure rises to between $4.0 and $6.0 billion each year. Whatever the amounts are, in the interest of good fiscal management, and in the interest of protecting its shareholders, it behooves management to account for these losses as accurately as possible. And yet it continues to deny these numbers whenever they are raised by outside critics.

This denial of reality must end. It is time for management to admit that it is losing billions of dollars to fraud, embezzlement, and theft. It is time for management to make every effort possible to determine the extent of these losses so that effective action can be taken to reduce them—action that includes more than just talking about governance, holding anti-corruption conferences, and nibbling at the edges with occasional revelations of fraud investigation cases. It can be done if the will to do it exists.

A TIME FOR ACTION

How can we translate the will to account for these losses into action? Obviously, no one can ever know just how much has been stolen down to the last penny. But there are ways to obtain sufficient information so that general levels of fraud, embezzlement, and theft can be established on specific projects, in specific sectors, and in specific countries. Information that can be used to arrive at reasonably accurate estimates of the losses incurred. Information that would be at least as accurate as anything else the Bank puts forth in the myriad economic studies and reports it produces each year to justify its lending program. An understanding of how much is being lost to corruption is the first step in finding ways to deal with the issue effectively. The following suggests how this might be accomplished.

Examinations of Local Project Accounts

In principle these are presently conducted. In reality, such examinations have been ineffective to date. It is imperative that qualified financial experts be assigned to supervise project accounts frequently and in depth to ascertain the integrity of those accounts. It is imperative that such supervision look beyond the normal accounting reviews to determine if standards of integrity have been met, such as (a) relevance to the project, (b) true market value, (c) vendor credibility, (d) appropriate quantities, and (e) any other indicators of malfeasance. If, for example, two transactions out of ten were shown to be fraudulent, one could conclude a 20 percent rate of corruption on the project. Three transactions would indicate a 30 percent rate, and so on. Other issues such as overpricing and substitution and/or the non-delivery of goods and services should also be factored in to determine the overall percentage of funds lost on a particular project.[2] If necessary, such samplings could be expanded to confirm the initial findings.

Review of National and International Contracts

Again, although such reviews are conducted in principle, they too have been ineffective to date. Reviews should be conducted both above and below the established Bank review and "no objection" levels to ensure compliance. It is imperative that qualified contract management experts conduct these reviews to verify that bid-rigging, kickbacks, and other forms of contract scams are not part of the process. As with the account reviews, the number of suspect contracts, the amounts of overcharging, the non-delivery of goods and services, and other forms of fraud would all be factored in to determine the general rate of corruption, which, in turn, could be translated into dollar amounts to quantify the Bank's losses in this area of procurement.

Random sampling of a number of projects within a given sector would be conducted as deemed necessary, as would a sampling of other sectors to determine the overall level of fiduciary risk posed to the Bank within a given country. By knowing how much is being stolen each year, it can only be hoped that management, the Bank's shareholders, and the donor community will finally find the courage to take the necessary actions to stem these losses. And although management will most likely be inclined to much hand-wringing at the thought of conducting such exercises, they would not be all that difficult to carry out, as demonstrated in the previous chapters about the Gambian project investigation. The Gambia exercise, you will recall, uncovered rampant fraud perpetrated by government officials where, without exception, every transaction reviewed provided evidence of falsified bids, falsified invoices, gross overpricing, non-delivery of goods and services, procurement that could not be verified, and other fraudulent acts.

In the case of the four vehicles allegedly procured locally through ILT, for example, the full invoiced amount of roughly $100,000 was paid to an offshore account in the Bahamas, proper documentation did not exist, the supplier could not be located at the address shown on his invoice, and the vehicles could not be located or identified. How could anyone accept this as anything other than fraud? And how could anyone not conclude that the losses from corruption in this particular case were 100 percent? In other transactions there was enough compelling evidence to draw similar conclusions. Surprisingly, the project officials themselves admitted openly that perhaps 20 to 25 percent of the IDA credit had been diverted to other government agencies, despite a lack of evidence to support that claim. Hardly a legitimate explanation for the disappearance of roughly three million dollars.

Adding to these revelations was the fact that during my nine days in The Gambia, I had uncovered roughly $1.3 million in fraudulent transactions, representing an additional 10 percent of the credit. How much more might I have found had I remained longer, and why weren't these scams uncovered by earlier Bank supervision missions? Would it be totally unrealistic to conclude that the losses to corruption on this particular project were at least 35 percent and possibly even higher? Well, consider this. In 2003 the Bank produced a report on financial accountability in The Gambia that stated the following:

> In the Gambia, effective public financial management is promoted through a reasonably sound budget framework. However, there are a number of serious weaknesses, which create a high level of fiduciary risk. Fiduciary risk means here that *there is a risk that resources are not accounted for properly, that they are not used for intended purposes and that expenditure does not represent value for money*. There are also risks associated with the governance environment. These weaknesses include *poor resource allocation, non-compliance, limited execution, inadequate monitoring and scrutiny, insufficient capacity, lack of enforcement, non-transparency, and poor parliamentary oversight*. The Government's pledge to strengthen governance needs to be translated into measures to address these weaknesses. This report recommends the following recommendations for providing evidence that significant progress has been made towards the fundamental benchmarks in public financial management: 1) Strengthen linkages between policies and budget expenditures through updating sectoral public expenditure reviews (PERS) for education, health and agriculture & natural resources, and completing two new PERS in the infrastructure (transportation) and local government sectors. 2) Provide spending departments with indicative resource envelopes beyond the coming month/quarter to facilitate their planning and management. 3) Update the accounting records (including bank reconciliations), immediately address concerns with information

technology systems (OMICRON, WANG) and urgently close the annual accounts. 4) Issue audit opinions on financial statements for 1991-1999.[3]

Well, what do we have here? A government in which resources (funds) are neither accounted for nor used for the intended purposes, where expenditures do not represent value for money (paying more for goods and services than they are worth). A government in which resources are allocated poorly, where agreements (with donors) are not complied with, where execution (of programs, projects, and public services) is limited, where monitoring (of expenditures) is inadequate, and where transactions are not transparent (read fraudulent). What a revelation! Could this be true? How could we have lent roughly $275 million of IDA funds[4] over the past three decades to a government that posed such a "high" level of fiduciary risk? How could we have ignored those glaring red flags of corruption for all those years? And why can't we do more than merely propose the usual ineffective solutions, such as linking policies and budgets, conducting more studies, closing accounts, and issuing audit opinions—opinions that apparently hadn't been issued since 1991? None of those panaceas will prevent a single dollar from being stolen!

Again the double talk, again the heads in the sand, again avoiding reality and the truth. With all this, why can't the Bank's management report things as they really are? Even with the pablum they have served up above, it should be evident that corruption consumes a large portion of government resources in The Gambia. Can we say precisely how much? Not exactly, but it would be very difficult to make the case that it is less than 30 percent, and it is probably higher than that. Coupled with TI's 2004 Corruption Perception Index giving The Gambia a score of 2.8 out of 10,[5] it is clear that the Bank's managers, if they are truly serious about fighting corruption, should want to know just how much money is being stolen from their Gambia portfolio. And perhaps, just perhaps, this might give them pause to reconsider the commitment and integrity of their clients, and adjust their lending program accordingly.

Just how much money overall has been and is being stolen from the Bank's lending program? Has the Bank lost $100 billion to corruption, as some critics have alleged?[6] Or, is this just a fictitious figure with no basis in fact, as claimed by management? To date, neither side has presented conclusive evidence to support its claims, nor have any meaningful attempts been made to ascertain in credible terms just how large the figure is. But be assured, whatever it is, it is large by any standards and it has caused grievous harm to the Bank's mission.

In truth, the risk of losses due to corruption is as great as it has ever been and continues to increase bit by bit each year as new lending instruments are periodically created that make it easier to commit fraud.[7] The sooner management recognizes this fact, the sooner it will be able to honor its fiduciary responsibility to the Bank's shareholders, and perhaps put an end to the back and forth recriminations between the Bank's critics and its management about how much is actually lost to corruption. And while some will downplay the significance of this knowledge, it is only when we see the actual dollar figures that we can understand the depth of the problem. It is one thing to say corruption exists in the Bank's portfolio; it is quite another to say that three, or four, or five billion dollars were stolen last year. It's a sure bet that once the numbers are revealed, management will be forced to implement the drastic measures that it has so carefully avoided all these years. Is there any one of us who, after having our homes or businesses robbed, would not want to take inventory of our losses? And more to the point, would we not want to recover that which was stolen from us?

LOOKING FOR THE EVIDENCE

But who will search for these stolen dollars? In a very rough way, I've tried to show that such information could be gathered through a combination of accounting, auditing, and investigative approaches that would be accomplished through forensic sampling of procurement and disbursement activities in Bank lending operations. Coupled with inputs from other donor and nongovernment agencies, this would permit reasonably credible analyses of the extent of corruption by sector, by country, or by any other breakdown desired. The important thing here is that management be totally committed to the undertaking, whether through a newly found will to do so or by mandate from the Bank's shareholders. This, in turn, must be followed by the provision of adequate resources to do the job. Resources that include adequate budget and sufficient numbers of professionally qualified investigative personnel. Resources that, as I will discuss further on, might very well be diverted from some of the superfluous, unnecessary, and irrelevant intellectual activities that presently occupy so much of the Bank's time.

Finally, two remaining issues need to be addressed if the quantification of the Bank's losses to corruption is to be realized. The first is the provision of adequate authority to those carrying out the task, and the second is the elimination of bureaucratic obstacles that might impede the gathering of evidence or, worse, whitewash the resultant findings. It is essential that those entrusted with this task not be encumbered by a plethora of management gatekeepers who may have other agendas, a condition that has thwarted similar efforts in the past.

Those conducting these corruption reviews must be independent and free from interference if they are to succeed. But, knowing the Bank, knowing its management, knowing its bureaucracy, and knowing of all the conflicting internal agendas that abound, it is difficult to believe that such freedom of movement and authority could, or would, be provided by management. And while it is possible that such an undertaking could be accomplished internally by the Bank, there is most certainly a high degree of risk that it would start with great fanfare and then slowly but surely be rendered ineffective as it becomes marginalized by the bureaucracy. This fate has befallen efforts to fight corruption in the past.

It is reasonable to conclude that management has a vested interest in keeping the true extent of the Bank's losses to a minimum. If it were to be demonstrated that through neglect, indifference, and/or incompetence, billions of dollars had been stolen by the Bank's corrupt clients, it would seriously discredit the Bank, its management, and the managers' claims of intellectual leadership in the world of economic development. Thus, if the Bank's shareholders are to be provided with accurate and truthful information on this contentious subject, if they are genuinely concerned about the Bank's fiduciary responsibility, then it behooves them to think of a new approach.

In this regard, it is logical to consider whether the quantification of such losses could be more effectively carried out by external entities. In following this train of thought, there are numerous national and international NGOs that could undoubtedly carry out such an exercise. Transparency International, for example, has conducted many corruption-related surveys over the years and has established many national chapters that devote much time and effort to understanding and reporting on corruption issues. Who better to spearhead, or at least be part of, such an operation?[8] And if not TI, numerous other private organizations, both profit and non-profit, I believe, would be more than capable of performing such tasks without the inherent risk of bias that might compromise final reports vetted by Bank management.

One might also look to any number of government agencies among the donor nations for assistance. The Government Accountability Office, for example, an investigative arm of the U.S. Congress, is well qualified to provide assistance in this area, as are similar agencies in the other donor countries. It is clear that there are many qualified organizations outside the Bank that could provide the necessary expertise with integrity. Free of the natural bias and temptation to alter the results, free of the temptation to cook the numbers. And finally, with an honest assessment of how much is being lost to corruption, let us hope that the Bank's shareholders and its management would at last begin to work toward an increased commitment to fiduciary responsibility, a commitment that has for so long been overlooked.

NOTES

1. Average annual disbursements over the six-year period 1997–2002 (*World Bank Annual Report 2002,* tables 6.2–6.7).

2. This process would be very similar to the investigations presented in previous chapters.

3. World Bank, "Gambia—Country Financial Accountability Assessment," Report 26046. Available on the World Bank website.

4. *World Bank Annual Report 2004,* vol. 2, p. 99.

5. With ten being free of corruption and zero being highly corrupt.

6. This issue was raised at hearings held in 2004 by the U.S. Senate Committee on Foreign Relations chaired by Sen. Richard G. Lugar. It has also been raised publicly on a number of occasions by Prof. Jeffrey A. Winters of Northwestern University, among others.

7. Increases in disbursements through special accounts, increased use of tranche releases, and adjustment lending without adequate oversight are prime examples of this.

8. While this may, or may not, fall within TI's mandate, I believe it has the network, the motivation, and the capacity to make a serious contribution in this area.

21

• • • • • • •

So Easy to Steal

Throughout this book I have tried to show how easy it is to steal from the World Bank. If we accept that the theft of Bank funds is widespread and amounts to billions of dollars each year, then we must recognize management's obligation to reverse these losses. Management cannot continue to treat this issue as an intellectual exercise whereby discourse substitutes for action. Yes, anti-corruption conferences and all the rest are fine, but they don't appear to deter corrupt government officials. Investigations conducted by the Department of Institutional Integrity have had some impact, but they have yet to slow down the thousands of fraudulent acts committed against the Bank each day. The debarment of firms engaged in bribes and kickbacks is commendable, but so far only a few small fish have been punished, while the bigger fish are merely inconvenienced for a little while, if at all. All these things are positive first steps in the fight against corruption, but they must be followed by more aggressive action if the Bank is ever to regain its credibility. It is time for management to stop talking and do the things it should have done decades ago. It is time to make things more difficult for the thieves. And where best to begin than to rethink the purpose and management of the special accounts.

CLOSING THE SPECIAL ACCOUNT LOOPHOLE

The use of special accounts was questioned as far back as 1976. At that time special-account disbursements were about 9 percent; now, thirty years later, they hover around 60 percent, which in dollar terms comes to roughly $12 billion each year. Twelve billion dollars going out the door annually—and no one has a clue where it has gone or if it was disbursed for valid purposes. It is unconscionable that management has chosen to ignore the warnings about these accounts for a full three decades.

This method of disbursement has only served to make it easier for corrupt government officials to embezzle and defraud ever larger sums from project loans as the use of the special accounts has increased. And while theoretically logical as a financial management tool, in practice they have become nothing more than private piggy banks for public officials. But how can these accounts be used for their intended purposes while preventing, or at least minimizing, their abuse? To answer this question, let us first consider the basic weaknesses of the special accounts.

Ignoring past project failures and pervasive country implementation issues, project disbursement schedules tend to be based upon optimistic assessments of how much foreign exchange will be needed locally to achieve project objectives. Based upon this optimism, large sums are transferred from the Bank into the locally managed special accounts. With all sorts of implementation delays—some legitimate and many contrived—these funds remain dormant in the account, drawing interest. This interest can be considerable, yet it is never properly accounted for. This convenient loophole was approved long ago by the Bank's management based upon the logic that "it is their money and they should be allowed to manage it." That philosophy would be sound, except for the fact that management doesn't identify to whom they are referring. Is it the government, or is it the government officials who control those accounts? I submit that it is the latter, with millions of dollars being siphoned off annually from interest accounts that function below the Bank's radar.

But why should that be important as long as the original amounts dedicated to the project are still intact? Well, first, if the funds are sitting idle so they can draw interest, then they are not being used to finance project activities. Second, there is the matter of counterpart funds provided by the government as its contribution to the project. Frequently falling far short of the original estimates made during appraisal, counterpart funds, while often only a small percentage of overall project costs, are critical to project success. Representing the government's financial commitment to the project, they are key to keeping project implementation on track by paying for expenditures incurred locally. But it is often the case that counterpart funds are not provided in the amounts or the time frames agreed upon during loan negotiations. And so, while the government reneges on its commitment to provide counterpart funds, the government officials in charge divert the interest that is "their money" into their own pockets.[1]

A second and much larger issue is the amount of funds initially placed in the special accounts. Determined during project appraisal, and agreed upon at negotiations, these amounts are often much larger than what is actually needed to keep the project on schedule. Appraisal disbursement schedules typically ignore disbursement failures on previous projects while painting rosy scenarios at board presentations. And so, two million dollars may go into a special account when two hundred thousand would be more appropriate under the circumstances.

Further complicating this issue is the manner in which management has addressed the problem of "disbursement lag,"[2] which has festered for decades, with management constantly seeking to distance itself from the awful truth that it has failed to conduct honest assessments of borrower commitment, competence, and integrity when presenting loans for board approval. This lack of honesty has resulted in the loss of billions of dollars each year as corrupt government officials find themselves happily drowning in oceans of special account money. And how has management sought to resolve this problem? Not by tighter control over these funds. Not by stricter auditing. Not by factoring in past financial management failures. Not by considering the degree of corruption within the government. And certainly not by reducing the amount of funds being disbursed in such a careless manner.

Rather, management has created the illusion that the problem has been solved by obtaining promises from borrowers that "they will do better in the future," by releasing funds in tranches,[3] by having borrowers sign anti-corruption pledges, and so on. Smoke and mirrors to hide the fact that despite all the anti-corruption rhetoric, despite all the warnings in the past, management is allowing 60 percent of its disbursements, twelve billion dollars each year, to go out the door without adequate accountability or oversight. Management would do well to revisit the 1976 audit report of special accounts and heed the advice contained therein.[4]

A CALL FOR RESTITUTION

Imagine this: A person entrusted to manage the accounts of a large corporation has embezzled several million dollars. He has put some of this stolen money into offshore bank accounts and has used the rest to buy a spacious villa, an expensive sports car, and other luxury items. After an exhaustive investigation, there is enough evidence to prosecute the culprit. But wait! Management and shareholders of the corporation do not wish to press charges! The few million he has taken were only a small fraction of their total annual sales, and it would be a public relations nightmare if this were all brought out in the open.

No, it would create too many problems to have him return what he stole. So they let him keep his offshore accounts, his villa, his car, and all the rest. To make a big fuss over it would just be an embarrassment. Their solution is simple: ignore the theft and pretend that the money has been used for legitimate purposes.

That, my friends, is the response management has taken with regard to funds stolen from the Bank's portfolio. Granted, the above scenario is oversimplified, but it accurately reflects what happens whenever investigations carried out by the Department of Institutional Integrity find that fraud has been committed against Bank-funded projects.[5] If the findings of those investigations are kept confidential, there is little chance that anything further will be done to pressure the responsible authorities to prosecute the criminals or to seek restitution. If the findings are reported openly, further action might be taken, but it is never directed against the actual culprits. Rather, it is the borrower government, and ultimately the poor, that will be asked to repay the stolen funds. Is this the way it should be? Are we to let the thieves keep their loot and pretend that we have done our duty?

While all their intellectual anti-corruption exercises have some value, management's refusal to take harsher measures only strengthens the conviction of the criminals that they can continue their corrupt ways with impunity. If their crimes are exposed—

and that is a rare occurrence—what punishment can they expect? At the worst, if a government official is found to have stolen from a Bank-funded project, he might lose his job. More likely, he would just be transferred to another position in government. The government would not prosecute him, nor would it seek to recover the stolen funds or other assets belonging to the culprit.[6] Depending upon the severity of the crime, the amount of public exposure it has received, relations with the borrower, and other factors, the Bank might declare misprocurement, cancel relevant portions of a loan, or even cancel an entire loan. Going further, management might ask the borrower to return an amount equal to that stolen to the Bank. And as a last resort, when the extent of corruption in a particular country can no longer be ignored, the Bank might even suspend all lending for a while.

But this is not the same as stealing from a corporation. The thieves have stolen money that belongs to their government and, by extension, to the general population. Money that was borrowed from the World Bank to improve life for the masses. Money that was supposed to be used to alleviate poverty. It is unconscionable that the government and the general population should then be asked to repay these stolen funds to the Bank while allowing the thieves to keep their ill-gotten gains. This is asking the victims to pay for the crime and does nothing to deter the criminals from further criminal acts.

So, how should we redress this situation? Quite simply, when it has been found that Bank funds have been stolen, the Bank must exert all its influence on the borrower to prosecute the guilty parties. When they are found guilty, the bank accounts and other assets belonging to the criminals should be seized and used as restitution to the project, the borrower, or the Bank, as determined by the injured parties. The thieves cannot be allowed to keep what they have stolen, and every effort must be made to ensure that this does not happen. To do less only makes a mockery of all that the Bank professes in the fight against corruption.

THE CORRUPTER AND THE CORRUPTED

In the previous chapters I have provided evidence of the complicity of government officials in the corruption equation, but at the risk of going too far, please allow me some final comments on the subject. In the past decade the Bank has made much ado about greedy contractors, consultants, and suppliers who, we are asked to believe, have tempted honest government officials with bribes and kickbacks. And indeed, there is little doubt that some firms and individuals do operate in this manner and do seek out officials who are willing participants in defrauding their governments. But having said that, I believe that there are many more firms and individuals that are basically honest and would prefer to compete for government business on an even playing field.

The scheming and manipulation of the bidding and award process by government officials is a nightmare for anyone attempting to bid competitively for government contracts. I base this assessment on the hundreds of private businessmen I have met over the years who have complained bitterly about the obstacles they faced when attempting to do business with government agencies in the Third World.[7] I base this assessment on the all too numerous complaints I have received from representatives of qualified firms who have submitted what should have been winning bids, only to have them rejected in favor of an unqualified bidder who wins the award at a higher price. And while there are those in the Bank who tend to dismiss these complaints as "sour grapes" from losing bidders, I have found that more often than not, such complaints have merit.

This observation is supported by the many allegations of bid-rigging that have been investigated and substantiated by the Bank's Department of Institutional Integrity in recent years. And in those cases where legitimate bidders were successful,[8] their problems were only beginning, as government officials made endless attempts to extract kickbacks at every turn throughout the life of the contract.[9] The following is a brief example.

WE CAN HELP YOU GET THE CONTRACT[10]

While filling in for a colleague who was away on vacation, I was contacted by the British Embassy regarding a matter that had been referred to them by a UK distributor of textbooks. The matter concerned the procurement of approximately $25 million worth of university textbooks through a Bank-funded project in Nigeria. It was alleged that the distributor had been approached by an individual claiming to represent certain government officials in the National Universities Commission (NUC) who were in a position to award the contract to whomever they pleased. The representative presented a number of confidential project documents to prove his relationship with the NUC officials and stated that he could ensure the contract award for a finder's fee. The finder's fee was to be 15 percent ($3.75 million) of the contract amount and would allegedly be shared among the project officials involved in the award. Upon being told that the distributor would not pay such a fee, the representative again contacted the distributor and alleged that the NUC officials would be willing to accept 10 percent ($2.5 million), but nothing less. Still refusing to cooperate with this extortion attempt, the distributor sought help from the Bank through the British Embassy.

Knowing there were only a few international firms qualified to bid on such a large book order, and anxious to win the contract award, the British distributor had submitted a very competitive bid based upon a low profit margin. It was technically qualified, and it offered the lowest prices. Nine days after learning of this situation from the British Embassy, I was contacted by the representative of a U.S. distributor who had also submitted a bid. It had been advised by an unnamed consultant that it would soon be invited to go to Nigeria to "negotiate" the award of the bid.

Ten days after that, the U.S. distributor was advised that "Bank procedures had prevented the negotiation of the bid award, but as there were only three bidders short listed, the Nigerians had decided to split the procurement into three awards." I passed this information on to my colleague and management, who in turn intervened to get the bid award back on a transparent track. But the government officials, ever determined, had other plans. And those plans centered around a divide-and-conquer scheme in which sub-contracts would become the vehicle by which the NUC officials would enrich themselves and their accomplices.

Let's be clear about what is involved here. This is ICB (international competitive bidding) procurement, for which the lowest technically qualified bidder should receive the award. If, in the course of providing goods and services, a winning bidder uses sub-contractors, this fact, and the qualifications of the sub-contractors, should be known up front at the time of bid submission. But that was not how it would be in this case, and shortly thereafter, both the British and the U.S. distributors received identical letters dated February 15, 1991, from NUC:

> I am pleased to inform you that as a result of the bid evalua-tion made on your bid as procurement agent for Books un-der the above credit facility, your company has been successful. A meeting of a representative of your organiza-tion with the Executive Secretary of the National Universi-ties Commission has therefore been scheduled for Monday, 25th February, 1991 to discuss this development.
>
> It is very important that a representative of your organi-zation to this crucial meeting is senior enough to take on-the-spot decisions on behalf of the company as there may not be time for any representative to consult his/her organi-zation on any issues that may be discussed at the meeting before agreements are reached.

And so it began. With only ten days' advance notice, each dis-tributor went to Lagos thinking it had won the $25 million book contract. Upon their arrival at NUC, both were handed letters dated February 15, 1991, that were almost identical to the earlier letters they had received of the same date. The one exception? In the sec-ond letter, instead of stating "your company has been successful," it now stated "your company has been short listed." They were politely told that the first letters had been written in error. But what a difference one word can make! Now in the same room with the NUC officials and two unqualified Nigerian book dis-tributors, the British and U.S. distributors quickly learned that if they wanted any business with NUC, they would have to share the award with the other bidders.

I will spare you many of the details regarding the back-and-forth communications between the parties concerned as this mat-ter dragged on for months. The two international distributors tried in vain to win the award honestly while pleading for assis-tance from the Bank. The Bank made an initial effort to keep the procurement transparent, but in the end, allowed the government officials to succeed with their scheme by not pursuing the obvious fraud that was committed after the award was made to the British distributor.

And this is how it played out. The British distributor had clearly submitted the winning bid, and NUC reported to the Bank that it had been awarded the $25 million contract. The award was approved by the Bank. But, unbeknownst to the Bank, that award was made on the condition that the other three bidders—the U.S. firm and the two Nigerian firms—would share in the business as sub-contractors. The British firm would get 50 percent, the U.S. firm would get 15 percent, and the Nigerian firms would get 20 percent and 15 percent respectively. And so it was that 35 percent ($8.75 million)—more than twice the original finder's fees solicited by the NUC officials—was awarded to the two unqualified Nigerian firms. In the end, much of what the Nigerian firms were to deliver to the universities was never accounted for, and neither was the money that was paid to them.

So yes, by all means, let us expose and debar those corrupt firms and individuals who prey on Bank-funded projects. Let us prevent them from doing business with the other multilateral banks. Let us turn them over to national authorities for prosecution and the restitution of their ill-gotten gains. But let us not forget: *Corruption cannot take place without the active involvement of government officials!* And let us insist that our borrowers mete out the same treatment to those government officials who are the driving force behind these scams, and who have profited handsomely from their crimes. When found guilty, they must be punished like any other criminals, and their stolen wealth, whether in offshore accounts or in real property, must be recovered. The World Bank—in living up to its fiduciary responsibilities to its shareholders, in living up to its commitment to the poor, and in living up to its claim of leadership—can do no less.

NOTES

1. This is not necessarily in the form of cash. Using funds from interest accounts to pay for overseas junkets, furnish private villas, or buy vehicles has the same effect.

2. This has always been a matter of concern for management, because it reflects the often huge disconnects between promises made during appraisal and failures on the ground.

3. Typically done, for example, when a new policy is enacted (but never mind if it is not enforced) or some other action is taken by the government in accordance with the loan agreement.

4. Internal Auditing Department, "Report on an Audit of Bank Loans and IDA Credits," September 29, 1978, p. 2, para. 5; p. 22, para. 67.

5. Such findings may also come from normal operational audits.

6. There have been a few rare cases where the criminals were prosecuted, but they hardly represent a change in the benign position usually taken when these crimes are exposed.

7. While it is outside the purview of the Bank, we all know this phenomenon is not limited to third-world countries.

8. A legitimate result is usually because of a conscientious task manager or procurement adviser holding firm to maintain the integrity of the bidding process.

9. Typical methods involve pressure on the contractor to award subcontracts to favored individuals or shell companies for services that are never provided; the inclusion of vehicles, overseas junkets, and other emoluments; and the demand for bribes to pay for the processing of invoices.

10. Parts of the following account have been previously published in Steve Berkman, "The World Bank and $100 Billion Question," in *A Game As Old As Empire,* ed. Steven Hiatt (San Francisco: Berrett-Koehler, 2007). Used with permission.

22

· · · · · · ·

The Essence of Knowledge

Figure 22–1. Cartoon by Marc Roesch

Somewhere in my travels I came across this cartoon depicting some of the absurdities of economic development as practiced by the World Bank and other donors.[1] As is so often the case, it contains a considerable degree of truth as it makes fun of the ludicrous quest for irrelevant information, a quest often engaged in by the great minds within the Bank's bureaucracy.

Knowledge is a wonderful thing when it can be put to good use, but when studies serve no purpose other than to keep certain individuals employed, one is obliged to weigh the cost of such efforts against the benefits received. It is all well and good if our objective is to acquire knowledge for its own sake, but if our objective

249

is to help the poor, then perhaps we need to revise our strategy. The Bank has produced untold thousands of studies, reports, and working papers. And while some of these exercises may represent a valid use of Bank resources, more often than not they do nothing to improve the quality of life for those who live in poverty.

Bank staff have written thousands upon thousands of intellectually inspired economic sector studies, country assistance strategy papers, and poverty reduction strategy papers. They have written about urban development, agriculture, education, road maintenance, public administration, private enterprise, and any other topic remotely connected with development economics. They have studied and written about poverty, the environment, social safety nets, labor markets, financial markets, infant mortality, demographics—and anything else one can think of. Project appraisal reports contain analyses of country and sector conditions that also add to the Bank's vast library of knowledge. So, after five decades and billions of words put on paper, is there anything that the Bank does not know? Is there anything that it has not written about? What elusive bit of truth about poverty has the Bank yet to uncover, and at what point does all this intellectual activity reach its limit of effectiveness? When does too much knowledge interfere with getting the job done?

Diverting attention from the many failures connected with the Bank's lending operations, management's consuming obsession with the acquisition of knowledge has seriously compromised its ability to manage its portfolio effectively. I have often been amazed at the frequency with which Bank reports profess that "we" do not know enough about this or that topic and that further studies are needed. Oblivious to the fact that these topics have been studied ad nauseam in the past, the economist managers of the Bank continually push for still more studies, more things to give them an excuse to avoid facing the disasters within the Bank's portfolio. How can they profess to be ignorant of all these things while at the same time proclaiming their intellectual leadership in the world of economic development?

There is something very wrong here, for these people were hired for their expertise. They were supposed to know all this when they came to the Bank. Why hire them for their expertise and then pay them to learn on the job? All the while consuming more and more of the Bank's resources while diverting attention from its failures, management has found a convenient way to distance itself from the dirty and high-risk work of development lending. Claiming to be at the forefront in the fight against poverty, it has found a way to advance individual careers without being held accountable for the disasters those same individuals have helped to create.

So, where do we go from here? Obviously, there will always be a need for research, analysis, and study of issues that are germane to the Bank's mission. But we must ask ourselves, to what extent do these exercises complement that mission, and to what extent do they compromise it? I have observed over the years that the best way to avoid taking action, and the risk it may entail, is to study the problem, form a committee, or write a report—anything that will keep you from being held accountable if things don't work out. And when you have exhausted those options, you may begin the process all over again. For the World Bank, and the people who manage it, this is unconscionable, and it needs to change.

Economic development is not rocket science; it is time for the Bank's management to back away from many of the absurd quests for knowledge it has pursued in the past. The Bank has no business being a "repository of knowledge" while billions of people are struggling to survive under appalling conditions. It has no business wasting its shareholders' money for esoteric studies that have no practical value. We know much more than we need to know in order to address the real issues of poverty and development, and should we need to know more, we can always turn to academia for help. The universities are, after all, best qualified to carry out that task, and it would free the Bank for more important tasks such as paying attention to its portfolio and its fiduciary responsibilities. Tasks such as increasing the supervision of lending operations. Tasks such as actively ensuring that the funds it provides to its borrowers are used for the purposes intended.

So, what would a reduction in the quest for knowledge mean for the Bank? Once management and the bureaucracy got over the shock of even considering such a concept, they might just find that it would not bring the Bank to its knees, nor would it compromise the Bank's true mission. Yes, they might find that some individuals are not adding real value to the Bank's work. And they might find that the Bank can be more effective with fewer bureaucrats running around pretending they are at the forefront of the fight against poverty. They might also find that being freed from the never-ending meetings to prepare and review reports, studies, strategy papers, and the like will allow them to direct their time and resources to improving the management of the Bank's lending portfolio. And while difficult for some to accept, it might be that less contemplation and more action can return the Bank to the path from which it has strayed.

But where to draw the line? Where to find a more appropriate balance between the intellectual and the practical? Obviously, there is no quick and easy formula for such a change in the Bank's culture. But I believe it is urgently necessary to begin the process nevertheless. Intellectual fat abounds within the Bank, and there is no question in my mind that it could easily be cut by at least one-third to one-half without seriously affecting the Bank's mission. Research that focuses upon esoteric topics far removed from the lives of the poor should be left for academia. Studies that have no direct connection to improving the delivery of services to the public should not be undertaken.

But who will do the triage? Is management capable of performing surgery upon itself? Perhaps, if pressed to do so by its shareholders, but it is more likely that it would impede the process rather than support it. And so, we might again consider calling upon others to review and evaluate the Bank's entire program of knowledge acquisition and management to determine new parameters for such activities. If the Bank can call in outside expertise, as it has so often done in the past to advise on its periodic reorganizations, it would not be inappropriate to do the same regarding this counterproductive obsession with knowledge. And who best to take on such an assignment than a consortium of universities and possibly concerned NGOs? Such an arrangement would relieve management of the responsibility for this distasteful task and would permit a healthy trimming of the intellectual fat. And with the fat gone, the Bank would be better positioned to return to its mission of alleviating poverty and more effective in managing its portfolio.

NOTE

1. Marc Roesch, December 1992.

23

• • • • • • •

Reporting the Truth

Like many of my former colleagues, I came to the Bank in complete awe of the institution, an institution renowned as a world
leader in economic development. One only had to read the Bank's
annual reports to know that this was true. But with time, it gradually became clear that much of what we did was more about maintaining the facade of success and leadership than it was about
actually achieving substantive results. And it soon became obvious that we had to be careful about what was told to the outside
world if we were to maintain this facade. We could write about
the most esoteric topics, the most mundane issues, and anything
else connected with economic development. We could report on
the wonderful dialogues we were having with our clients. We could
prepare charts showing how much money had been disbursed
each year. We could compile data showing road usage or the number of children attending school. We could publish photographs
of workers at a power plant, a farmer sitting on a new tractor, or
women standing around a village well.

But it was all window dressing, for in reality the dialogue with
our clients was just so much hot air that seldom, if ever, translated
into substantive results. Statistics were "cooked" to show how
much we were alleviating poverty. Photographs were taken in
showplace locations that had nothing to do with reality, while the
empty buildings, the broken equipment, and the decaying infrastructure were hidden from view. Smoke and mirrors used to create the illusion of overwhelming success in project and adjustment

lending, while hiding the glaring failures that prevailed through-out the Bank's portfolio.

In all fairness, these transgressions are not unique to the Bank; most entrenched bureaucracies are prone to subverting the truth in order to protect their vested interests. But we should not allow this fact to deter us from corrective action if we are sincere about our mission to alleviate poverty. So why is the Bank's management unable to admit that not all lending is beautiful? Why is it unable to admit that some governments are so corrupt that any money loaned to them is a complete waste of the Bank's time and effort? Worse, it won't make a penny's worth of difference for the poor. Why is it unable to admit that lending without a demonstrated commitment by the borrower is throwing money down a rat hole? Why is it unable to admit that some of the Bank's esteemed clients are nothing more than thieves in government clothing?

None of this comes out when one reads the annual reports produced by the Bank, reports that heap praise on the Bank, its management, and all the wonderful things supposedly accomplished year in and year out. True accountability is thrown out the window as we are inundated with mind-numbing statistics, pie charts, bar charts, and graphs of all kinds to show us what a brilliant job the Bank is doing in the fight to alleviate poverty. Meanwhile, the uncomfortable facts concerning the real mess within the Bank's portfolio remain hidden from the reader.

A brief review of the *World Bank Annual Report 2004* will help demonstrate management's lack of interest in presenting any unpleasant facts that may challenge its stories of success. And when those unpleasant facts cannot be avoided, they are presented in language that renders them inconsequential in the mind of the reader. Yes, there are some problems out there, but look at all the meetings and conferences we've held to discuss them! In "Fiscal 2004 Highlights,"[1] we learn that the Bank has:

- Held a global conference on poverty reduction.
- Approved 245 lending operations totaling $20 billion.
- Held the Annual Bank Conference on Development Economics.
- Addressed the UN Security Council and called for a War on AIDS (address by the Bank's president).

- Joined in partnership with several UN and NGO groups to provide generic drugs for HIV/AIDS to poor countries.
- Published the first *Global Monitoring Report.*
- Implemented the statistical capacity building program to "help developing countries strengthen statistical systems, institutional capacity, and planning."
- Conducted a review of its activities in middle income countries.
- Worked to simplify and modernize its lending policies and procedures to make it easier for clients to borrow.
- Worked with the UN to produce the "Joint Iraq Needs Assessment."
- Advised that its Post Conflict Fund is now benefiting thirty-six countries.
- Created a new $25 million trust fund for low-income countries under stress.
- Launched negotiations for the fourteenth IDA replenishment.
- Held the global Development Marketplace, in which 183 finalists presented proposals for solving development problems.
- Launched Global Economic Prospects 2004: Realizing the Development Promise of the Doha Agenda, a detailed overview of the world economy.
- Met with participants at the Youth, Development, and Peace Conference (the president and a managing director were present).
- Conducted the annual meetings of the Bank's shareholders.
- Launched its infrastructure action plan.

Well, that's certainly an impressive list, but is there really any direct link between all this talk and introspection, all these conferences and the rest, and actually getting results on the ground? Is that it? Is that what economic development and the alleviation of poverty is all about? It is clear that the Bank's management believes it has accomplished great things and that it is at the cutting edge of development. But is it?

It is interesting that many of the accomplishments Bank managers are touting are about meetings, conferences, reviews, working on this, advising on that, launching another nobly named quixotic exercise, creating easier ways to move money—and anything else that keeps them from taking concrete action for which they might be held accountable. And while one could certainly applaud the efforts to provide generic drugs for HIV/AIDS, it is difficult to comprehend exactly how all these other efforts will ultimately translate into benefits for the man, woman, or child on the streets of Lagos, Dacca, or Port au Prince. Yes, they have approved 245 lending operations totaling $20 billion, but where, in this overview of their accomplishments, do we find even the slightest mention of dysfunctional governments, failed projects, and the ugly specter of corruption permeating the Bank's portfolio? And where in all this have they given us anything by which their accomplishments can be measured? Has anyone other than themselves established any objective criteria by which the Bank may be judged?

Now, let us look beyond these highlights of what the Bank accomplished in 2004. Surely it is not all bad, and surely some noteworthy things have been accomplished. But lending money for development is not, in and of itself, noteworthy unless that money has produced measurable results. And this is where the Bank faces a serious dilemma. Did the Bank's money really reach the poor, or was most of it sucked up by all those in between the Bank and the intended beneficiaries—the consultants, the contractors, the suppliers, and the government officials managing those funds? How much of it actually translated into real benefits for the poor? How many dollars did it take to put a shovel in the hands of a farmer, a book in the hands of a child, or a box of bandage in the hands of a nurse? How much did it cost to achieve ten dollars' worth of progress? Was it ten dollars, or a hundred dollars? Was it a thousand? No one really knows. Nor does anyone appear to care. All we hear from the Bank is that it has approved loans, disbursed money, held conferences, published reports, and joined partnerships.

And although one finds subtle hints of problems of great magnitude throughout the annual report, it is difficult to put one's finger on just exactly what those problems are. Problems that are quickly buried under mountains of praise for the Bank's alleged achievements. A report that is overrun with mission statements that typically define what the Bank does, but not what it has accomplished. A report that is more boiler plate and platitudes than substance. A report that does little to expose the underlying issues that plague economic development in general, and the Bank's portfolio in particular. A few excerpts from the report illustrate the extent to which the hard realities of the whole business are avoided. For example, in regard to the Bank's development agenda, we read:

> The International Bank for Reconstruction and Development (IBRD) and the International Development Association (IDA) together make up the World Bank, an international financial organization whose mission is to fight world poverty. The Bank helps client countries achieve sustainable development by harnessing resources and forming partnerships with others, including development institutions and civil society organizations.[2]

A noble statement, but the big question is never answered. How successful has the Bank been in achieving its mission? And, although it will be implied throughout the report that the Bank has been responsible for many good things in the development arena, one is hard put to find any concrete evidence to support such implications. Then, after being told that developing countries have made much progress in recent decades,[3] we learn that

> *The success stories of many developing countries prove that progress is possible when countries have good policies and the support of partners.* But progress has been uneven. Slow growth, low educational achievement, civil disturbances, and poor health remain obstacles for many countries.[4]

Well, which countries have made progress, and which haven't? If we remove South Korea, China, Brazil, and the small number of other successes, we are left with a lot of countries where the alleviation of poverty for the masses is still a distant vision. And while, as a minor afterthought, we learn of slow growth, low educational achievement, and the rest, where do we learn about the ravages of corruption and dysfunctional governments? Aren't these two latter factors among the main obstacles to progress?

Throughout the report other noble topics abound. Development goals for the millennium, addressing global priorities, combating communicable diseases, fostering trade and regional integration, improving the environment, improving governance and resolving conflict, building the climate for investment, and on, and on, with one profound statement after another.

> One key to reducing poverty is investing in people—by improving access to education and health services and providing other social interventions that benefit vulnerable groups.[5]

> The most effective development strategy is one that is country owned and country led, promotes economic growth, and ensures that poor people participate in and benefit from their country's development. Reducing poverty effectively depends on many factors. Foremost among these are a conducive development climate and the participation of all people in their country's development. These two pillars form the basis of the Bank's strategy, set forth in the Strategic Framework in 2001.[6]

By merely reading these all-too-obvious statements, we are expected to believe that Bank managers have stumbled upon some heretofore unknown wisdom. Do they really have to tell us this after decades of development failures? Do we really need the Bank's experts to share these pearls of wisdom with us? Filling the pages of the report with these empty statements does nothing to enlighten us and has the perverse effect of diverting our attention from issues that are much more crucial to achieving the Bank's mission. Issues that center on the Bank's fiduciary responsibility, its adherence to Article III of its Articles of Agreement, and the corrupt and dysfunctional status of many of its clients.

This is not to say, however, that the annual report totally ignores the many obstacles to development. It is just that those obstacles are never presented in a clear and unambiguous manner. They are whitewashed into the background. They are there, but they are not connected with anything the Bank does or has done. For example, in presenting the Millennium Development Goals put forth by the donor community, we learn of the eight lofty objectives to be achieved by the year 2015: eradicate extreme poverty; achieve universal primary education; promote gender equality and empower women; reduce child mortality; improve maternal health; combat HIV/AIDS, malaria, and other diseases;

ensure environmental sustainability; and develop a global partnership for development. But there is a caveat here. Hidden within a few paragraphs on the Bank's monitoring progress is the following comment based on the findings of the June 2004 *Global Monitoring Report*:

> Its findings present the sobering assessment that, while the first goal of halving poverty will likely be met globally, given current trends, most countries will not meet most of the goals.[7]

So, what are we saying here? Has the donor community set goals that cannot be met? And if they can't be met, wouldn't it behoove us to identify the specific reasons for this rather large disconnect between our goals and reality? Could it be that we really haven't a clue about how to achieve these goals? Could it be that there is only so much one can hope to accomplish when dealing with corrupt and dysfunctional governments that are run by individuals who have other agendas? What is going on here?

Throughout the annual report one finds paragraph after paragraph filled with innocuous statements that tell us little, if anything, about the true state of affairs within the Bank's portfolio. Nor does the report provide any substantive indications of what the Bank is doing to improve the situation. We learn that the country assistance strategy (CAS) is "the business plan that guides Bank activities in a client country."[8] We learn that "the Board discussed six Transitional Support Strategies (TSS) for post-conflict settings" and that "15 Country Assistance Strategies and CAS Progress Reports were prepared,"[9] and on, and on, and on. A single paragraph on corruption was the only reference to one of the most serious issues facing the Bank today.

What are we to make of all this obfuscation? While Bank officials were convening all those conferences, writing all those CAS reports, their dear friends and clients were busy robbing billions from World Bank loans and credits. Yet there is not even the slightest hint in the annual report that this rampant thievery is going on, or that it exists at all within the Bank's portfolio. Where in this report of over one hundred pages is anything to inform us of the Bank's poor handling of its fiduciary responsibility? Where is anything to inform us of the very real failures of so many of its lending operations? How can Bank management deal with the hard issues if it refuses to recognize them? Where is the truth?

It would be foolish to expect the Bank's management to hang all its dirty laundry out for the world to see, but a much greater degree of honesty and openness is necessary if the Bank is to address the problems within its portfolio. The Bank's shareholders, the donor community, and those struggling to survive in the Third World deserve nothing less. The Bank is, after all, not the only player on the development scene, and it should not bear full responsibility for all the development failures we have seen over the past several decades.

The Bank's management should not be afraid to stand up and tell the world what is really going on with so many of these dysfunctional governments. It should not be afraid to admit that the Bank's assistance, whether financial or intellectual, cannot always achieve the lofty objectives touted in the annual reports. So why pretend otherwise? All too often the money is stolen and the advice is ignored. So what purpose is served by covering up these ugly facts? I believe that it would be more beneficial to expose them than to suppress them. Better to offend thousands of corrupt government officials than to betray the millions living on a dollar a day. Better to be seen as honest and credible than as an apologist for dysfunctional governments and the thieves who run them.

So how can the Bank's annual report be improved so that it becomes more than just smoke and mirrors? How can it be changed so that it serves as a meaningful source of information for its shareholders, its borrowers, and the donor community? To begin with, Bank managers must stop looking at this annual event as a marketing exercise. One would be hard put to find any informed reader of the annual report who does not know what the Bank does or what its mission is. So perhaps they might begin by cutting back on all the timeworn boiler-plate paragraphs that tell the same story year in and year out about what they do and how they do it. And then we come to the difficult stuff.

Is there anyone who doubts that the Bank's portfolio contains more problems than the Bank has previously been willing to admit? If that is the case, then it behooves management to be much more forthright about the problems than it has been in the past.

Sweeping problems under the carpet does not resolve them, and the time for honest reporting is long overdue.

So let us ask, what would be the harm in devoting a chapter in the annual report to portfolio issues? A chapter that would tell us why certain projects are not succeeding, or more honestly, why they are failing. Could it be that certain projects were over-designed? Or perhaps certain borrowers weren't really committed to implementing them in the first place? Or maybe the government was just too corrupt and dysfunctional to make them work? Such a chapter could identify problem projects by name, with detailed discussions of cause and effect.[10] It could discuss overdue project audits, accounting problems, policies that were not implemented, difficulties in achieving sustainability, the reasons for loan cancellations, and all the other issues associated with projects that are not succeeding. What could be wrong with that?

Next, what would be the harm in devoting a chapter to anti-corruption efforts? Corruption has, after all, been identified by the Bank as a serious obstacle in the path to development. So why not devote a chapter to it? It could still pay homage to the many studies, research activities, conferences, and workshops that were conducted to enlighten the world on the dangers of corruption, but more important, this chapter would serve to expose the true nature of the myriad crimes perpetrated against Bank-funded operations. And while I'm certain that management would shudder at the thought, such exposure would at last shake off the cloud of uncertainty over the subject and permit appropriate corrective actions to be taken.

In essence, such a chapter would consist of a substantive report on the investigative findings and associated work conducted by the Department of Institutional Integrity and other Bank units working in this area. The reporting would cover numbers and types of allegations received, fraud investigations conducted and their findings, amounts of money stolen, legal actions taken by the Bank and the borrowers, and any other related issues that would motivate the donor community, committed leaders of developing countries, and honest persons everywhere into doing whatever is necessary to reverse the increasing spread of these criminal acts.[11] It is difficult to fight an enemy you don't know, and such information would go a long way toward resolving that issue. I have no doubt whatsoever that such a chapter would be read avidly by readers of the annual report.

In addition, and I believe this to be extremely critical, the Bank *must* report on the recovery of stolen funds. As I have stated previously, management's will to recover those funds is egregiously lacking. It is not enough to investigate the theft of Bank funds and then debar this firm or that consultant while still allowing the individuals involved to keep the loot. It is not enough to uncover instances of fraud and embezzlement while still allowing government officials, often the facilitators of the crimes, to keep their offshore accounts intact. And while the recovery of stolen Bank funds can be difficult to carry out, it is not impossible if the governments concerned are committed to doing so.

When fraud has been proven, it is not enough to ask a government to return an amount equal to that which has been stolen. It is not enough to cancel a portion of a loan. It is not enough to threaten not to lend to this or that sector until a better accounting system is installed. When fraud has been proven, the Bank *must* insist that the government prosecute, punish, and recover the assets of the guilty individuals in the same manner it would for any other criminals. And while management will undoubtedly argue that this is not within the Bank's purview, it must be done, and it must be reported. It is time for management to accept the challenge and do what is right, if for no other reason than to honor its professed commitment to the poor souls living under corrupt third-world regimes.

Finally, the annual report must return to its pre-1986 days and include a chapter about bank management and the Bank's staffing structure. As stated earlier in this book, prior to 1986, the Bank included information on overall staff levels and senior management positions down to the director level. Information that the Bank's management was not afraid to publish two decades ago, but which it subsequently decided was not fit for public consumption. While seemingly insignificant to some, this information provides insight into the effectiveness of the institution by permitting one to see where staff resources are being concentrated and the prevailing ratios between staff and management. Information that could reveal much about management's true agendas. So why, one might ask, did management phase out this topic after 1986, and why can't it be included in future annual reports?

In the format of the 2004 annual report there is an introductory section that presents an overview of the Bank, its board of executive directors, and the Bank group. Within this section are subsections that briefly explain the bank's "strategic framework," its role in "poverty reduction," its "country programs," its "global programs and partnerships," its "fiduciary responsibility," and its "administrative budget." The last two topics, taking up two short paragraphs of two sentences each, hardly provides the reader with anything by which to assess the management of the Bank. In this regard I would propose expanding the information presented in this introductory section to include the following discussion of management:

- Reference to the criteria by which Bank oversight and fiduciary responsibility are measured, for example, human and financial resources (staff years and budget) applied to project supervision, knowledge management, portfolio auditing, project evaluation, and the preparation of lending instruments.
- An organization chart and associated tables showing numbers of staff in each department, numbers of staff by job description, and numbers of supervisors/managers up through senior management.

The inclusion of this information in the annual report would, I am sure, be derided by management as totally unnecessary. But the very fact that it wishes to hide this information only encourages one to believe that it has a probative value for determining management's effectiveness in running the Bank. If, for example, it were shown that x amount had been budgeted for portfolio auditing, while $2x$ had been budgeted for knowledge management, one might conclude that management was not quite as committed to fiduciary issues as it claimed to be. Conversely, if the budget numbers were reversed, the Bank's credibility on these issues would be strengthened. The same reasoning applies to other issues as well. If the staff/management ratios, the skills mix, and the other factors were to show an aggressive focus on addressing the Bank's primary mission, so much the better for management. This information is all readily available in the Bank's computerized data bases, so why not include it in the annual report? What's the harm in that?

NOTES

1. In *World Bank Annual Report 2004*, vol. 1, pp. 12–13.

2. Ibid., p. 14.

3. Claims of progress are accompanied by vague numbers showing increases in life expectancy and decreases in illiteracy and the numbers of people living in extreme poverty—numbers that do not always represent actual conditions.

4. *World Bank Annual Report 2004*, vol. 1, p. 14.

5. Ibid., p. 29.

6. Ibid., p. 17.

7. Ibid., p. 15. Most of the progress in achieving this goal is expected to come from China and a few other countries, while a large portion of the Third World is expected to remain mired in poverty.

8. Ibid., p. 18.

9. Ibid., p. 19.

10. This information is readily available from internal Bank reports.

11. As an aside, the Bank frequently mentions that it works with Transparency International. It would be interesting if the Bank were to include TI's Corruption Perception Index in the annual report so that readers might compare Bank and IDA loans made to the different countries against TI's ratings.

24

• • • • • • •

Money Can't Buy Happiness

It would be wonderful if the World Bank could alleviate poverty merely by lending $20 billion dollars each year. But sadly, money alone cannot eliminate economic hardship for the millions of people suffering under corrupt and dysfunctional governments. For, without a demonstrated commitment by those charged with managing those loans, it is guaranteed that the money will disappear with little to show for it. Without a commitment to use the money with integrity, those loans merely become a conduit by which corrupt government elites enrich themselves at the expense of the governed. The history of Bank lending over the past several decades has shown this to be true. And this truth continues to plague Bank managers, raising serious contradictions between their self-proclaimed image of leadership and the lending failures they make every effort to hide.

And so we have the dilemma facing management, the board of directors, and the Bank's shareholders. Should the Bank continue to lend billions without regard for the integrity or competence of the governments to which it entrusts those funds? Should it continue to lend billions for projects that are beyond the capacity of its borrowers to implement? Should it continue to lend billions to egregiously corrupt regimes that have shown no genuine interest in improving the lives of their citizens? Should it continue to lend when there is considerable evidence to show that past lending has done little to improve the lives of the poor? Logic tells us that no concerned person would answer these questions in the affirmative, leaving us to ask why, after all these years and all those failed projects, management continues to deny the obvious? Why is it so afraid to reconfigure the Bank's portfolio to more manageable and potentially more successful lending levels?

Caught between a proverbial rock and a hard place, management has spent decades mired in its culture of profligate lending while refusing to acknowledge that money by itself cannot buy happiness. Pointing to statistics that are often "cooked," biased, or otherwise manipulated, it may occasionally admit that perhaps progress hasn't been all that great but will mitigate such statements by suggesting that things would have been much worse if the Bank hadn't intervened with its frequently ill-conceived loans. The truth is that we don't really know how much worse things might have been without those loans and the debt that goes with them. And besides, what choice did management have? The Bank was created to lend money, and if that money should go to the corrupt regimes of Marcos, Suharto, Mobuto, and the rest, so be it. But it does not have to be that way.

Rather than financing large projects that create a feeding frenzy for corrupt government officials, it would be more logical to support smaller projects with clearly defined and easily measured objectives. For the most part large projects with overly ambitious objectives are a recipe for disaster, with too many individuals and too many conflicting agendas for the Bank to supervise effectively. The Bank has never been able to deal with the local management chaos that frequently occurs in these kinds of projects, and it never will. Responding to this dilemma, management will claim that "it is their money" and that the only way "they" will learn to manage their own affairs is for the Bank to stand back and let them learn by trial and error. The Bank has been doing this for decades, and it hasn't worked! It is merely management's way of avoiding any responsibility for the failures engendered by its willful disregard for the risks involved when making those loans in the first place. We have met our lending targets for the year, and that's all that matters.

And so, we must question the necessity of making large loans that promise to solve many, if not all, development issues in one sector or another yet ultimately fail to deliver on those promises. It has not worked in the past, and it will not work in the future. Therefore, let us ask what is wrong with lending small? What is wrong with first successfully completing a hundred kilometers of highway construction before attempting to do a thousand kilometers and failing? What is wrong with first successfully building, equipping, and staffing a few health clinics rather than trying to build several hundred that have no chance of becoming functional due to the sheer size of the undertaking? What is wrong with building upon small successes to create sustainable growth? With all its collective intellectual acumen, why hasn't management learned from past experience that big is not necessarily better, and that over the long term, smaller projects carefully supervised will bring more sustainable results? The simple answer is that to do so would prevent management from achieving its lending targets, and that would not please the gods of lending.

So, let us consider the consequences of eliminating lending targets from the Bank's management plan. Lending targets that are nothing more than empty promises made in advance that the Bank's borrowers are able and willing to use Bank loans effectively to improve the lives of the poor. Lending targets that foster a supply-driven process that should really be demand driven. Let management forget about how much money it *must* lend each year, and concentrate upon how much money it *can* lend to governments that are truly committed to using it for the common good. Let management focus upon smaller projects based upon thorough risk analyses with truly measurable criteria for success. Smaller projects that can be expanded with subsequent loans once it has been established that they have succeeded. Smaller projects in which the impact of mistakes can be minimized and corrective action can be taken before moving on. And if, in the process, the Bank does not lend as much as it had anticipated, so be it. For it might just be that something would be achieved, with less money wasted, less money stolen. The Third World might be less indebted. And what would be wrong with that?

LENDING FOR CORRUPTION

What better example of an oxymoron is there than the concept of lending money to corrupt governments to fight corruption? It is, after all, like lending money to the mafia to encourage it to fight crime. And best of all, it is the mafia's victims that will be asked to pay the loans back. And what a sweet deal it is!

Of course, I am exaggerating somewhat, for the situation is considerably more complicated than that. Nevertheless, there are some similarities, and it is critical that the Bank's management exercise extreme caution when lending to corrupt governments. Yes, corruption exists in varying degrees in government institutions everywhere. But we are not talking about the civil servant who steals paper clips from the office or overcharges for dinner on his travel expenses. We are talking about the rampant, pervasive, and wholesale theft of government resources by government officials. Billions of dollars stolen through fraud, embezzlement, bid-rigging, bribes, and all the other scams I have discussed. Billions of dollars entrusted to thieves, billions of dollars that will have to be paid back by future generations of the poor or absorbed by the taxpayers of the donor nations.

And so, what is the Bank and its management to do about this dilemma? One could say that *all* governments are corrupt and that therefore the Bank should not lend to any of them. But this conclusion ignores the Bank's potential for good works. It ignores the role the Bank can play in the alleviation of poverty, provided its management can shed the inwardly focused lending culture that has led the Bank astray over the past several decades.

It follows that the Bank must redefine the criteria by which it lends to its borrowers. Lending to fight corruption must be done with extreme caution, as those governments that may need it most may be those who are least committed to implementing anti-corruption measures. Money lent for a noble cause that may disappear through costly workshops, studies, and conferences about corruption, expensive overseas junkets, and other hyped-up exercises that do nothing to curtail the problem. For much the same reasons, lending for governance must also be done with extreme caution, as those in government may have little desire to change their ways.

In either case, whether it is for anti-corruption efforts or for improving governance, Bank funds should be lent with discretion and only after intensive risk analysis has been carried out. I have observed over the years that one of the most glaring fallacies of policy-based lending, whether for anti-corruption, governance, education, health, or anything else, is that it won't work unless there is serious commitment by the borrower. And more to the point, many of the policies that are conditional to the loans are things that the government could implement without funding from the Bank, if it truly had the will to do so. Does it really require Bank funds to pass a law criminalizing fraud? Does it really require Bank funds to pass a law calling for the restitution of monies stolen from the government? Does it really require Bank funds to mandate equal educational opportunities for girls? Does it really require Bank funds to pass laws reducing restrictions on small-scale enterprises? Government officials can move heaven and earth to enact laws and regulations that favor corrupt practices without assistance from the Bank, so why can't they do the same in reverse?

It therefore behooves the Bank to take a hard look at policy-based lending to ensure that it is more than just a bribe to government officials to get them to implement policies that they could do otherwise if they so desired. Bribes that allow them access to World Bank funds with little to hold them accountable if the policies are later ignored. And if this resulted in less lending by the Bank, what would be wrong with that?

BITING THE BULLETS

When I was a youngster I couldn't wait for Saturday, the day when all the kids in the neighborhood went to the local cinema. And we loved nothing more than to watch the old cowboy movies. The good guys on their white horses chasing the bad guys, the bank robbers, the runaway trains, the barroom shootouts, and all the rest. Our hearts pounded as we watched our heroes save the world from evil. And we loved it.

But it was almost guaranteed that at some point, one of the good guys would get wounded in a gunfight and would have to have the offending bullet removed. As we all watched tensely, he would be given a shot of whiskey and a bullet from his gun belt. He would drink the whiskey and then place the bullet between his teeth, biting down hard as one of his companions dug into his wound searching for the piece of lead embedded in his body. I never could figure out exactly why he had to bite the bullet, but it appeared that it took his mind off the pain during the operation.

What I have proposed in this chapter are several bullets that need to be bitten by the Bank's management if it is sincere in returning the Bank to its stated mission of alleviating poverty. And while biting these bullets will by no means resolve all the problems of development lending, I submit that they will address several of the Bank's most fundamental shortcomings in achieving that mission. Shortcomings that, as I have tried to present throughout this book, have a much greater negative impact upon third-world development than management would have us believe. Shortcomings that once addressed, it is to be hoped, will allow the Bank to continue its mission more successfully over the next fifty years. And perhaps the poor will suffer just a little bit less economic hardship in the process. And what would be wrong with that?

25

• • • • • • •

Taming the Gods of Lending

During my twelve plus four years with the Bank I observed the disastrous effects that bureaucratic mismanagement has had on the institution. Effects that reach into every corner of the Bank, reducing the dedication, intelligence, and experience of its staff to the lowest common denominator as they struggle to do their best against all odds. Faced with mind numbing bureaucratic tasks that have nothing to do with economic development or alleviating poverty, endless meetings, myriad deadlines, reorganizations, office moves, and a host of other irrelevant activities, it is amazing that Bank staff have any time left for the real work at hand. To compound the problem, staff members are often faced with the impossible task of trying to achieve meaningful project outcomes while working with corrupt and dysfunctional borrower institutions.

Against this background, choices have to be made, individual careers have to be weighed against personal convictions, and professional judgment has to give way to bureaucratic expediency. It is here that we find the huge disconnect between what Bank staff members are capable of, and what they are actually able to achieve. It is here that we find the disillusionment and despair among those who have come to the Bank thinking they would "make a difference," only to learn that maintaining the illusion of the Bank's infallibility takes precedence over all else. And gradually, without realizing it, they become hostages to the system as their moral and professional convictions become subservient to the bureaucracy. Hostages who have to compromise their professional principles if they wish to keep their jobs. Frustrated, they either leave the Bank or accede to the inevitable, doing whatever is necessary to appease the gods of lending. Either way the Bank loses, as the talents and experience of its employees are lost or wasted on meaningless efforts that do little to advance the Bank's mission.

And so, where does that leave us? We see a Bank smothered by its own bureaucracy, unable to deliver on the promises it has made to the poor, unable to adhere to reasonable standards of fiduciary responsibility, unable to explain its lending failures, and unable to account for the billions stolen from its portfolio. Poorly managed and constantly in a state of counterproductive flux, it has yet to find an effective modus operandi by which to assist developing nations. Its management has shamelessly fostered a lending culture that has enriched countless corrupt government elites in the Third World while keeping the poor mired in poverty. And while this record is not obvious from reading the self-congratulatory reports emanating from the Bank, it is nevertheless closer to reality than the Bank would dare to admit. This leaves one to ask, in terms of achieving its mission objectives, how effective is the Bank's management? How would it be graded by an unbiased and objective observer? I submit that on a scale of one to ten, it would surely be somewhere below five—and that, my friends, is not very good for an institution that claims to be a world leader at the cutting edge of all things.

All of this is sufficient cause to conclude that the Bank has outlived its usefulness, that maybe fifty years is enough, and that the Bank should be closed down. But this is unrealistic. To begin with, it just isn't going to happen. There are way too many powerful parties that have a vested interest in keeping the institution alive, and they will not be persuaded otherwise. More important, the Bank does indeed have a critical role to play in the development arena, and the fact that it has done so poorly in the past is not necessarily justification to shut its doors. It is, after all, not the institution that is at fault; the fault lies with those who have managed it over the years. It is management that has brought the Bank to its present state, and it is management that should be held accountable, not the institution. It is perhaps time to consider major changes in the Bank's management. Not the usual panaceas of the past—the reorganizations, the game of musical chairs, the rolling out of new slogans, and all the other smoke-and-mirror tactics—but a true changing of the guard that would bring in fresh blood with a more appropriate skills mix for the job at hand. Fresh blood that would not be encumbered by all the baggage of the past. Fresh blood that would not expend its efforts covering up past mistakes but would focus upon the problems of the present. Fresh blood that could truly revitalize the Bank. And what would be wrong with that?

THE GOOD AND THE BAD

Throughout this book I have tried to present those shortcomings that have the most immediate impact upon the Bank's mission. Shortcomings that my colleagues and I faced day in and day out, year in and year out, as we tried to keep Bank-funded projects on track in Africa and elsewhere. Tasks that were not made any easier by the Bank's bureaucratic mismanagement and our borrowers' dysfunctional government agencies. It is not all bad, however, and although rarely in Africa, there have been success stories elsewhere. I have not chosen to present those successes for three reasons. First, those successes, wherever and whatever they were, have been publicized endlessly by management, and they will no doubt be rolled out again in an attempt to refute what I, and others, have said to the contrary. Second, I believe that those successes are far outweighed by the many failures within the Bank's portfolio, thus making them more the exception than the rule. And third, although I worked on over one hundred projects during my tenure at the Bank, I never had the pleasure of witnessing a truly successful and sustainable outcome on any of them, and so I had no point of reference upon which to discuss success stories.

Indeed, there are a number of things that I have left out or only made passing mention of: the debacle of structural adjustment lending through which billions of dollars have disappeared without a trace; the mismanagement of trust funds; the cases of fraud, embezzlement, and extortion committed by a small number of Bank staff; the aiding and abetting of corruption by certain United Nations agencies; and the flawed lending in the social sectors that facilitates corruption much more than it helps the poor. These things will have to be left for another time, or perhaps for another author. And besides, I do want to end on a somewhat positive note.

ALL IS NOT LOST

It must appear that I consider the Bank to be beyond redemption, but this is not so. I firmly believe that all is not lost. No institution is perfect, after all, and the Bank cannot be expected to perform miracles at every turn, nor can it be expected to be right all the time. The fact that it has fallen far short of its potential does not mean that it cannot do better, and during the past ten years there have been indications that improvements are indeed possible.

Bank presidents have come and gone, while the bureaucracy has strengthened its control over the institution. It is my belief that the Robert S. McNamara presidency led to the birth of the "economic-manager syndrome" that has evolved into the bureaucratic and self-serving lending culture that exists today.[1] Subsequent presidents from Clausen to Conable to Preston appear to have been more the puppets of management than forceful leaders with their own vision of where they wanted to take the Bank.

This changed dramatically in 1995 with the arrival of James Wolfensohn, who appeared to be concerned about the Bank's neglect of its fiduciary responsibilities, and was committed to doing something about it. It was Wolfensohn who gave birth to the Bank's anti-corruption crusade in spite of management's opposition. The Wolfensohn presidency also brought the creation of the Department of Institutional Integrity and a new focus upon corruption and its impact on the Bank's mission. Things that I would never have expected to happen prior to 1995. And while I have presented a number of issues throughout this book that still prevent the Bank from achieving its mission, I will be the first to admit that it is a different Bank from the one I left in 1995.

But different does not necessarily mean that all is well. Wolfensohn began what I believe to be a sea change for the Bank by shaking it vigorously, by opposing the bureaucracy, and by addressing the corruption issue for the first time. There are still many problems to overcome if the Bank is to serve well its shareholders, its borrowers, and the poor. Unfortunately, management has not demonstrated a willingness to address these problems in the past, and it will remain for strong presidents to lead the way. Hopefully, the tradition of a strong presidency, initiated by Wolfensohn, will continue in the coming years. And this is a good sign.

In 2005, Wolfensohn retired from the Bank and was replaced by Paul Wolfowitz, the former deputy secretary of the U.S. Department of Defense. Notorious as one of the architects of the Iraq War, his appointment was resented by many within the Bank. Wolfowitz continued his predecessor's anti-corruption campaign with even more vigor, which fueled the resentment of the bureaucracy even more. Only two years into his presidency, he was ousted by the board of directors over a personal scandal and has recently been replaced by Robert Zoellick, a former official of the U.S. Department of State with extensive international experience.

It remains to be seen how the Bank will fare under Zoellick's leadership. I wish him every success. But that success will ultimately depend upon his ability to assert his control over the bureaucracy and tame the gods of lending. And that will not be easy, for I fear the bureaucrats may have been emboldened by the Wolfowitz affair. Nevertheless, with strong leadership it remains possible to turn the Bank around from the bloated bureaucracy it has become, endlessly occupying itself with irrelevant activities that have nothing to do with the alleviation of poverty, ignoring its fiduciary responsibilities, and accountable to no one.

Let us hope that the talent, experience, and dedication of its staff will be freed from the mindless bureaucratic diversions that prevent them from truly serving the poor. Let us hope that the Bank will return at last to its mission and its rightful place as a leader in economic development. Remembering that *nowhere is it written that the World Bank has an obligation to lend money to corrupt and dysfunctional governments,* let us hope that the gods of lending will return to serving the people and not the corrupt government elites that rule them. And that will be a good thing.

NOTE

1. Based upon discussions with older colleagues who were present, it was during McNamara's tenure that the Young Professional Program began. This program was the entry point for a majority of the economists who have spent their entire careers at the Bank, rising to upper management and to de facto control of all that the Bank does.

About the Author

Following a varied career in industry and technical education, Steve Berkman joined the World Bank's Africa Region group in 1983. Providing advice and assistance with capacity building and institutional development issues on Bank-funded projects, he worked in all the major economic sectors throughout the region. Soon realizing that the Bank's lending program was exposed to high risk from corruption, his attempts to convince management of the extent of the problem were given little credence until the arrival of President James Wolfensohn in 1995. Retiring in that same year, Berkman was called back from 1998 to 2002 to assist with the establishment of an Anti-Corruption and Fraud Investigation Unit, during which time he was lead investigator on a number of corruption cases in Africa and Latin America. He has given presentations at various international anti-corruption forums and has provided assistance to the U.S. Senate Committee on Foreign Relations for the enactment of legislation to reform the multilateral development banks and Senate passage of the United Nations Convention against Corruption.

Index

management accepting, 164, 229
management admitting/ denying losses form, 230–31
management's punishment for, 242–43
management v. staff on, 145–46
NBTE, review showing, 91–92
in NEPA, 64–65, 70–71
in Nigeria, 79
Nigeria, World Bank aiding in, 29–30, 41
Pakistan, IDA credit, risks of, 166
poverty alleviation and, 43
PREM's report on, 142
in project appraisal process, 55
project size impacting, 266–67
public officials and, 152
report prepared on, 121–22
risk of losses from, 235
of SALs, 76
SA's history with, 239–40
solutions for reviews on, 236–37
solutions needed for alleviating, 224–25
in staff, 150
staff frustrations with, 271–72
staff, IADIU uncovering, 154–55
third world governments and, 5–6, 224, 244
Wolfensohn's investigations in, 6, 23
Wolfensohn's plan for, 143
Wolfensohn v. management on, 149
Wolfensohn v. staff on, 150–51

World Bank addressing, 140–41, 149–50, 153, 159–61, 247
World Bank admitting, 143–44, 161, 169–70, 235
World Bank Annual Report 1997 discussing, 144
World Bank, borrowers prosecuting, 243, 262
World Bank dealing with, 4–5, 121–22
World Bank management divided, investigation on, 139–40, 155–56, 229–30
World Bank publicity of, 161–63
in World Bank's African portfolio, 117–18
of World Bank's annual reports, 254–55
Corruption and Fraud Investigation Unit (CFIU), 157
Cote d'Ivoire, 223
counterpart funds
corruption common to, 241
failures/weaknesses in use of, 240–41
The Gambia, Kalley Trading Enterprise fraud with, 197
for NBTE, 92
NBTE, lack of, 103–4
shortage problems with, 52
country assistance strategies (CASs), 49
definition of, 259
country departments (CDs), in AFR, 17
country program divisions, of EAP, WAP, 11–12
"Country Strategy Note," for Nigeria, 28–29

for Argentina public sector
  governance, 165
borrowers' project commitment and, 48–49
borrowers, solutions for, 268–
  69
Congo, risks of corruption
  with, 165
corruption, estimated losses
  for, 166, 173
corruption fought with, 267–
  68
document preparation for,
  51
economic development,
  challenges with, 222–23
ERR assessment failures,
  approving, 53
failures of, 266
IBRD, IDA, cumulative totals
  of, 43
Kainji Multipurpose Project
  and supplementary, 59
management, adjustments for
  targets of, 267
management's agendas with,
  48
for NBTE, 92
for NEPA, 57
NEPA, appraisal report for,
  59–62
poverty affected by integrity
  of, 265
poverty not reached by, 256
projects, evaluations on, 47
projects repeated and, 49–
  50
solutions needed for pressure
  on, 226–27
World Bank, challenges
  facing, 265–66
of World Bank to Nigeria, 29

local competitive bidding (LCB)
  DFR, fraud in housing/
    furnishing for, 124–26
  The Gambia explaining
    corruption in, 216–17
  Ghana, ICB compared to, 123
losses
  estimation tools for, 231
  The Gambia, corruption and,
    233–35
  loans, corruption, estimated,
    166, 173
  management admitting/
    denying corruption and,
    230–31
  risk of corruption causing,
    235
  solutions for examination/
    review of, 231–37

Managed Information Systems
  (MIS), 151
management. *See also* economic
    management
  Africa success v. career
    advancement in, 45
  Africa, World Bank's prob-
    lems with, 22–23
  annual reports, structure of,
    262–63
  borrowers, financial prob-
    lems with, 116–17
  Cameroon, World Bank
    problems with, 30
  corruption, acceptance of,
    164, 229
  corruption, losses admitted/
    denied by, 230–31
  corruption, punishment of,
    242–43
  corruption, staff v., 145–46
  corruption, Wolfensohn v., 149

The Gambia, difficulties with,
174
The Gambia, SA fraud by
officials of, 193–94, 195f.
identification of, 47–50
loan evaluations for, 47
loans, borrowers commit-
ment to, 48–49
loans for repeated, 49–50
management, results prob-
lems with, 47
in Nigeria, SA fraud, 110–
12
planning neglected in, 50
preparation of, 50–54
process of, 45–46
success contradictions with,
45–47
in Uganda, SA fraud, 113–15
project teams
composition of, 51
ERR, SAR manipulated by,
52–53
planning ignored by, 51–52
supervision missions of, 83
PRT. *See* project-related training
public-administration specialists,
low levels of, 26–27
public expenditure reviews
(PERS), 233
public officials
corruption with, 152
third world, objectives of, 3–4
public sector governance, Argentina, loans for, 165

reorganization
of AFR, 14
of ECN, NDA into NEPA, 59
of IADIU, INT, 157–58
management affected by, 11,
13–14
real change v., 272–73

World Bank, 1987 cause of,
12–13
World Bank, 1987 cost of, 13
World Bank, 1987 transitional
problems from, 14–15
World Bank's problems with,
10–11, 40
report. *See* ACFIU Gambian
report; annual report(s);
performance rating
reports; project audit
reports; Project Comple-
tion Report; Staff Ap-
praisal Report
review(s). *See also* annual review
of project portfolio;
midterm review
for ICB, NCB, 232
losses, solutions for, 231–37
NBTE, corruption found in,
91–92
solutions for corruption and,
236–37
risks
of corruption causing losses,
235
of corruption with Congo
loans, 165
of corruption with Haiti, IDA
credit, 166–68
of corruption with Pakistan
IDA credit, 166
ECN, ignorance of, 57–58
NDA assessment, ignoring,
58
NEPA, ignorance of, 72–73
Rodriguez, Fritz, 151
Russia, 166

SACs. *See* structural adjustment
credits
SALs. *See* structural adjustment
loans

Also from Kumarian Press...

International Development:

The Search for Empowerment: Social Capital as Idea and Practice at the World Bank
Edited by Anthony Bebbington, Michael Woolcock, Scott Guggenheim, and Elizabeth Olson

Nation-Building Unraveled? Aid, Peace, and Justice in Afghanistan
Edited by Antonio Donini, Norah Niland, and Karin Wermester

The Poor Always Pay Back: The Grameen II Story
Asif Dowla and Dipal Barua

Capitalism and Justice: Envisioning Social and Economic Fairness
John Isbister

New and Forthcoming:

Creating Credibility: Legitimacy and Accountability for Transnational Civil Society
L. David Brown

Surrogates of the State: NGOs, Development, and Ujamaa in Tanzania
Michael Jennings

World Disasters Report 2007: Focus on Discrimination
Edited by Yvonne Klynman, Nicholas Kouppari, and Mohammed Mukhier

Peace through Health: How Health Professionals Can Work for a Less Violent World
Edited by Neil Arya and Joanna Santa Barbara

Visit Kumarian Press at **www.kpbooks.com** or call **toll-free 800.232.0223** for a complete catalog.

green press
INITIATIVE

Kumarian Press is committed to preserving ancient forests and natural resources. We elected to print this title on 30% post consumer recycled paper, processed chlorine free. As a result, for this printing, we have saved:

13 Trees (40' tall and 6-8" diameter)
4,810 Gallons of Wastewater
9 million BTU's of Total Energy
618 Pounds of Solid Waste
1,159 Pounds of Greenhouse Gases

Kumarian Press made this paper choice because our printer, Thomson-Shore, Inc., is a member of Green Press Initiative, a nonprofit program dedicated to supporting authors, publishers, and suppliers in their efforts to reduce their use of fiber obtained from endangered forests.

For more information, visit www.greenpressinitiative.org

Environmental impact estimates were made using the Environmental Defense Paper Calculator. For more information visit: www.papercalculator.org.

Kumarian Press, located in Sterling, Virginia, is a forward-looking, scholarly press that promotes active international engagement and an awareness of global connectedness.